TOP 10
ANDALUCÍA
AND THE COSTA DEL SOL

Top 10 Andalucía and the Costa del Sol Highlights

The Top 10 of Everything

CONTENTS

Andalucía and the Costa del Sol Area by Area

Streetsmart

Within each Top 10 list in this book, no hierarchy of quality or popularity is implied. All 10 are, in the editor's opinion, of roughly equal merit.

Title page, front cover and spine *The grand Alhambra palace overlooking Granada*
Back cover, clockwise from top left *Spanish tapas; Roman bridge, Córdoba; Nerja beach; Alhambra, Granada; Old Town, Malaga*

The rapid rate at which the world is changing is constantly keeping the DK Eyewitness team on our toes. While we've worked hard to ensure that this edition of Andalucía and the Costa del Sol is accurate and up-to-date, we know that opening hours alter, standards shift, prices fluctuate, places close and new ones pop up in their stead. So, if you notice we've got something wrong or left something out, we want to hear about it. Please get in touch at **travelguides@dk.com**

Welcome to
Andalucía and the Costa del Sol

Flamenco, wine, tapas, beaches, sunshine: all the things that make Spain one of the best-loved and most visited countries on Earth is concentrated in the region of Andalucía. But this beguiling region is also home to some of Europe's most romantic cities, its most important wetlands reserve and second-highest mountain range, offering a wealth of outdoor pursuits from hiking to skiing. With DK Eyewitness Top 10 Andalucía and the Costa del Sol, it's yours to explore.

Andalucía's three great cities – **Granada**, **Seville** and **Córdoba** – are repositories of Spain's historical identity and symbols of the area's Moorish past, with world-class heritage sites such as the **Mezquita** in Córdoba, Granada's **Alhambra** and Seville's **Cathedral**. Other must-sees are **Jerez de la Frontera** and its sherry *bodegas* and **Ronda**, with its location above the **Tajo** gorge, while **Baeza** and **Úbeda** are well-preserved towns full of Renaissance architecture. In between are the famous *pueblos blancos* (white villages) that dot the hilltops.

Along the sun-drenched **Costa del Sol**, cultural and culinary riches are concentrated around **Málaga**, **Marbella** and **Gibraltar**. Between the dramatic "rock" and the ancient city of **Cádiz** lies the gorgeous **Costa de la Luz**, popular with Spanish tourists and windsurfers.

Whether you're visiting for a weekend or a week, our Top 10 guide brings together the best of everything the region has to offer. The guide has useful tips throughout, from seeking out what's free to finding places off the beaten track, plus seven easy-to-follow itineraries, designed to tie together a clutch of sights in a short space of time. Add inspiring photography and detailed maps, and you've got the essential pocket-sized travel companion. **Enjoy the book, and enjoy Andalucía and the Costa del Sol**.

Clockwise from top: **The Alhambra, Granada, Sierra de Aracena, Alcázar, Seville, Cabo de Gata nature reserve, Andalucían wall tiles, Ronda atop the Tajo gorge, La Mezquita, Córdoba**

Exploring Andalucía and the Costa del Sol

The region offers a dizzying range of sights, sounds, flavours and fun. To start you off, here are ideas for a four- and seven-day tour.

Four Days in Andalucía

Day ❶
MORNING
Follow the dramatic winding A397 up through the coastal mountains of the Serranías Penibéticas to lunch in **Ronda** *(see pp30–31)*. Take in the architecture of the bullring, palaces and the view from the Puente Nuevo.
AFTERNOON
Drive to **Cádiz** *(see pp26–7)* and wander the backstreets of the medieval Barrio del Pópulo; don't miss the Catedral Nueva and the coastal promenade.

The Catedral Nueva sits proudly above Cádiz seafront.

Day ❷
MORNING
Explore the **Parque Nacional Doñana** *(see pp36–7)*, catching the birdlife at dawn. Next visit **Jerez de la Frontera** *(see p106)* to sample the local sherries.
AFTERNOON
Enjoy the back-road route north via the *pueblo blanco* of **Arcos de la Frontera** *(see p106)* to **Seville** *(see pp84–93)* and its **Cathedral** and **La Giralda** *(see pp18–19)*.

Day ❸
MORNING
Visit Seville's **Real Alcázar** *(see pp20–21)* before driving on to the white village of **Carmona** *(see p96)*, then on to **Córdoba** *(see pp22–3)*.
AFTERNOON
Tour **La Mezquita** *(see pp24–5)*, the **Judería** *(see p22)* and the **Alcázar de los Reyes Cristianos** *(see p23)*.

CÓRDOBA

Córdoba

4 — 4

3 3

Seville Carmona

SEVILLA

Parque Nacional de Doñana

2 2

Arcos de la Frontera

1 1

Ronda

MÁLAGA

Málaga

Cádiz Jerez de la Frontera Serranías Penibéticas Marbella

CÁDIZ Mediterranean Sea

Atlantic Ocean

Sierra de Cazorla is a vast and diverse reserve.

The impressive Alhambra is a complex of Moorish fortresses and gardens.

Key
— Four-day itinerary
— Seven-day itinerary

Baeza ○ *Úbeda*
Sierra de Cazorla
JAÉN
Granada
Sierra Nevada
Vélez-Málaga *Nerja*

0 kilometres 40
0 miles 40

Arcos de la Frontera is dramatically situated on a cliff edge.

tearooms. Afterwards, visit UNESCO-listed **Úbeda's Pottery Quarter** *(see p35)*, pretty plazas and Renaissance and Plateresque buildings.

Day ❺
Go for a short hike in the **Sierra de Cazorla** *(see p61)* and look out for birds of prey. Spend the evening in beautifully preserved **Baeza** *(see p34)*, another UNESCO-listed site.

Day ❻
Discover the **Sierra Nevada** *(see pp38–9)*, Europe's second-highest mountain range after the Alps. If it's summer, see the Valle de Lecrín's olive, almond and citrus groves; in winter, you can go skiing.

Day ❼
Take the A41 south, along the western edge of the **Sierra Nevada** *(see pp38–9)* and enjoy the beach at Nerja before visiting the market town of Vélez-Málaga on **the Costa del Sol** *(see pp32–3)*.

Day ❹
Head to **Granada** *(see pp116–123)* to see the architectural complex and gardens of **the Alhambra** *(see pp12–13)* and **Generalife** (summer palace) *(see pp14–15)*, then finally relax on the beach at **Nerja** *(see p33)*.

Seven Days in Andalucía

Days ❶–❸ as above
Day ❹
Start at **the Alhambra** *(see pp12–13)*, then explore the **Albaicín** quarter *(see pp16–17)*, taking in the churches, Moorish baths and Moroccan

Top 10 Andalucía and the Costa del Sol Highlights

The impressive Puente Nuevo spans El Tajo gorge at Ronda

🔟 Andalucía Highlights

The diverse and politically semi-autonomous region of Andalucía has a population of 8.4 million and embodies what is thought of as typically Spanish. Memories of a visit here will be colourful, joyous and deeply stirring, and will likely include flamenco, remote white villages, sierras and sunny beaches.

1 Moorish Granada

Andalucía's 1,300-year-old Moorish heritage evokes pure Romanticism that is hard to equal. The delicate art and architecture are among the most splendid in Europe *(see pp12–17)*.

2 Seville Cathedral and La Giralda

These two chief wonders of Seville beautifully embody the juxtaposition of the Moors and their Christian successors *(see pp18–19)*.

Real Alcázar, Seville 3

A mix of styles is evident in this luxurious palace, mostly built by Moorish artisans for Christians *(see pp20–21)*.

4 Córdoba and La Mezquita

This was once the most important Islamic city in Europe, a fact that is illustrated by the architectural masterpiece of La Mezquita, the Great Mosque *(see pp22–5)*.

Cádiz 5

Said to be Europe's oldest constantly inhabited city, Cádiz retains a mysterious aura. Its golden-domed cathedral is spectacular *(see pp26–7)*.

0 kilometres 50
0 miles 50

Jabugo • Aracena • Cazalla de la Sierra
Minas de Riotinto • Lora del Río
Gibraleón • HUELVA
Huelva • 2 3 Alcalá de Guadaira
Parque Nacional de Doñana 9 Seville SEVILLA
Jerez de la Frontera • Arcos de la Frontera
CÁDIZ
Cádiz 5 San Fernando
Costa de la Luz Algeciras

6 Ronda

The largest of the *pueblos blancos* scattered throughout the region, Ronda is split by El Tajo gorge. It is also reputed to be the birthplace of the modern style of bullfighting (see pp30–31).

The Costa del Sol 7

From the wealthy yachting-set enclaves to package deals for families, this famous expanse of sand has something for everyone (see pp32–3).

Baeza and Úbeda 8

Both of these exquisite towns in Jaén Province offer world-class Renaissance architecture set in perfectly preserved historic centres (see pp34–5).

9 Parque Nacional de Doñana

The vast delta of the Guadalquivir River is one of the world's most vital nature reserves; without it birdlife throughout Europe would be seriously compromised (see pp36–7).

The Sierra Nevada 10

Europe's second-highest mountain range after the Alps offers its southernmost ski resort, a wealth of wildlife for trekkers, and dozens of remote traditional villages along its southern slopes (see pp38–9).

⭐ Moorish Granada: the Alhambra

The great complex of the Alhambra is the best-preserved medieval Arab palace in the world and, with nearly two million visitors annually, it is also the most popular monument in Spain. Built on the Sabika Hill overlooking the city of Granada, its most distinctive phase began in the 11th century as the *qa'lat al-Hamra* (Red Fort) of the Ziridian rulers. From the 13th to almost the end of the 15th century the kings of the succeeding Nasrid dynasty embellished the site in a most spectacular fashion.

The Alhambra, backed by the Sierra Nevada

1 Puerta de la Justicia

Built in 1348, the "Justice Gate" **(above)** horseshoe arch makes use of Arab defensive techniques – a steep approach combined with four right-angled turns – intended to slow down invading armies.

2 Puerta del Vino

The "Wine Gate" – so called because it was used as a wine cellar in the 16th century – marks what was once the main entrance arch to the Medina (market).

3 Plaza de los Aljibes

From these ramparts, visitors can enjoy superb views of Granada. The giant cisterns *(aljibes)* underneath were built by the Christian successors.

4 Alcazaba

Although largely in ruins, this fortress is well worth a look. Don't miss climbing up onto the Torre de la Vela for views of the Sierra Nevada.

5 Palacio de Carlos V

This Italian Renaissance palace **(left)** is the masterpiece of Pedro Machuca, a student of Michelangelo. Inside are the Museo de Bellas Artes and the Museo de la Alhambra, with its fine collection of Nasrid art.

6 Palacios Nazaríes

The Nasrid palaces are built of simple brick, wood and stucco, so as not to compete with the creations of Allah.

Plan of the Alhambra

Generalife

7 Palacio de Mexuar

The most poorly preserved of the three palaces, this was the most public space, dedicated to judicial and bureaucratic business. The original structure dates from 1365, but in the 16th century the Christians converted it to a chapel.

9 Palacio de Comares

Built in the mid-14th century, this area constituted the Serallo, where the sultan would receive dignitaries and deal with diplomatic issues. Inside is the Salón de Embajadores, the main throne room of the Alhambra. In front of the palace is the Patio de Arrayanes **(right)**.

10 Palacio de los Leones

Dating from the late 1300s, this palace was the Harem, the private zone reserved for the sultan and his family. The fountain with 12 lions, in the central courtyard of the palace, may represent the 12 signs of the zodiac, the 12 hours of the clock, or the 12 tribes of Israel.

8 Partal

As you leave the Alhambra, stroll through the gardens with their watercourses laid out in an area that used to have palaces of its own. All you can see of them now are five porticoed arches **(above)**. This area leads up to the Generalife *(see pp14–15)*.

NEED TO KNOW

MAP S2

The Alhambra: 958 02 79 71; open Apr–mid-Oct: 8:30am–8pm daily, 10–11:30pm Tue–Sat; mid-Oct–Mar: 8:30am–6pm daily, 8–9:30pm Fri & Sat; closed 1 Jan, 25 Dec; adm €14, €14.85 (online), €8 (night visits); www.alhambradegranada.org

Museo de la Alhambra: open mid-Mar–mid-Oct: 8:30am–2:30pm Tue–Sun; mid-Oct–mid-Mar: 8:30am–2:30pm Sun & Tue, 8:30am–8pm Wed–Sat; closed Mon, 1 Jan, 25 Dec

▪ Snacks and drinks are available, but taking water is a good idea.

▪ Visitor numbers are restricted, so book tickets online in advance.

Moorish Granada: Generalife

The Torre de los Picos

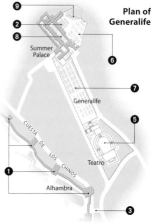

Plan of Generalife

1 The Towers

Following the gardens of the Partal (see p13) as you walk towards the Generalife, you will encounter a number of restored Moorish towers built into the wall. The Torre de los Picos, Torre del Cadí, Torre de la Cautiva, Torre de las Infantas, Torre del Cabo de la Carrera and Torre del Agua are all worth a look for their fine detail, as well as for the views they command. The Torre de la Cautiva and the Torre de las Infantas are twin tower-palaces with richly decorated rooms.

2 Patio de los Cipreses

The Court of the Cypresses is also known as the Patio of the Sultana, for this is where Zoraya,

the wife of Boabdil (see p43), is said to have secretly met her lover, the chief of the Abencerrajes clan. The sultan had the chief's men massacred upon discovery of the infidelity. A 700-year-old cypress tree commemorates the trysting place.

3 The Hill of the Sun

A footbridge flanked by two towers takes you over to the hill that rises above the Alhambra. A vast summer palace once stood here, amid an enormous garden, which predated the Alhambra by more than a century, although little of it remains today.

4 The Name of the Garden

The word Generalife is generally considered to be a corruption of the Arab phrase *Djinat al-Arif*, which can be translated as ``the Architect's Garden" (referring to Allah) or simply the "Best" or "High" garden. The Darro River was diverted 18 km (11 miles) to provide water for this lush sanctuary.

Patio de los Cipreses

HISTORY OF THE ALHAMBRA

The castle was the last bastion of al-Andalus, the Moorish hegemony that, at its height, included almost the entire Iberian Peninsula. By 1237 the Christians had reconquered all but this emirate. The Moors managed to flourish for some 250 years longer, only falling to the forces of King Fernando and Queen Isabel in 1492 (see p42). The Generalife was the summer palace where the Moorish leaders could escape political life and the bustling city below and relax in the landscaped grounds. After centuries of neglect, and attempts by Napoleon's army to blow up the palace, the structures were preserved in the early 19th century, after the American writer Washington Irving inspired the world with his *Tales of the Alhambra* (see p55).

5 Teatro
As you climb the hill, you will encounter the amphitheatre, nestled into a tree-lined hollow. Dance performances and musical concerts are offered here as part of an annual festival of the arts.

6 Jardines Altos
As you reach the entrance to the upper gardens, you will encounter the Patio de Polo, where visitors would leave their horses before ascending to the palace.

Wisteria in the Jardines Altos

On this level there is a series of fountains and formal plantings, joined by walkways and copses.

7 Jardines Nuevos
It is clear the "New Gardens", also called the Lower Gardens, owe little to Moorish taste. Hedges and formal patterns echo Italian style, but the sound of running water creates an atmosphere in keeping with the Moorish ideal. In Islam, Paradise is defined as an oasis – a water garden full of blossoms.

Patio de la Acequia fountains

8 Patio de la Acequia
The "Court of the Long Pool" is the most famous water spectacle of the garden. Perfectly proportioned pools are set off by rows of water jets. At one end stands one of the complex's most harmonious buildings, the Sala Regia, with its decorated arcades and airy portico.

9 Escalera del Agua
These staircases above the palace, also known as the Camino de las Cascadas, have handrails that double as watercourses. It is best viewed in spring.

10 Leaving the Gardens
As you exit the gardens you will pass along the Paseo de las Adelfas and the Paseo de los Cipreses, lined respectively with oleanders and cypresses. Back to the Hill of the Sun, stroll down the pretty Cuesta del Rey Chico to the Albaicín (see pp16–17).

Moorish Granada: Albaicín

Mudéjar-style Iglesia de Santa Ana

1 Iglesia de Santa Ana
MAP R2 ■ C/Santa Ana 1

At the end of Plaza Nueva stands this 16th-century brick church in Mudéjar style, built by Muslim artisans for Christian patrons. Inside the main chapel is a coffered ceiling in the Moorish tradition. The bell tower was originally a minaret.

2 Paseo de los Tristes
MAP S2

The broad tree-lined esplanade follows the course of the river upstream. It once accommodated tournaments, processions and funeral cortèges, but now bars and restaurants dominate the scene.

3 Casa de Castril
MAP R2 ■ Carrera del Darro 43 ■ 600 14 31 41 ■ Open Jul–Aug: 9am–3pm Tue–Sun; Sep–Jun: 9am–9pm Tue–Sat, 9am–3pm Sun

This ornate 16th-century mansion was originally owned by the secretary to King Fernando and Queen Isabel. Since 1879 it has served as the Archaeological and Ethnological Museum, displaying artifacts from Granada's past, from the Paleolithic era up until the Reconquest in 1492. The remarkable collection is displayed across three galleries and around the central courtyard.

4 Iglesia de San Pedro y San Pablo
MAP R2 ■ Carrera del Darro 2

Across from the Casa de Castril, this church, built in the 1500s, graces an attractive spot on the banks of the river. From here you can see the Alhambra dominating the landscape.

5 Real Chancillería
MAP Q2 ■ Plaza del Padre Suárez 1

The austerely impressive Royal Chancery dates from 1530, built shortly after the *reconquista* as part of the futile attempt to Christianize this Moorish quarter. The palace is attributed to architect Diego de Siloé.

Real Chancillería, now the high court

6 El Bañuelo (Baños Árabes)
MAP R2 ■ Carrera del Darro 31 ■ 958 57 51 31 ■ Open daily

Dating from the 11th century, these are the best preserved Moorish baths in Spain. They comprise several rooms that were used for changing, meeting, massage and bathing.

The old Moorish baths of El Bañuelo

El Mirador de San Nicolás, offering fine views of the Alhambra

7 El Mirador de San Nicolás
MAP R1

In front of the Iglesia de San Nicolás, this magnificent terrace has such lovely views of the Alhambra and the Sierra Nevada that it has long been dubbed El Mirador ("The Lookout Point") de San Nicolás. The views are extraordinary at sunset, when the Alhambra glows softly ochre and the often snowcapped Sierra Nevada radiates pink in the distance.

8 Plaza Larga
MAP R1

From the Paseo de los Tristes follow Calle Panaderos to reach this busy market square, where you'll mostly find produce stalls as well as cheap restaurants and bars. The square sports an Islamic gateway with a typically angled entrance as part

Map of Albaicín

of what remains of the upper fortifications. This is the Arco de las Pesas – if you pass through it you will come to the Albaicín's most popular square, Plaza San Nicolás.

9 Tearooms

As you wander around the labyrinth of whitewashed houses and tiny sloping alleyways of the Albaicín quarter you will encounter many tearooms – a Moroccan tradition that is very much alive in this quarter. Possibly the best one, La Tetería del Bañuelo (see p122), consists of a series of rooms set amid delightful gardens. Here you can sip your minty brew, nibble honeyed sweets and contemplate the timeless panorama.

10 Moroccan Shops

Check out the hilly streets off Calle Elvira, especially Caldería Vieja and Caldería Nueva, for typically Moroccan shops. The scene is indistinguishable from what you would find in Morocco itself, with the colourful wares spilling out onto the pavements (see p120).

SACROMONTE GYPSY CAVES

Leaving the Albaicín quarter to the north, follow the Camino del Sacromonte to reach the hill of the same name. The so-called "Holy Hill" is most noted for the presence of some 3,500 caves traditionally inhabited by gypsies (see p50). For more than six centuries, the zone has been known for zambras and impromptu gypsy fiestas of flamenco music and dance, and visitors have always been welcome to witness these cultural celebrations. Today some 80 per cent of the caves are still occupied and several of them continue to operate as venues for flamenco tableaus.

🔟 ⭐ Seville Cathedral and La Giralda

In 1248, after some 500 years of Islamic rule, Seville was reconquered by Christian forces, who warned the Moorish inhabitants against damaging the city's magnificent edifices. Pragmatically, the conquerors simply rededicated the huge Almohad mosque to the Virgin and for about 150 years used it as their principal place of worship. In 1401, the building was demolished. It took just over a century to erect a new cathedral of unprecedented proportions on its rectangular base.

1 Exterior and Scale

In sheer cubic vastness, Seville Cathedral (right) is the largest Christian church (see p86) in the world, and there's a certificate from the Guinness Book of Records on display here to prove it. It measures 126 m (415 ft) by 83 m (270 ft) and the nave rises to 43 m (140 ft). The best place to take it all in is from La Giralda.

2 Cathedral Paintings

There are around 600 paintings throughout the cathedral, from the entrance pavilion to the sacristies, together with sculptures from the 17th-century Sevillian School, which included artists Bartolomé Esteban Murillo, Francisco de Zurbarán and Francisco Pacheco.

3 Puerta del Perdón

The "Gate of Forgiveness" is set in a crenellated wall and is the main entrance to the one surviving part of the mosque. The arch and bronze doors are a masterpiece of Almohad art, carved with 880 Koranic inscriptions. Sculpted Renaissance elements include a bas-relief of the Expulsion of the Moneychangers from the Temple.

4 Sacristía de los Cálices

Part of the cathedral's treasury is housed here. The anteroom displays the Tenebrario, a 7.8-m (25-ft) Plateresque candelabrum used during Holy Week. Inside, the star turns are a painting by Goya of Seville's patron saints, Justa and Rufina, as well as canvases by Zurbarán, Jordaens and other Masters.

5 Sacristía Mayor

The Main Sacristy (left) is dominated by a dome, designed in the 16th century. The centrepiece of the sacristy is a 450-kg (990-lb), 3-m (10-ft) silver Baroque monstrance created by Juan de Arfe.

6 Patio de los Naranjos

The Courtyard of Orange Trees was the place where ritual ablutions were performed before entering the mosque for prayer.

7 Interior

The vast Gothic arches that line the nave inside the cathedral are so high that the space within the building is said to have its own independent climate.

8 La Giralda

This grand tower **(below)** is the symbol of Seville, built between 1172 and 1195 *(see p86)*. It takes its name from the weathervane on top, called *El Giraldillo*.

SEMANA SANTA FESTIVITIES

Seville's Holy Week celebrations *(see p80)* are Andalucía's richest. Here, 61 *cofradías* (brotherhoods) compete to bear aloft the most well-dressed Virgin in mourning and an image from the Passion of Christ. Floats are carried by *costaleros* (bearers), while the processions are led by *nazarenos* – penitents in hoods and robes.

Plan of Seville Cathedral

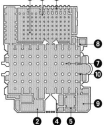

9 Sala Capitular

The Chapter House contains Murillo's *Immaculate Conception* in the vault and has a lavish marble floor.

10 Capilla Mayor

The main altar's *tour de force* is its 15th-century *retablo* – the world's largest altarpiece **(below)**. Composed of gilded carved wood, it features some 45 Biblical scenes employing some 1,000 figures.

NEED TO KNOW

MAP M4 ▪ Plaza Virgen de los Reyes ▪ 954 21 49 71 ▪ www.catedralde sevilla.es

Open 10:45am–5pm Mon–Sat, 2:30–6pm Sun; services: check website for timings

Adm €10 online (10 per cent increase in price if bought on-site; includes access to La Giralda); audio guides €5 (€4 in app format)

Guided tours and rooftop tours available in English (check website for details)

▪ For great views, head to the rooftop bar at EME Catedral Hotel *(see p140)*.

▪ It's an easygoing climb up La Giralda, on ramps.

🔟 ⭐ Real Alcázar, Seville

This extensive complex embodies a series of palatial rooms and spaces from various ages. The front towers and walls are the oldest surviving section, dating from AD 913 and built by the Emir of Córdoba, Abd ar-Rahman III, most likely on the ruins of Roman barracks. A succession of caliphs added their dazzling architectural statements over the ensuing centuries. Then came the Christian kings, particularly Pedro I in the 14th century, and finally the rather perfunctory 16th-century apartments of Carlos V.

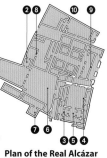

Plan of the Real Alcázar

1 Puerta del León

The entrance gate into the first courtyard **(above)** is flanked by original Almohad walls. Note the Gothic and Arabic inscriptions on the interior façade.

2 Sala de Justicia

Here and in adjacent halls and courts is some of the purest Mudéjar art commissioned by Alfonso XI of Castile around 1330 and executed by craftsmen from Granada. The star-shaped coffered ceiling and fine plasterwork are quite exquisite.

3 Patio de las Muñecas

The intimate Courtyard of the Dolls was the private living room of the palace and supposedly gets its name from two faces carved into the base of one of the arches.

4 Patio de las Doncellas

The Courtyard of the Maidens **(above)** commemorates the annual tribute of 100 virgins delivered to the Moorish rulers by the Christians. Look out for the fine *azulejos* (tiles).

PEDRO I

Few Spanish kings have received such contradictory press over the centuries as Pedro I (1350–69). Called both "the Cruel" – el Cruel – and "the Avenger" – el Justiciero – he killed his own brother in order to consolidate his position and flaunted his cohabitation with his mistress María de Padilla. The Alcázar we see today is almost entirely the result of Pedro's rebuilding programme, primarily so that he and María would have a cosy place of retreat.

5 Salón de Embajadores

The most brilliant room in the entire Alcázar, its crowning glory is the dazzling dome of carved, painted and gilded wood **(above)**, constructed by craftsmen from Toledo and completed in 1366.

6 Patio de la Montería

The Hunting Courtyard has 14th-century Mudéjar decorative work – a perfect mix of cultural influences.

7 Casa de la Contratación

The halls in the House of Trade are where Fernando and Isabel met with the explorers of the Americas.

8 Patio del Yeso

The secluded Courtyard of Plaster, greatly restored, is one of the few remnants of the 12th-century palace. The delicate stucco work features scalloped arches **(right)** and is set off by a garden with water channels.

9 Palacio Gótico

In a refurbished 13th-century Gothic structure built by Alfonso X the Wise, this palace has a rather inharmonious Renaissance style.

10 Gardens

Moorish touches such as fountains, pools, orange groves, palms and hedgerows abound in these gardens **(left)**. Concerts and events are held here on summer evenings.

NEED TO KNOW

MAP M4 ■ Patio de Banderas ■ 954 50 23 24 ■ www.alcazarsevilla.org

Open 9:30am–7pm daily (Oct–Mar: to 5pm); closed 1 & 6 Jan, Good Friday, 25 Dec

Adm: €13.50 (€14.50 with online booking fee); €5.50 (for Royal Bedroom); free Mon (Apr–Sep: 6–7pm, Oct–Mar: 4–5pm)

■ A flow-control entry system allows a limited number of people into the Alcázar every half hour. To avoid long waits, visit at off-peak times.

■ There are dramatized 30-minute evening tours with re-enactments of the Alcázar's history; book tickets in advance.

TOP 10 ⭐ Córdoba

This city is a jewel in Andalucía's crown. The main sight is undoubtedly the Great Mosque, La Mezquita – one of the unsurpassed masterpieces of world architecture. In addition to the mosque and its incongruous but splendid cathedral within, other sights here include fine monuments and palaces from every age, art and history museums, one of Andalucía's greatest archaeological repositories, and a museum dedicated to the history of the bullfight.

4 Palacio de los Marqueses de Viana

A former noble residence (14th- to 18th-century), the museum includes preserved period rooms and furnishings.

Museo Taurino 5

Dedicated to bullfighting, this museum is home to a fine collection of art on the theme. Its spectacular exhibits showcase the history of the bullfight, the rearing of the bulls as well as important figures in bullfighting.

1 Judería

The city's ancient Jewish quarter **(above)**, dates back to the time of the Roman Empire. Its narrow alleyways, brilliantly whitewashed and hung with flowerpots, are graced with beautiful Moorish patios. This district also has Andalucía's only medieval synagogue.

2 Plaza del Potro

This small but elegant square, adorned with a 16th-century fountain, was once Córdoba's livestock market.

3 La Mezquita

The world's third-largest mosque (see pp24–5) remains a place of immense grandeur and mystical power.

NEED TO KNOW

MAP D3

Alcázar and Baños: Campo Santo de los Mártires; 957 42 01 51; open summer: 8:30am–2:30pm Tue–Sat, 9:30am–2:30pm Sun & hols; winter: 8:30am–8:45pm Tue–Fri, 8:30am–4:30pm Sat (to 2:30pm Sun); adm Alcázar €5, Baños €3

Museo de Bellas Artes: Plaza del Potro 1; 957 10 36 59; open summer: 9am–3pm Tue–Sun; winter: 9am–9pm Tue–Sat (to 3pm Sun); adm €1.50

Museo Arqueológico: Plaza Jerónimo Páez 7; 957 35 55 17; open hours same as Museo de Bellas Artes; adm €1.50

Palacio de los Marqueses de Viana: Plaza Don Gome 2; 957 49 67 41; open summer: 9am–3pm Tue–Sun; winter: 10am–7pm Tue–Sat (to 3pm Sun); adm €10

Museo Torre de la Calahorra: Puente Romano; 957 29 39 29; open May–Sep: 10am–2pm & 4:30–8:30pm daily; Oct–Apr: 10am–6pm daily; adm €4.50

Museo Taurino: Plaza de Maimónides; 957 20 10 56; open 8:45am–3:15pm Tue–Sun & hols; closed Mon; adm €4; www.museotaurinodecordoba.es

Map of Córdoba

7 Museo Arqueológico

Housed in a Renaissance mansion is this excellent archaeological museum. One highlight is the 10th-century Moorish bronze of a stag, which was found at Medina Azahara *(see p125)*.

MULTICULTURAL TRADITION

Córdoba's brilliance owes much to its rich multicultural history. Its most important edifices are emblematic of the cross-fertilization of Islamic, Christian and Jewish cultures. In the 10th century, Córdoba was the spiritual and scientific centre of the Western World, due to its policy of religious tolerance *(see p42)*. After the *reconquista*, many non-Christian thinkers were banished and the city fell into decline.

8 Puente Romano

Crossing Río Guadalquivir, this bridge **(left)**, has Roman foundations. A statue in the middle honours Archangel Raphael, said to have saved the city from the plague.

9 Museo de Bellas Artes

A former 16th-century charity hospital is now the city's main art museum. It has a collection of works by local painters and sculptors, as well as paintings and drawings by masters such as Goya, Ribera, Murillo Valdés Leal and Zurbarán.

6 Museo Torre de la Calahorra

Part of a Moorish castle that controlled access to the city, the tower now houses the Roger Garaudy Three Cultures Museum, which explains how all religions lived side by side in medieval Córdoba and houses exhibits from the time **(right)**. There are great views of the city from the tower.

10 Alcázar de los Reyes Cristianos

This fortified palace, built in 1328, was used by the Inquisition (1500s–1820) and as a prison (until the 1950s). Today it is tranquil, with gardens, water terraces and fountains **(left)**. Also visit the Baños del Alcázar Califal, the Arab baths, which are adjacent.

🔟 ⭐ La Mezquita, Córdoba

Although it has officially been a Christian site for almost nine centuries, La Mezquita's identity as a mosque is inescapable – notwithstanding the cathedral insensitively placed in its centre like a huge spider in its web. As with the Alhambra, Emperor Carlos V can be blamed for this aesthetic transgression. Overriding the wishes of Córdoba's mayor, Carlos authorized the cathedral's construction in the 16th century, although he deeply regretted his decision when he saw the completed travesty.

① The Caliphal Style

The mosque was begun by Caliph Abd el-Rahman I in AD 786. La Mezquita constitutes the beginning of the Caliphal architectural style, combining Roman, Gothic, Byzantine, Syrian and Persian elements.

② Puerta del Perdón

Originally the mosque had many entrances, designed to let in light. The Gate of Forgiveness (1377) is now the only one open to all **(above)**.

③ Torre del Alminar

A minaret once stood where the belfry now is **(right)**. Built in 957, it was enveloped in this Baroque bell tower.

④ Interior

The plan of the interior **(above)** is that of a so-called "forest" mosque, with the rows and rows of variegated columns (856 remaining) and arches designed to resemble palm trees. Unlike Christian churches, based on earlier Roman basilicas with their focus on the central enthroned "judge", the Islamic aim is to induce a meditative state for prayer.

5 Patio de los Naranjos

The delightful Courtyard of the Orange Trees would have been used by worshippers to perform ritual ablutions before they went to prayer.

6 Recycled Columns

Great ingenuity was required to achieve the rhythmic uniformity inside, since most of the columns used in construction were recycled from Roman, Visigothic and other sources. They were a hotchpotch of varying sizes, so the longer ones had to be sunk into the floor. To reach the desired height, a second tier was then added.

7 Capilla de Villaviciosa and Capilla Real

One of the more grand Christian additions, the Villaviciosa Chapel **(above)**, built in 1377, has exuberant Mudéjar arches. Next to it, the Royal Chapel has stucco work and *azulejos* (tiles).

A SPIRITUAL SITE

This magnificent edifice was not the first religious structure to be built on this spot. The Caliph bought the land from the Christians, who had built the Visigothic Cathedral of St Vincent here. In its last years, that building had been divided by a partition, so that it could serve the needs of both Christian and Muslim communities. The Visigothic structure, in its turn, had been constructed on top of a Roman temple, and its columns are still visible in La Mezquita.

Mihrab 8

Dating from the 10th century, this is the jewel of the mosque. An octagonal chamber set into the wall, it was to be the sacred focal point of prayer, directed towards Mecca. No amount of ornamentation was spared. Emperor Nicephorus III sent artisans from Constantinople to create some of the finest Byzantine mosaics in existence **(right)**.

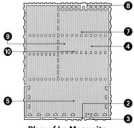

9 Cathedral

In 1523, some 60 of the 1,013 columns were removed from the mosque to make way for the cathedral.

10 Choir Stalls

The Baroque choir stalls date from 1758, and the exquisite carved mahogany depicts Biblical scenes.

NEED TO KNOW

MAP D3 ■ C/del Cardenal Herrero 1, Córdoba ■ 957 47 05 12 ■ www. mezquita-catedraldecordoba.org

Open Mar–Oct: 10am–7pm Mon–Sat, 8:30–11:30am & 3–7pm Sun & hols; Nov–Feb: 8:30am–6pm Mon–Sat, 8:30–11:30am & 3–6pm Sun & hols

Adm adults €8; children aged 10– 14 €4; under 10s free; 8:30–9:30am Mon–Sat free entry (no groups)

■ Last admission is 30 minutes before closing, but try to allow at least an hour to do the site justice.

■ El Caballo Rojo *(C/Cardenal Herrero 28; 957 47 53 75)*, located across from the Puerta del Perdón, is a local favourite serving dishes inspired by the Moors. The terrace offers views of the mosque.

Plan of La Mezquita

🔟 ⭐ Cádiz

The gorgeous city of Cádiz inspired the poet Lord Byron to praise its heavenly blue setting. Nowadays it is one of Andalucía's under-visited treasures. According to ancient chronicles, the city was founded by the Phoenicians as Gadir ("Fortress") in 1104 BC, giving it a good claim to being Europe's oldest. Under the Romans it became Gades and was notable as the city where Julius Caesar held his first public office.

Map of Cádiz

3 Barrio del Pópulo

The Barrio del Pópulo is the medieval heart of the city, which still retains its three 13th-century gates. The main entrance of the surviving 18th-century city wall, the Puerta de Tierra (left), marks the boundary between the old city and the modern part of Cádiz.

1 Iglesia de Santa Cruz and Teatro Romano

In the midst of the Barrio del Pópulo are ruins of a Roman theatre and church dating from 1260.

2 Hospital de Mujeres

This Baroque former hospital's main attraction is El Greco's *Extasis de San Francisco*.

4 Plaza de las Flores

Also known as the Plaza de Topete, this square (right) was the sight of a Phoenician temple.

5 Torre Tavira

The camera obscura in this tower, the city's highest at 46 m (150 ft), offers great views (above).

6 Oratorio de la Santa Cueva

This Neo-Classical chapel has an upper church with Ionic columns. Three frescoes by Goya depict miraculous moments from the life of Christ.

7 Catedral Nueva

The "New Cathedral" **(above)** was begun in 1722. The bell tower, or Torre de Poniente (western tower), offers superb views of the city below.

8 Museo de Cádiz

Archaeological finds and Baroque paintings are the museum's forte. Exhibits include Roman shipwreck finds and a pair of 5th-century BC Phoenician sarcophagi, showing Greek and Egyptian influences.

10 Museo de las Cortes de Cádiz

A mural in this museum eulogizes Cádiz as the birthplace of liberalism. On 29 March 1812, Spain's first liberal constitution was drawn up here; it played a huge role in shaping modern European politics.

9 Plaza San Juan de Dios

On the edge of the Barrio del Pópulo is this 16th-century, palm-fringed plaza **(below)**. Facing the port, it forms the hub of city life *(see p58)*.

LOS CARNAVALES

The vibrant Carnaval celebrations in this port town are the most exhilarating in all of Spain *(see p80)*. In fact, so dear is this annual blow-out to *gaditanos* (as the locals call themselves) that it was the only such event in the country that Franco's forces failed to suppress during the decades of dictatorship. The festival's various traditions date back to the 15th century, when the town had a Genoese enclave, though some claim there is also a strong Cuban influence.

NEED TO KNOW

MAP B5

Catedral Nueva & Torre de Poniente: 956 28 61 54; open 10am–3pm Tue–Thu, 10am–7pm Fri & Sat, 2–6:30pm Sun; adm €6 (includes the cathedral and the tower)

Torre Tavira: C/Marqués del Real Tesoro 10; 956 21 29 10; open 10am–6pm daily (May–Sep: to 8pm); adm €7

Hospital de Mujeres: C/Hospital de Mujeres 26; 956 80 70 18; open summer: 8am–1:30pm Mon–Fri; winter: 10am–1:30pm & 5:30–8pm Mon–Fri

Museo de Cádiz: Plaza Mina; 856 10 50 23; open mid-Jun–mid-Sep: 9am–3pm Tue–Sun & hols; mid-Sep–mid-Jun: 9am–9pm Tue–Sat (to 3pm Sun & hols); adm €1.50 (free for EU members)

■ Book hotels up to a year ahead for Carnaval.

TOP 10 ⭐ Ronda

This is the most famous of the *pueblos blancos* – a scattering of evocative hamlets that reveal their Moorish roots between Málaga, Algeciras and Seville. Ronda is the only town in the wildly mountainous region of the Serranía de Ronda. Located just half an hour's drive from the Costa del Sol, Ronda has managed to retain its timelessness and charm, no matter how busy it gets. Its natural setting is so spectacular that the views alone make it a must-see experience.

① El Tajo and Puente Nuevo

Ronda perches upon a sheer outcrop that is split by a precipitous cleft, El Tajo, 100 m (330 ft) deep **(right)**. The spectacular 18th-century Puente Nuevo bridge links the old city, La Ciudad, with the new.

② Casa del Rey Moro

A visit to the gardens of this 18th-century mansion, built on the foundations of a Moorish palace, will provide superb views.

④ Palacio del Marqués de Salvatierra

The carved stone portal outside this private 18th-century mansion features four squat figures that may represent South American Indians.

③ Baños Árabes

These wonderfully preserved Moorish baths **(above)** date from the 1200s or early 1300s. The multiple barrel vaulting pierced with star-shaped lunettes is typical of such structures, but the octagonal brick columns supporting horseshoe arches are highly original.

NEED TO KNOW

MAP D5

Casa del Rey Moro: C/Cuesta de Santo Domingo 9; open May–Sep: 10am–9:30pm daily (gardens only); adm €7; www.casadelreymoro.org

Baños Árabes: Barrio de Padre Jesús; 656 95 09 37; open 10am–6pm Tue (to 7pm Wed & Thu, to 8pm Fri); 10am–2pm & 3–8pm Sat; 10am–3pm Sun, Mon & hols; adm €3.50

Palacio de Mondragón: 952 87 08 18; opening hours same as Baños Árabes; adm €4

Plaza de Toros: C/Virgen de la Paz 15; 952 87 41 32; adm €8; www.rmcr.org

Museo Lara Coleccionismo: C/Armiñán 29; 952 87 12 63; open Jun–Oct: 11am–8pm daily; Nov–May: 11am–7pm daily; adm €4; www.museolara.org

Iglesia de Santa María la Mayor: Plaza Duquesa de Parcent; 952 87 40 48; open 10:30am–2pm Mon & Wed–Sat; adm €4.50

Previous pages *The Alhambra with a backdrop of the Sierra Nevada*

6 Palacio de Mondragón

One of Ronda's most beautiful palaces dates from 1314. Some of the original mosaic work, a magnificent Mudéjar ceiling and shady inner courtyards **(left)** can still be seen. Part of the palace is now the city's archaeological museum.

THE ORIGINS OF BULLFIGHTING

The creation here of the Real Maestranza de Caballería (Royal Academy of Knights) in 1572 set the stage for the birth of bullfighting. The Maestranza trained Spain's aristocracy to ride and students on horseback would challenge wild bulls. Legend tells that when one rider fell from his horse and was attacked by a bull, a bystander distracted the animal by waving his hat. The man's grandson, Pedro Romero (1749–1839), perfected the art.

Map of Ronda

5 Puente Viejo and Puente de San Miguel

The Puente Viejo (Old Bridge) dates from 1616 and may be a rebuilding of a Roman span across the gorge, though it is believed by some that its pedigree is Moorish, like the Puente de San Miguel.

7 Minarete de San Sebastián

This 14th-century tower is all that remains of a Nasrid mosque and the church of San Sebastián that was built on top of it.

8 Plaza de Toros

Inaugurated in 1785, Ronda's bullring **(left)** was constructed in limestone in an elegant double-tiered sweep; it is the widest in the world and one of the oldest in Spain. Ronda is the birthplace and spiritual home of Spanish bullfighting, and houses a museum – the Museo Taurino – dedicated to the tradition.

9 Museo Lara Coleccionismo

With over 2,000 works, this museum holds the largest private collection in Spain. Objects include cultural artifacts, antique clocks, weapons and scientific instruments.

10 Iglesia de Santa María la Mayor

Much of this church includes a 13th-century mosque, notably the base of the Mudéjar belfry.

⭐ The Costa del Sol

The former fishing villages of the "Sun Coast" welcome millions of international visitors each year – not counting the estimated 300,000 expats who call the coast home. The winning formula is 320 sunny days a year, warm waters and beaches, a good selection of museums, and good-value entertainment options. Heavy on neon and tower blocks, most of what's here has little to do with local culture, but what is exuberantly Andalucían is the verve with which visitors enjoy themselves in the sun – and party well into the night.

① Estepona

The first major resort on this coast is an excellent quieter choice, with 19 km (12 miles) of beach. In the *casco antiguo* (old town), Plaza Las Flores retains considerable charm.

Marbella ②

The 15th-century Plaza de los Naranjos is the heart of old town Marbella *(see p65)*, Spain's most expensive resort. Nearby Puerto Banús is the town's glittering marina **(right)**, where you can admire the fabulous yachts and glimpse luxurious lifestyles.

⑤ Mijas

Visit this beautiful little village nestled in the mountains **(left)** for views of the coast, as well as the maze of old Moorish streets filled with charming shops in its tiny squares.

③ Fuengirola

This large resort is the most family-orientated, with a good beach and a seafront promenade. There is a restored 10th-century Moorish castle.

Benalmádena ④

This resort comes in three parts: the old town inland; the beach and port area **(right)**; and Arroyo de la Miel, a lively suburb.

6 Torremolinos

Torre de los Molinos (Tower of the Windmills) refers to a Moorish watchtower that was once sur-rounded by 19 flourmills. The ancient Torre Vigia is still here, but today it is a hotspot for family vacations. It also has the largest LGBTQ+ scene in the region.

7 Málaga

Andalucía's second largest city **(above)** has invested €100m in the arts in the last ten years and has outposts of Paris's Pompidou Centre and the State Russian Museum – part of a "mile of art". The redeveloped waterfront has given Málaga *(see p104)* dozens of new dining options.

8 Torre del Mar

Favoured by Spanish families, this resort is less tawdry than others to the west. It has a wide sandy beach backed by a tree-lined promenade *(see p65)*.

FRANCO'S DREAM

It was General Franco, Spain's dictator until 1975, who had the idea of transforming the impoverished fishing villages into the "Florida of Europe". He enacted his plan in the 1960s with money loaned by the US, in return for the right to build nuclear bases on Spanish soil. The jet-set glamour and cheap package deals were a runaway success and by the 1970s the area was an aesthetic and environmental disaster. Since the 1980s, steps have been taken to clean it up.

9 Vélez-Málaga

This market town has beautiful Mudéjar features and a lively annual flamenco guitar competition every July.

10 Nerja

The white-washed town of Nerja **(above)** sits on attractive, verdant cliffs with quiet pebble beach coves below *(see p65)*.

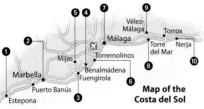

Map of the Costa del Sol

Estepona · Marbella · Puerto Banús · Mijas · Benalmádena · Fuengirola · Torremolinos · Málaga · Vélez-Málaga · Torrox · Torre del Mar · Nerja

---

NEED TO KNOW

MAP D5–E5

Estepona: Tourist office, Plaza de las Flores; 952 80 20 02

Marbella: Tourist office, Glorieta de la Fontanilla; 952 76 87 60

Fuengirola: Tourist office, Paseo Jesús Santos Rein 6; 952 46 74 57

Benalmádena: Tourist office, Avda Antonio Machado 10; 952 44 24 94

Mijas: Tourist office, Plaza Virgen de la Peña 2; 952 58 90 34

Torremolinos: Tourist office, Paseo Marítimo de La Carihuela; 608 20 88 71

Málaga: Tourist office, Plaza de la Marina 11; 952 92 60 20

Nerja: Tourist office, C/Carmen 1; 952 52 15 31

⭐ Baeza and Úbeda

These two Jaén Province towns, only 9 km (5.5 miles) apart, are like matching jewel boxes overflowing with Renaissance architectural treasure, and so were awarded the title of UNESCO World Heritage Sites in 2003. Of the two, quiet Baeza has managed to stay almost completely out of the modern age, while Úbeda is now a thriving town with many seasonal attractions. Nevertheless, its stunning historic district is, if anything, the more spectacular.

Plaza del Pópulo, Baeza ①

The town's most charming area, the Plaza del Pópulo, is in the midst of Renaissance edifices. It is also called the Square of the Lions, after its fountain, which has four stone lions and a female figure **(right)**.

② Puerta de Jaén, Baeza

A section of the ancient wall, the Jaén Gate, supports an additional arch with coats-of-arms set above.

③ Plaza Santa María and Catedral, Baeza

Several glorious 16th-century structures, including the cathedral, front this square. One of the many masterpieces by Renaissance architect Andrés de Vandelvira, the cathedral was originally a Gothic church, built over a mosque in the 13th century.

④ Paseo de la Constitución, Baeza

The 16th-century Alhóndiga (Corn Exchange) has elegant three-tiered arches, while the Torre de los Aliatares is a remnant of the old wall *(see p59)*.

⑤ Palacio de Jabalquinto, Baeza

One of the most unusually decorated palaces, the 15th-century Palacio de Jabalquinto **(left)** is sprinkled with coats of arms and stone studs in Isabelline Plateresque style *(see p47)*.

6 Plaza San Lorenzo, Úbeda

The Casa de las Torres features two vast square towers with gargoyles, while the Church of San Lorenzo rests on the parapet of the old wall.

Plaza de San 7 Pedro, Úbeda

Visit the patio of the Real Monasterio de Santa Clara, the town's oldest church **(right)**, where the nuns will sell you their distinctly Arabic *dulces* (sweetcakes). The Palacio de la Rambla is another Vandelvira creation, now home to a luxury hotel *(see p145)*.

ARCHITECTURE OF THE SPANISH RENAISSANCE

Spanish Renaissance architecture divides into three periods: Plateresque, Classical High Renaissance and Herrerean. The first refers to the carved detailing on silverwork (*platero* means silversmith), a carry-over from the late Gothic style popular under Queen Isabel. The High Renaissance style is noted for its symmetry and its Greco-Roman imagery. Herrerean works are very sober, practically devoid of decoration.

10 Plaza de Vázquez de Molina, Úbeda

Notable on this square is the Capilla del Salvador **(below)**. The Plateresque main front marks a high point in the Spanish Renaissance *(see p45)*.

8 The Pottery Quarter, Úbeda

Passing through the Puerta del Losal, a splendid 13th-century Mudéjar gate, takes you into the town's age-old pottery quarter *(see p128)*. Here, modern ceramic artists renowned all over Spain and beyond ply their ancient trade **(above)**.

9 Plaza del Primero de Mayo, Úbeda

The variety of riches here includes the Iglesia de San Pablo, displaying an array of styles, the 15th-century Casa Mudéjar – now an archaeological museum – and the 16th-century Ayuntamiento Viejo, with its superb arcades.

NEED TO KNOW

MAP F2

Baeza: Tourist office, Casa del Pópulo, Plaza del Pópulo; 953 77 99 82; open 9am–7:30pm Mon–Fri, 9:30am–3pm Sat, Sun & hols; www.ubedaybaezaturismo.com.

Úbeda: Tourist office, Plaza Andalucía 5; 953 75 01 38; open 9am–3pm Mon–Fri, 9:30am–3pm Sat, Sun & hols; www.turismodeubeda.com

■ In Úbeda, have a drink in the courtyard of the **Parador Condestable Dávalos**, a 16th-century palace located at the town centre *(see p142)*.

■ Baeza's **Restaurante Juanito** *(Avda del Alcalde Puché Pardo 57, 953 74 00 40)* is a good place to try regional food.

■ The Úbeda potters are all located along Calle Valencia; look for the workshops of the premier ceramists, the Tito family.

TOP 10 ⭐ Parque Nacional de Doñana

Established in 1969, the Parque Nacional de Doñana is an important wetland reserve and a prime site for migrating birds. It covers more than 2,470 sq km (954 sq miles) and its wide variety of ecosystems, rare fauna and abundance of bird life are so vital to the overall environmental stability of Western Europe that it is designated a UNESCO Biosphere Reserve. It yields up its natural wonders gradually, but a trip to western Andalucía is not complete without a visit here.

① Setting and History
Located at the estuary of the Guadalquivir River, the area probably owes its present pristine condition to the fact that it was set aside as a hunting preserve for the nobility in the 16th century.

④ Habitats
The park features three distinct kinds of ecosystem: dunes **(left)**, *coto* (pine and cork forests and scrubland) and *marisma* (wetlands), which in turn comprise marshes, salt marshes, lagoons and floodplains.

White storks fly over Doñana's wetlands

② Guided Tours
All-terrain vehicles depart from the Visitor Centres twice daily with itineraries dependent on the time of year. The marshes dry up during the summer months, limiting birdwatching, but this increases the chance of seeing rare mammals.

⑤ Fauna
The endangered pardel lynx **(right)** is the emblem of the park. At least 300,000 birds make their home here, including the flamingo and the purple gallinule. Around 25 pairs of the very rare Iberian eagle also survive here.

③ El Rocío's Romería
This town **(below)** is the focal point of one of Spain's largest festivals, the Romería del Rocío *(see p80)*. The four-day pilgrimage leading up to Whitsun winds its way through the park. Thousands honour the Virgin of El Rocío.

⑥ Visitor Centres
Visitor Centres, such as Centro de Información La Rocina, offer exhibitions as well as planned trails, with rest areas and birdwatching options.

Flora (7)

Umbrella pines and cork-oaks flourish here and both types of tree provide crucial nesting sites for birds. Wild flowers in the dunes and scrubland areas include the bright pink spiny-leafed thrift **(right)**, besom heath, yellow gorse and the bubil lily.

ECOLOGICAL ISSUES

Despite vigilant efforts to protect the park, in 1998 a Río Tinto mining toxic waste storage reservoir burst, dumping pollutants into the Guadiamar River, one of the wetlands' main tributaries. Thankfully, the poisonous wave of acids and heavy metals was stopped just short of the park, but damage was done to its border areas. As a result of this disaster, strict measures are enforced to prevent further pollution.

(10) Bird Shelter

The Centro de Visitantes El Acebuche, the main visitor centre, is set on a lagoon. At the eastern end there is an aviary where rescued birds receive intensive care. It's an opportunity for visitors to view some unusual species.

(8) El Palacio de Acebrón

This Neo-Classical style hunting lodge, built in 1961, has an exhibition on the history and ethnography of the region, and offers good views above. It is a starting point for a 12-km (8-mile) woodland trail nearby.

(9) Huts

Dating from the 18th century, these traditional huts **(right)** are found in the *pinares* (pine forests). Sometimes clustered into small villages, the uninhabited structures are made of pine frames covered with local thatch.

NEED TO KNOW

MAP B4 ■ For 4x4 guided tours 959 44 24 74

Doñana Reservas: 959 44 24 74; www.donanareservas.com; open two tours daily, hours vary; tours adults €30, under-10s €15

El Rocío Turismo: C/Muñoz Pavón; 959 02 66 02

Centro de Visitantes El Acebuche: Ctra A483, 12 km (7 miles) from Matalascañas; 959 43 96 29

Centro de Información La Rocina: Ctra A483, 27 km (17 miles) from El Rocio; 959 43 95 69; open 9am–3pm & 4–9pm daily (mid-Jun–mid-Sep: to 3pm Sun)

■ The main visitor centre has a snack bar.

■ Bring binoculars, mosquito repellent, sunscreen and walking shoes – watch out for quicksand.

■ If you join in the Romería del Rocío, you will need a sleeping bag and food.

🔟 ⭐ The Sierra Nevada

The Sierra Nevada ("Snowy Mountains") include Spain's tallest peaks and are Europe's second-highest mountain range after the Alps. Until the 20th century, their only regular visitors were the so-called *neveros* (icemen), who brought back blocks of ice to sell in nearby Granada, and for years the only part the mountains played in a tour of the region was as the glistening backdrop to the Alhambra. They have now become popular in their own right – for trekking, skiing and exploring the remarkable collection of villages on their southern slopes, Las Alpujarras. The area was made a national park in 1999.

① Setting
Spain's highest peak, the Mulhacén (3,482 m/11,425 ft), is at the western end of the range **(right)**. To the south are fertile valleys.

② Flora and Fauna
Snowcapped most of the year, these heights are still rich in wildflowers. Some 60 varieties are unique here, such as a giant honeysuckle. Fauna include the ibex and the golden eagle.

③ Puerto del Suspiro del Moro
Heading south from Granada on the N323, you'll come to the spot known as the "Pass of the Moor's Sigh". Here, the bereft Boabdil (the last Moorish ruler in Spain), expelled by the Christians, is said to have looked back on his beloved city for the last time.

④ Barranco de Poqueira
This vast and gorgeous ravine is home to a stunning collection of tiny villages. Much loved by visitors seeking tranquillity, the remote site even has its own Tibetan monastery, founded in 1982. The ravine is an excellent place for easy day walks, and each town offers traditional local crafts.

⑤ Las Alpujarras
The southern side of the Sierra Nevada is a dramatic zone, home to a stunning series of white villages **(left)**. The architecture here is pure Moorish, almost identical to that found in the Rif Mountains of Morocco. Houses are flat-roofed, clustered together and joined by little bridges.

8 Skiing

The main ski resort, Sol y Nieve (which means "sun and snow"), is Europe's most southerly, and in operation from December to April or even May. The pistes and facilities **(left)** are good enough to have hosted the world Alpine skiing championships.

9 Valle de Lecrín

This bucolic valley is filled with almond, olive and citrus groves – the almond blossom is stunning in late winter.

10 Hiking

There is a paved road over the top of the range but the uppermost reaches have been closed to cars since the national park was established in January 1999. In summer it's a hiker's paradise **(right)** – the second-highest peak, Veleta (3,470 m/11,385 ft), is a relatively easy 5-hour round trip.

BRENAN'S SOUTH FROM GRANADA

In the 1920s, British writer Gerald Brenan, a member of the Bloomsbury set, came to live in the village of Yegen in the eastern Alpujarras. A plaque in the town marks the house he lived in. He noted his experiences in his book *South from Granada*, a wonderful evocation of the place and its people, whose way of life is still largely unchanged. The 2002 Spanish film *Al Sur de Granada*, based on the book, is a delightful dramatization.

6 Órgiva

Made the regional capital in 1839, this town remains the area's largest. It's at its best on Thursday mornings, when everyone comes alive for market day, and you can find traditional local products **(above)**.

7 Lanjarón

Famous since Roman times for its mineral springs, the town is now a modern *balneario* (spa) and marks the beginning of the Alpujarras proper. Below the main street is a Moorish castle with great views over the gorge.

NEED TO KNOW

MAP F4 ■ Parque Nacional de la Sierra Nevada, Ctra A 395 – dirección Pradollano – km 23, 18196 Güéjar Sierra ■ 958 98 02 46

Sierra Nevada Club (skiing): Plaza de Andalucía 4, Monachil; 902 70 80 90; www.sierranevada.es

■ Lovers of *jamón serrano* (mountain ham) must try the delicious snow-cured version from the town of Trevélez.

■ Extra sun protection is vital here. Hikers and trekkers should have good walking shoes, something to wear against the wind and binoculars.

■ Petrol stations are a rarity in Las Alpujarras. Coming from the west, Órgiva is a good place to fill up.

■ Enjoy Sierra Nevada views from Torre de la Vela in the Alhambra *(see pp12–13)*.

The Top 10 of Everything

Patio de las Doncellas (Courtyard of the Maidens), Real Alcázar, Seville

Moments in History

1 Bronze Age Developments

The Iberian (Tartessian) civilization got its strongest start when bronze began to be smelted and worked in Andalucía around 2500 BC. Some early tribes built the oldest megalithic tombs (dolmens) in western Europe.

2 Phoenician and Greek colonies

Attracted by the area's mineral wealth, the Phoenicians founded a trading post in around 1100 BC at what is now Cádiz, while the Greeks established a toehold near Málaga in 636 BC. The two maintained a mercantile rivalry until Carthage, a former Phoenician colony, dominated the region.

3 Roman Spain

The first Roman town in Spain, Itálica (see p97), was established in 206 BC; Rome finally wrested the entire region from the Carthaginians in 201 BC. Due to abundant local produce, Andalucía became one of the empire's wealthiest outposts.

4 Arab Domination

Some 700 years later, when the Roman Empire began to come apart, tribes from northern Europe laid claim to the peninsula. The Vandals and then the Visigoths ruled for some three centuries. Political instability and conflict over rightful succession in AD 710 led to the enlistment of Muslim armies from North Africa. The Moors saw their chance and within 10 years they had taken over.

5 Moorish Sophistication

The Moors were custodians of the best features of Roman civilization: religious tolerance, scientific and philosophical thought, engineering and art (see pp48–9). In the 10th century, Córdoba became the largest and wealthiest city in Europe under the Caliphate of Abd ar-Rahman III.

Moorish La Mezquita, Córdoba

6 Reconquista

The dissolution of the Caliphate in 1031 marked the beginning of the end for Moorish Spain. Some 30 *taifas* (principalities), jostling for political hegemony, proved no contest for the Christians. The eight-month siege and *reconquista* of Granada in 1492 was the most poignant loss.

Itálica's Roman amphitheatre

Columbus sets sail for the Americas

7 Expedition to America
Christopher Columbus set sail for the Americas in 1492. The result was a wealth of gold and silver from the new empire for Spain.

8 Imperial Collapse
Colonial losses that began in 1713 following the War of Spanish Succession reached their *dénouement* with Spain's defeat in the Spanish-American War of 1898. In Andalucía this long decline meant grinding poverty and mass emigration.

9 Franco and the Civil War
The Spanish Civil War (1936–9) was ignited by a military coup led by General Francisco Franco. On 18 July 1936 the war began when Nationalists took Cádiz, Seville and Granada. Then followed the grim years (1939–75) of Franco's dictatorship.

General Francisco Franco

10 Seville Expo '92
The World Fair in 1992 celebrated the quincentenary of Columbus's seafaring expedition to the Americas. It brought 42.5 million visitors and a sprucing up of Seville, but left bankruptcy in its wake. After more than a decade of difficulties, numerous efforts to improve the city have resulted in a boom in tourism once again.

TOP 10 HISTORIC ANDALUCÍAN FIGURES

1 Melkarth
The Phoenician's name for Hercules, whom legend claims to have founded Andalucía.

2 Trajan
One of the greatest Roman emperors (AD 98–117) was a native of Itálica.

3 Hadrian
Emperor Trajan's successor (AD 117–38) was a great builder, emphasizing Rome's Classical Greek roots.

4 Abd ar-Rahman III
The Syrian Emir (AD 912–61) established al-Andalus, an autonomous caliphate.

5 Isabel and Fernando
Isabel of Castilla and Fernando of Aragón (1479–1516) were dubbed "The Catholic Monarchs".

6 Boabdil
The final Moorish ruler (r.1482–92) lost Granada to the Catholic Monarchs.

7 Emperor Carlos V
His reign (1516–56) left Spain nearly bankrupt, but with cultural legacies such as his palace in Granada (see p12).

8 Felipe V
Felipe V (1700–46) had his court in Seville until a claim to the throne by Archduke Charles of Austria led to the War of Spanish Succession.

9 Felipe González
A native of Seville, this left-wing leader (1982–96) brought rapid change to Spain and to Andalucía.

10 María Soledad Becerril Bustamante
Bustamante (b 1944) became the first woman elected to serve as the Commissioner of the State in 2012.

Boabdil at the Alhambra, 1492

TOP10 Places of Worship

1 Mosque, Almonaster la Real

MAP B3 ▪ Ayuntamiento ▪ 959 14 30 03 ▪ Open 9am–8:30pm daily

Virtually unchanged for 1,000 years, this is one of Andalucía's few surviving rural mosques (see p56). Inside, it has the oldest *mihrab* (Mecca-facing prayer niche) in Spain.

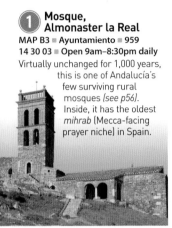

Mosque, Almonaster la Real

2 La Colegiata de la Asunción, Osuna

Set on a hilltop, this massive Spanish Renaissance church dominates the town (see p96). Its austere façade is relieved by a fine Plateresque portal, the Puerta del Sol. The many treasures inside include five masterpieces by José de Ribera, a Crucifixion sculpture by Juan de Mesa, beautiful Renaissance ornamentation and a wonderful Baroque altarpiece.

3 Oratorio de San Felipe Neri, Cádiz

MAP B5 ▪ Plaza San Felipe Neri ▪ 662 64 22 33 ▪ Open 10:30am–2pm & 4:30–8pm Tue–Fri, 10:30am–2pm Sat, 10am–1pm Sun ▪ Adm

As the commemorative plaques adorning the façade reveal, this fine Baroque church is one of the most significant buildings in Spain. On 29 March 1812, Spanish patriots defied a Napoleonic blockade and met here to compose the country's first constitution. The document's liberal ideas have inspired fledgling democracies ever since.

4 Monasterio de San Jerónimo, Granada

MAP F4 ▪ C/Rector López Argueta 9 ▪ 958 27 93 37 ▪ Open 10am–1:30pm & 4–7:30pm daily ▪ Adm

This Renaissance magnum opus is largely the creation of Diego de Siloé, one of the great masters of the age. The façade's upper window is flanked by sinuous mythological animals and medallions. The altar is complex and monumental, consisting of row upon row of high reliefs framed by columns.

Monasterio de San Jerónimo, Granada

Cristo, is brought out for the faithful to kiss. This is believed to be the cloth that St Veronica used to wipe Christ's face on the road to Calvary. A miraculous impression of the holy face is said to have been left upon it.

8 Seville Cathedral

The vast cathedral is Seville's most striking architectural masterpiece. It has soaring columns, precious artworks and the world's largest altarpiece *(see pp18–19)*.

9 Capilla Real and Catedral, Granada

Although not without aesthetic merit, these two structures *(see pp116–7)* are more about Christian triumph and royal ego than they are about spirituality. At the Royal Chapel's sarcophagi, note how Queen Isabel's head presses more deeply into her marble pillow than that of King Fernando – said to indicate greater intelligence. In the cathedral is the equestrian statue *El Matamoros* ("The Killer of Moors") by Alonso de Mena.

Moorish arches inside La Mezquita

5 La Mezquita, Córdoba

This spectacular mosque *(see pp24–5)* may have been savagely reconsecrated but visitors can still see its Byzantine mosaics and other exquisite marvels.

6 Iglesia de San Mateo, Lucena

MAP E3 ■ Open 7:30am–1:30pm & 6:30–9pm daily

It's intriguing to find one of the masterpieces of Andalucían Rococo design in this industrial town – Lucena was famous for having been a virtually independent Jewish enclave during Moorish rule. The gem of this 15th-century church is its 18th-century octagonal sacristy and the decorative dome.

7 Catedral de Jaén

The cathedral was primarily the work of famed Renaissance architect Andrés de Vandelvira *(see p127)*, although the west façade was designed later, decorated with Baroque sculptures by Pedro Roldán. Each Friday, at 10:30am–noon and 5–6pm, one of Spain's holiest relics, the Reliquía del Santo Rostro de

Granada cathedral's lavish interior

10 Çapilla del Salvador, Úbeda

Designed by Siloé and Vandelvira, this masterpiece of Andalucían Renaissance was commissioned as a family pantheon and is still privately owned *(see p35)*. The sacristy is the highlight, employing caryatids and atlantes as columns and pilasters. It was once embellished by a Michelangelo sculpture, a sad casualty of the Spanish Civil War.

🔟 Alcázares, Palacios and Castillos

1 Real Alcázar, Seville

This sumptuous palace (see pp20–21) and extensive gardens constitute a world of royal luxury. The architectural styles are a blend of mainly Moorish traditions – note the lavish use of the horseshoe arch, glazed tilework and wood ceilings.

2 Palacio de las Dueñas, Seville

MAP M1 ▪ C/Dueñas 5 ▪ Open 10am–6pm daily (to 8pm in summer) ▪ Adm ▪ www.lasduenas.es

Built between the 15th and 16th centuries, this luxurious palace is the official city residence of the Duke of Alba. In addition to its magnificent architecture, which is a combination of Gothic and Moorish styles, Las Dueñas is also home to a vast collection of art and a beautiful garden.

3 Fortaleza de la Mota, Alcalá la Real

MAP E3

This Moorish castle crowns the hill above the town (see p127). Created by Granada's rulers in the 8th century, it incorporates 12th-century structures and earlier elements, since the town dates from prehistoric times. After the Christian reconquest in 1341 (see p42), additions to the fortress continued till the 16th century. The keep houses a visitor centre.

Fortaleza de la Mota, Alcalá la Real

Decorative tiles, La Casa de Pilatos

4 La Casa de Pilatos, Seville

Few palaces are more opulent than this 16th-century mansion (see p85). Featuring a mix of Mudéjar (Christian-Islamic), flamboyant Gothic and Renaissance styles, it is also adorned with Classical sculptures, including a 5th-century BC Greek Athena and Roman works. A noble residence to this day, the mansion is filled with family portraits and antiques.

5 Palacio del Marqués de la Gomera, Osuna

MAP D4 ▪ C/San Pedro 20 ▪ 954 81 22 23

Now a hotel and restaurant, this 18th-century palace is a striking example of the Spanish Baroque style. The family escutcheon crowns the carved stone doorway.

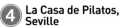

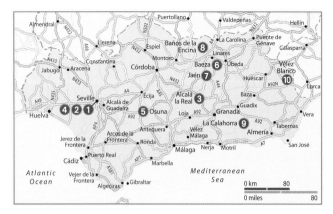

horseshoe-arched main gate bears an inscription dating its construction to AD 967. Some 14 square towers provide vistas far and wide.

Palacio de Jabalquinto, Baeza

6 Palacio de Jabalquinto, Baeza

The façade of this 15th-century palace *(see p34)* defies categorization, while the gallery and the patio evoke the Renaissance style.

7 Castillo de Santa Catalina, Jaén

MAP F3 ■ 953 12 07 33 ■ Open Jul–Sep: 10am–2pm & 5–9pm Mon–Sat; Oct–Jun: 10am–6pm Mon–Sat; Jan–Dec: 10am–3pm Sun ■ Adm (free entry 5–9pm Wed)

Restored by the Christians, this 13th-century castle towers above the town and affords spectacular views.

8 Castillo de Burgalimar, Baños de la Encina

MAP F2 ■ Cerro del Cueto, Plaza de Santa María 1 ■ 953 61 33 38 (visit by appt) ■ Opening hours vary, check website for details ■ Adm ■ www.bdelaencinaturismo.com

This Moorish castle is one of the best-preserved in Andalucía. Its

9 Castillo de La Calahorra

MAP F4 ■ 958 67 70 98 ■ Open 10am–1pm & 4–6pm Wed ■ Adm

One of the few castles built after the Christian reconquest, this was also one of the first in Spain to be built in Italian Renaissance style. Despite its intimidating setting and exterior, the inner courtyard is exquisite.

Castillo de Vélez Blanco

10 Castillo de Vélez Blanco

MAP H3 ■ 607 41 50 55 ■ Open 10am–2pm & 4–6pm Wed–Sun (May–Sep: 5–8pm)

This has the grace of a fairy-tale castle. Unfortunately, it was gutted in the early 1900s, but a reconstruction of one of the patios gives you some idea of its original splendour.

🔟 Aspects of Moorish Heritage

1 Religious Tolerance
Although non-Muslims had to pay a special tax and wear distinctive clothing, Moorish policies towards Jews and Catholics were generally easy-going. There was greater repression after the fundamentalist Almohads came into power in the 12th century, but on the whole, the various faiths were well integrated for many centuries.

Moses Maimonides

2 Music
The Moors can be credited with the early development of the guitar *(see pp50–51)*, which they adapted from the four-stringed lute. The Middle Eastern musical forms they imported were also to have an effect later on flamenco.

3 Gardens
Moorish gardens make prominent use of water, which is especially important to people from a perpetually arid land. It was sprayed, channelled, made to gurgle and fall, to please the ear and eye. Jasmine, honeysuckle and roses are just a few of the many flowers the Moors brought to the region.

4 Philosophy
Great minds of Andalucía, such as the Moor Averroës and the Jew Maimonides, were considered among the most advanced thinkers of their age. The former almost single-handedly preserved the writings of Aristotle, while the latter's writings sought to reconcile Biblical faith and reason.

5 Crafts
The hand-tooled leather of Córdoba, silver and gold filigree jewellery, pottery, silk and embroidered goods and inlaid creations all owe their existence to the Moors' 800-year rule.

6 Agriculture
Inheriting many of their techniques from the Romans, the Moors were masters of agricultural engineering. Their system consisted of three main elements: the aqueduct, the waterwheel and the irrigation channel. Thereby, they were able to cultivate vast areas, often building ingenious terracing on slopes. They also introduced many crops, including bitter oranges, lemons, almonds, rice, cotton, asparagus and mulberry trees (to feed silk-worms).

The lush Partal gardens with their watercourses at the Alhambra

Moorish calligraphy, the Alhambra

7 Art and Architecture

Moorish art and architecture is full of signs and symbols and often incorporates calligraphy into its designs, quoting the Koran or poetry. The point was to inspire viewers to reflect upon the unity of all things under Allah, whose power and perfection could never be equalled by the achievements of man.

8 Science

Moorish scientists excelled in the fields of metallurgy, zoology, botany, medicine and mathematics. Moorish inventors also developed revolutionary devices such as the astrolabe and the quadrant, both used for navigation. Arabic numerals were introduced by them, as well as algebra (from *al-jebr*, meaning "reuniting broken parts") and the algorithm.

A brass astrolabe

9 Food

The simple fare that had existed prior to the Moorish incursion – centred around olives, wheat and grapes – gave way to flavours such as almonds, saffron, nutmeg, pepper and other spices.

10 Language

Modern Spanish language is full of everyday terms that come from Moorish heritage – the word for "left" *(izquierda)* is almost pure Arabic, as is any word beginning with the prefix *al-* (the).

TOP 10 MOORISH SITES

1 Moorish Granada
The spectacular Alhambra palace is the gem of Spain's Moorish heritage, while the adjacent Generalife offers sumptuous gardens (see pp12–15).

2 Vejer de la Frontera
The most Moorish of the *pueblos blancos (see p57)*.

3 La Mezquita, Córdoba
This vast mosque (see pp24–5) marked the beginning of the Arab-Hispanic style known as Caliphal.

4 Baños Árabes, Ronda
These Moorish baths (see p30) feature Arabic-style horseshoe arches.

5 Medina Azahara, Córdoba
Sadly now in ruins, this once splendid palace (see p125) epitomized the city's glory in the 10th century.

6 Almonaster la Real
This village's mosque is one of Andalucía's finest, with great views from the minaret (see p98).

7 Alcazaba, Almería
One of the largest surviving Moorish fortresses in the region (see p119).

8 Alcazaba, Málaga
Remains of the original Moorish walls and tower can still be seen (see p104).

9 Las Alpujarras
The villages on the slopes of the Sierra Nevada (see pp38–9) retain distinctive Moorish architecture.

10 Real Alcázar, Seville
The front towers and gateway of Seville's royal palace (see pp20–21) retain their Moorish origins.

Moorish tiling, Real Alcázar

🔟 Aspects of Gypsy Culture

Dancers performing flamenco, which is closely associated with Andalucía

1 Origins

Gypsies (Roma) arrived in Eastern Europe in the 14th century and in Andalucía in the 15th century. Linguistic research shows that their language, Romany, was related to ancient dialects from northern India. Why they left India is unclear, but it was possibly to escape conflict with invading Muslim groups.

2 Cave-dwellings

In remote hills and mountains, gypsies escaped Christian persecution by turning caves into homes. Although flooding and other natural mishaps have crushed these communities and forced many out, some gypsies return to their former dwellings to perform lively flamenco shows for visitors.

Inside a cave-dwelling

3 Dance

Similarities between Middle Eastern and North African dance forms and flamenco are obvious. But using the feet to create rapid staccato rhythms, combined with expressive arm and hand gestures, clearly resembles traditional kathak dancing from northern India, revealing flamenco's true roots.

4 Song

Despite some persecution in Andalucía, many gypsies stayed, and developed a unique strain of music, flamenco, which draws on Arabic, Jewish and Byzantine sources, as well as their own Indian traditions. Similar to the American Blues, it is the raucous, rhythmic music of the dispossessed and marginalized, full of pathos and catharsis. The word flamenco is probably a corruption of the Arabic *felag mengu* (fugitive peasant).

5 Guitar

The six-stringed flamenco guitar can be traced back to the medieval lute. It is lighter, shallower and less resonant than a classical guitar, and can be played extremely fast. A plate below the sound hole is used for tapping out rhythms.

Flamenco Legends

A few people who advanced the art include singers El Fillo and La Niña de los Peines; guitarist Paco de Lucía; and dancers La Macarrona and Carmen Amaya.

Sevillanas

This strident dance, with clapping rhythms, has been infused with the flamenco spirit. It is danced with enthusiasm at festivals.

Horses

Andalucían gypsies have a reputation for their ability to train their steeds. To watch a gypsy horseman putting an animal through its paces is to witness an amazing display of communication between man and beast.

Riders at the April Fair, Seville

History

Although Roma have been marginalized throughout their history, they found a more congenial civilization in Andalucía than anywhere else. The culture was decidedly Middle Eastern and not dissimilar to that of their native land. With the Christian reconquest, however, "pagan" Roma were forced into hiding or to continue their wanderings.

Performances

Historically, flamenco is an improvised performance that arises spontaneously from a gathering, but the rule these days tends towards scheduled spectacles. Still, if the mood is right, these events generate a great deal of emotion.

TOP 10 FLAMENCO VENUES

Performers at El Arenal, Seville

1 Tablao El Arenal, Seville
MAP L4 ▪ C/Rodo 7 ▪ www.
tablaoelarenal.com
Come for the first-class performances.

2 Peña La Bulería, Jerez
MAP B5 ▪ C/Empedrada 20 ▪ 856
05 37 72
Club named after a fast flamenco style that originated in Jerez.

3 Museo de Baile Flamenco
MAP B5 ▪ www.museodelbaile
flamenco.com
Shows staged in an intimate setting.

4 Juan Villar, Cádiz
MAP B5 ▪ Paseo Fernando Quiñones
▪ 956 22 52 90 ▪ Open Tue–Sun
(performances Fri)
A good peña for genuine flamenco.

5 Puro Arte
MAP B5 ▪ Calle Madre de Dios 10,
Jerez de la Frontera ▪ 660 03 04 20
Book ahead for authentic flamenco.

6 Casa de la Memoria, Seville
A museum, gallery and cultural centre with performances (see p91).

7 Tablao Flamenco Cardenal, Córdoba
MAP D3 ▪ C/Buen Pastor 2
▪ www.tablaoflamencocardenal.es
Enjoy authentic flamenco shows.

8 Venta El Gallo, Granada
MAP F4 ▪ Barranco de los Negros 5
▪ www.cuevaventaelgallo.es
Professional performances. Book early.

9 La Peña Platería, Granada
MAP F4 ▪ Placeta de Toqueros 7
▪ www.laplateria.org.es
One of Spain's oldest peñas.

10 La Canastera, Almería
MAP G4 ▪ C/Cordoneros 5 ▪ 662 14
32 31 ▪ Performances 10pm Thu & Sat
Skilled amateurs dance flamenco.

Museums and Galleries

① Museo Arqueológico Antiquarium, Seville

MAP M2 ■ Plaza de la Encarnación ■ 955 47 15 80 ■ Open 10am–8pm Tue–Sat, 10am–2pm Sun & public hols ■ Adm

This subterranean museum, situated below the extraordinary Metropol Parasol structure in Plaza de la Encarnación, showcases the fascinating archaeological remains found in 1973 when the Parasol complex was being built. Extensive Roman ruins date from the Tiberius era onwards (around 30–600 AD) and there is a Moorish house dating back to the 12th–13th century.

② Museo de Bellas Artes, Seville

Housed in an exquisite former convent, this art museum (see p87) is second only to Madrid's famed Prado. Paintings include early works by Velázquez, and important pieces by Zurbarán, Ribera, El Greco, Murillo, Valdés Leal and Vásquez.

Museo de Bellas Artes, Seville

③ Museo Automovilistico y de la Moda, Málaga

Edificio de La Tabacalera, en Avenida Sor Teresa Prat 15 ■ 951 13 70 01 ■ Open 10am–2:30pm & 4–7pm daily ■ Adm ■ www.museoautomovil malaga.com

This museum has an excellent private collection of classic cars, with models from automobile designers like Ettore Bugatti, Giuseppe Figoni, Firestone and Labourdette. There is also a section dedicated to haute couture.

Exhibit at the Museo Automovilistico

④ Museo Picasso, Málaga

This is the world's third-largest museum dedicated to the modern master, and honours Picasso's wish for his native city (see p104) to have a part of his artistic legacy. With over 187 paintings, including some major canvases, the collection here covers eight decades of the artist's career and gives an idea of the breadth and depth of Picasso's work.

⑤ Centre Pompidou, Málaga

MAP S5 ■ Pasaje Doctor Carrillo Casaux ■ 951 92 62 00 ■ Open 9:30am–8pm Wed–Mon ■ www. centrepompidou-malaga.eu

This offshoot of the renowned Parisian art museum has some unusual and thought-provoking pieces and features artists such as Francis Bacon, Frida Kahlo, René Magritte and Pablo Picasso. Exhibitions are divided and displayed as per themes.

Journey Through the Human Body exhibition, Museo Parque de las Ciencias

⑥ Museo Parque de las Ciencias, Granada

This dazzling science park *(see p118)* is home to a range of inter-active exhibitions on such topics as the human body, outer space, the environment and technology.

⑦ Museo Municipal, Antequera

This museum is located in a striking 18th-century ducal palace *(see p104)*, which means that many of the exhibits simply cannot compete with the context. Two that do, however, are the life-size 1st-century AD Roman bronze representing a naked young man, possibly Ganymede, cupbearer to the gods, and a life-like carving of St Francis of Assisi in wood by Pedro de Mena, a 17th-century Andalucían master.

⑧ Museo de Cádiz

A Neo-Classical mansion houses Cádiz's main museum *(see p27)*, a rich mix of archaeological treasures and fine art. The museum features artifacts from the city's ancient cultures, including jewellery, pottery and small bronzes, but most notably a pair of 5th-century BC marble sarcophagi. Among the art are works by Zurbarán, Rubens, Murillo and Cano. An ethnological collection features pieces that high-light aspects of the city's culture.

⑨ Museo Arqueológico, Córdoba

A small 16th-century Renaissance mansion *(see p23)* is home to this excellent collection, highlighting the city's importance in Roman times. In fact, the mansion was built over a Roman structure and there is an ancient patio to prove it. A sculpture of the Persian god Mithras, found at Cabra, is particularly fine. Other parts of the collection focus on Iberian finds and Moorish artifacts.

Patio of the Museo Arqueológico

⑩ Museo Provincial de Jaén

The lower floor contains some truly extraordinary 5th-century BC Iberian stone sculptures. Found near the town of Porcuna, in the western part of the province, they show clear influences from Greek works. Upstairs, the museum *(see p127)* has some fine medieval wood sculpture.

🔟 Art and Cultural Figures

1 Andrés de Vandelvira
Andrés de Vandelvira (1509–75) was the quintessential architect of the Spanish Renaissance in Andalucía. His work spanned the three major phases of the style's predominance, from ornamental Plateresque, to Italianate Classical, to austere Herrerean. He can virtually be given sole credit for the architectural treasures in the town of Úbeda and many important edifices in Baeza *(see pp34–5)*.

2 Francisco de Zurbarán
The great painter (1598–1664) spent most of his life in and around Seville, where his art adorns many churches and museums. His works are noted for their mystical qualities, dramatized by striking *chiaroscuro* (light and shade) effects.

A King of Spain (c. 1645) by Cano

The Apparition of Saint Peter to Saint Peter Nolasco (1629) by Zurbarán

3 Velázquez
Born in Seville, Diego Rodríguez de Silva y Velázquez (1599–1660) left for Madrid in 1623 to become court painter to the king. His was the most remarkable talent of the Golden Age of Spanish painting, taking naturalism and technique to new heights. The works that remain in his home town were mostly religious commissions; his real genius lay in portraits.

Diego Velázquez

4 Alonso Cano
Architect, painter and sculptor, Granada-born Alonso Cano (1601–67) studied art and began his illustrious career in Seville before moving to Madrid, where King Philip IV appointed him as Royal Architect and Painter. He later returned to Granada, where most of his works can be seen today.

5 Murillo
Bartolomé Esteban Murillo (1618–82) was the most successful of the Baroque painters from Seville. He received countless commissions to produce devotional works, notably the many *Immaculate Conceptions* seen in Andalucía.

6 Pedro Roldán
Roldán (1624–99) was one of the chief proponents of the Spanish aspiration to combine painting, sculpture and architecture into unified works of art, such as the altarpiece in Seville's Hospital de la Caridad *(see p88)*.

7 Luisa Roldán

Seville-born Luisa Roldán (1652–1706), also known as La Roldana, was the first documented female sculptor in Spain. After creating wooden sculptures and statues for the Cathedral of Cádiz, she moved to Madrid where she became the Court Sculptor to King Charles II and Philip V.

St. Ginés de la Jara by Roldán

8 Manuel de Falla

Andalucían-born de Falla (1876–1946) was Spain's finest classical composer. One of his major works, *The Three-Cornered Hat*, has its roots deep in flamenco.

9 Picasso

Pablo Picasso (1881–1973) was born in Málaga, although he settled in France in 1909. His native land, with images of the bullfight and later of the horrors of the Franco era, featured in his work throughout his career.

Statue of Picasso, Málaga

10 Federico García Lorca

The Granada-born poet and playwright (1898–1936) was also an artist, musician and theatre director. Due to his sexuality and Socialist views, he was murdered by Franco's Nationalists at the start of the Spanish Civil War. His work shows his love for Andalucían culture.

TOP 10 WORKS INSPIRED BY ANDALUCÍA

1 Lord Byron
The English Romantic poet's fascination with Andalucía is chronicled in his *Don Juan* (1819).

2 Michael Jacobs
Factory of Light (2003) is a vivid, witty and informative account of life in the Andalucían village of Frailes, near Jaén.

3 Washington Irving
The American writer lived in Granada for some time and produced the hit *Tales of the Alhambra* (1832).

4 Chris Stewart
Former Genesis drummer wrote the funny and insightful *Driving Over Lemons*, a memoir about relocating to an Andalucían farmhouse.

5 Serafín Estébanez Calderón
This Málaga-born writer's *Andalusian Scenes* (1847) featured the first literary description of a gypsy festival.

6 Salman Rushdie
The British Indian author's *The Moor's Last Sigh* (1995) was inspired by the exile of Granada's last Moorish king.

7 Manuel Machado
The works of Machado (1874–1947), such as *Cante Jondo*, evoke a poetic passion for Andalucía.

8 Dalí and Buñuel
This Surrealist pair created the avant garde film *Un Chien d'Andalou* in 1928.

9 Ernest Hemingway
For Whom the Bell Tolls (1940) was based on the American writer's Andalucían experiences during Spain's Civil War.

10 Opera
Operas set in Andalucía include *The Marriage of Figaro* (1786, Mozart), *The Barber of Seville* (1816, Rossini) and *Carmen* (1875, Bizet).

Scene from *The Barber of Seville*

🔟 Villages

1 Almonaster la Real

From a distance, this lovely *pueblo blanco* in Huelva Province looks like a sprinkling of snow amid the green of the surrounding forests. The citadel (see p98) features one of the oldest mosques in the region, dating from the 10th century.

Monument on the cliff above Alájar

2 Alájar

Another pretty Huelva Province village (see p98), where the stone houses seem ageless. There are some nice Baroque churches too. More intriguing, however, is the mystical importance of the place, as seen in the hallowed caves and hermitage on the cliff above the town.

3 El Rocío

Deserted for the majority of the year, except for its handful of residents – who still customarily get around on horseback – this town (see p36) overflows with around one million pilgrims during the annual Romería. It's worth a visit at any time to take in its wonderful Wild West-style architecture, as well as to book a tour of the nearby Doñana nature reserve (see pp36–7).

4 Cazorla
MAP G3

Simple whitewashed cubes cluster around a citadel here, while birds of prey overhead remind you that this is the southwestern entrance to the Sierra de Cazorla (see p61). The town's position made it desirable for Moors and Christians, hence the castle in town and the ruined La Iruela, 1 km (0.5 miles) away.

5 Arcos de la Frontera

The historic part of this town (see p106) is from the Cuesta de Belén to the Puerta de Matrera – a zone that has been a beautifully preserved national monument since 1962. Central to the area is the Plaza del Cabildo, with ancient walls in evidence and set about with orange trees. Sadly, the castle below the square is not open to the public, but the terrace of the parador opposite is a fine place for a drink with a view.

reputation. It's a delight to see on the approach and offers fine views once there. The ruined castle, however, stands witness to tougher times. In the 15th century it was attacked continually, sought by both Muslims and Christians for its position guarding the access route to the Serranía de Ronda *(see p68)*.

Narrow street in Vejer de la Frontera

6 Vejer de la Frontera

This inland village *(see p107)* in Cádiz Province probably retains its quintessential Moorishness more than any other town in Andalucía. It stands gleaming white on a hill with a view of the coast, and its warren of maze-like alleys and byways is virtually indistinguishable from any North African town. Before the Spanish Civil War, women here wore a traditional veiled garment like the Muslim *hijab*, called the *cobijado*; now they are only worn during August festival.

7 Iznatoraf
MAP F2

This mountain eyrie of a place opens out onto 360-degree panoramas of the Cazorla highland. The best view is from the mirador above the cliff at the village's northern edge.

8 Zahara de la Sierra
MAP C4

The town's name means "flower" in Arabic and this quiet little hamlet *(see p105)*, scented with orange groves, lives up to its

9 Sabiote
MAP F2

This hamlet is a hidden gem, with medieval walls that are largely intact and one of the most impressive castles in the region. The castle, Moorish in origin, was restored by the famed architect Andrés de Vandelvira, who was born here.

Restored ruins of Sabiote castle

10 Castril
MAP G3

At the foot of an imposing stone outcropping and surrounded by the Parque Natural de la Sierra de Castril, this enchanting town dates back to Roman times. A mountain torrent surges below the idyllic hamlet.

The approach to Zahara de la Sierra

🔟 Paseos, Plazas, Parks and Gardens

1 Alcázar de los Reyes Cristianos, Córdoba

A major delight of Córdoba is the grounds of this fort-cum-palace dating back to the 14th century (see p23). The gardens are lavishly done in Moorish style, indulging in a profusion of colour setting off the sun-bleached stone walls and ancient carvings. Another tourist attraction nearby is Baños del Alcázar Califal, the 10th-century Arab bathhouse that uses the classical order of Roman baths, with cold, warm and hot rooms.

Alcázar de los Reyes Cristianos

2 Plaza San Juan de Dios, Cádiz

This is one of Cádiz's busiest hubs of commercial and social life. Lined with cafés, bars and palm trees, its chief adornment is the monumental Neo-Classical façade of the Ayuntamiento (town hall), along with several handsome towers (see p27). The square opens out onto the port, ensuring a constant stream of pedestrians and opportunities for hours of people-watching.

3 Parque Genovés, Cádiz

MAP B5

Lying along the west side of Cádiz, this swathe of landscaped greenery facing the seafront has paths for strolling along, some civic sculpture and interesting flora, including an ancient dragon tree originally from the Canary Islands. This is one leg of a two-part park, the other half curving around along the northern seafront.

4 Parque Zoológico, Jerez

MAP B5 ▪ C/Madreselva ▪ 956 14 97 85 ▪ Open 10am–6pm Tue–Sun (May–Sep: to 8pm) ▪ Adm ▪ www.zoobotanicojerez.com

Jerez's small zoo, set in botanical gardens, is also an active centre for the rehabilitation of regional endangered species or any injured animals. This is also the only chance you may get to see the elusive and extremely rare Iberian lynx, of which only an estimated 1,000 remain in the wild. A tourist train takes visitors through the park informing them about the flora and fauna.

5 Paseo Alcalde Marqués de Contadero, Seville

This central promenade is one of Seville's loveliest. Stretching along the riverfront, within sight of most of the major monuments, its tree-lined walkways make a pleasant break from the crowded city streets. The *paseo* is also pedestrianised so you don't have to worry about traffic as you stroll (see p89).

Paseo Alcalde Marqués de Contadero, Seville

A pavilion in Parque de María Luisa

6 Jardín Botánico la Concepción, Málaga

MAP E5 ■ Ctra N331 km 166, Málaga ■ 951 92 61 80 ■ Open 9:30am–4:30pm Tue–Sun (Apr–Sep: to 7:30pm) ■ Adm ■ www.laconcepcion.malaga.eu

Just north of Málaga lies this impressive botanical garden, the work of a 19th-century English woman, Amalia Livermore, and her Spanish husband, Jorge Loring Oyarzábal. The garden houses a collection of palms and plants from around the world. The grounds are also embellished with charming touches, such as a domed gazebo decorated with tiles and columns. Visitors can stay in the garden for an hour and a half after the closing time.

Jardín Botánico la Concepción

7 Plaza de la Corredera, Córdoba

MAP D3

Córdoba gave this 17th-century arcaded square a long overdue sprucing up for the tourist onslaught of 1992 (see p43), even putting in an underground car park. But it still retains some of its customary functions, including an open-air market on Saturday morning, in addition to the regular market in the building with the clock tower. The arches provide shade for cafés and tapas bars, from where you can admire the brick façades with wrought-iron balconies.

8 Parque de María Luisa, Seville

Seville's glorious main park was a gift to the city from a Bourbon duchess in 1893. It was redesigned for the 1929 Ibero-American Exhibition. Numerous lavish structures have been left behind, including the stunning Plaza de España (see p89) and several other fine buildings, two of which house local museums. The grounds are largely the creation of Jean-Claude Nicolas Forestier, the French landscape gardener who also designed the Bois de Boulogne in Paris.

9 Plaza Nueva, Granada

MAP Q2

Located at the base of both the Alhambra hill and Albaicín (see pp12–17), and providing views along the banks of the river that runs beneath the city, this is a great place to while away the time. There are street performers, and plenty of cafés with tables outside.

10 Paseo de la Constitución, Baeza

Baeza's hub for strollers and café-goers is this oblong central promenade that was built in the 16th century. Fountains grace its tree-lined length, and there are bars with shady seating. Interesting buildings by the square include La Alhóndiga, the former corn exchange (see p34).

Beaches

Playa Puerto del Mar, Almuñécar

1 Almuñécar

The main resort (see p119) on the Costa Tropical of Granada Province is a more relaxed alternative to the intensity of the Costa del Sol. The two central beaches are the Playa San Cristóbal and the Playa Puerto del Mar, separated by a headland. Good diving and windsurfing spots can be found along here.

2 Mazagón
MAP B4

Huelva Province's Costa de la Luz has several appealingly remote beaches, and Mazagón is one of them. Located 23 km (14 miles) southeast of Huelva, this low-key resort is surrounded by pines and has lovely dune beaches. Deserted in winter, it comes alive in summer, mostly with Spanish families, but there's plenty of empty expanse to find solitude.

3 Chipiona

Cádiz Province has some good beach resorts that lack some of the high tourism of further along the coast, and Chipiona (see p107) is one of the nicest. The beaches are excellent and the town has retained its age-old traditions. It's still a thriving fishing port, for example, as well as a renowned producer of the local sweet muscatel wine. In addition, historic attractions include the longest jetty in the Guadalquivir estuary, known as Turris Caepionis to the Romans and these days as Torre Scipio.

4 Tarifa

Cádiz Province's – and Europe's – southernmost point (see p107) is one of the best spots in the world for devotees of the West Wind. The wind rarely ceases blowing here, which makes it a top spot for kite- and windsurfing, but less ideal for sunbathers. Still, it is possible to find protected niches that shelter you from the wind, and the nightlife and sense of fun here are second to none.

Windsurfing off the beach at Tarifa

5 Marbella
MAP D5

The Costa del Sol's most exclusive town (see p32) naturally has several fine beaches to recommend. To the east there are Cabo Pino, a nudist beach, and Las Dunas, sand dunes beside a modern marina. To the west is a string of party beaches, good for barbecues and dancing, including Victor's Beach and Don Carlos, perhaps Marbella's best.

Sierra Blanca mountains, Marbella

6 Torremolinos
MAP E5

Considering that they are in the main Costa del Sol nightlife magnet, Torremolinos's beaches come as a pleasant surprise (see p33). Because of the steep streets, most of the action remains above as you make your way down to the sand.

7 Torre del Mar
MAP E5

Very much off the beaten track, this area (see p33) – frequented mostly by local Spanish families – has vast sandy beaches and a fun-filled waterpark nearby.

8 Nerja
MAP E5

This little town (see p33) is a favourite for those who want an alternative to the brash Costa del Sol. It's a welcoming spot, with a wonderful position on top of an imposing cliff with palm-fringed beaches below.

9 Ayamonte
MAP A4

Andalucía's westernmost town is located at the mouth of Río Guadiana, and just to the east are the beach resorts Isla Canela and Isla Cristina. Isla Canela has a long, broad beach and an array of bars, while Isla Cristina boasts a fine sandy stretch and a harbour.

10 Cabo de Gata
MAP H5

Almería Province offers some of the finest unspoiled beaches in the region, including the Cala de la Media Luna and the Playa de Mónsul. The main resort town in this natural park (see p61) is San José.

Playa de Mónsul, Cabo de Gata

🔟 Outdoor Activities and Sports

Horse riding in the Sierra Nevada mountains

provides surfers with sufficiently high waves. Mediterranean waves are the best for body-boarding or SUP (stand-up paddleboarding).

③ Hiking
FEDAMON: 958 29 13 40; www.fedamon.com
Andalucía's sierras range from verdant to desert-like and rocky, and are perfect for hiking *(see pp60–61)*. If mountaineering appeals, head for the Sierra Nevada. Maps and lists of refuges are available from the Federación Andaluza de Montañismo (FEDAMON).

① Horse Riding
Far and Ride (7 destinations in Andalucía): MAP C5; 0845 00 66 552 (from UK); +44 1462 701 110 (intnl); www.farandride.com ■ Rutas a Caballo Castellar de la Frontera: C/Principe Juan Carlos 30; 629 57 24 46; www.castellargp.es
Andalucía is renowned for breeding fine horses and offers a range of riding options, with trails and schools in every province.

④ Spelunking
MAP D5 ■ Team4you: Avda de las Naciones Unidas, Puerto Banús, Marbella; 952 90 50 82; www.team4you.es
The region has some of the world's most interesting caves, many of them commercially developed. For information and organized jaunts, contact Team4you.

② Windsurfing and Surfing
ION Club: MAP C6; 619 34 09 13; www.ion-club.net ■ Windsurf la Herradura: MAP F5; Paseo Marítimo 34; 958 64 01 43; www.windsurf laherradura.com
Tarifa is a magnet for windsurfers, while good possibilities can also be found along the Costa Tropical. For board surfing, the Costa de la Luz

⑤ Skiing
Sol y Nieve ski resort near Granada is the only possibility for skiing in Andalucía. Although a little too sleek compared to its Alpine cousins, it offers a variety of runs and, best of all, skiing *(see p39)* fairly late in the season.

⑥ Boating and Fishing
Andalucían Fishing Federation: 956 18 75 85; www.fapd.net ■ Andalucían Sailing Federation: Avda Libertad, Puerto de Santa María (Cádiz); 956 85 48 13; www.fav.es
With so many marinas along the coast, sailing is big in this part of Spain. For deep-sea and freshwater fishing, you will need to obtain a licence.

Windsurfing at Tarifa

7 Golf

So copious are the golf courses *(see p109)* that the Costa del Sol has often been dubbed the "Costa del Golf". Courses include everything from world masterpieces, designed by top golfers, to putting greens suitable for families.

8 Diving

Yellow Sub Tarifa: MAP C6; 956 68 06 80; www.divingtarifa.com ■ Centro de Buceo Isub: MAP H5; C/Babor 3, San José de Níjar; 950 38 00 04; www.isubsanjose.com

Off Gibraltar are many sunken ships, while the wilds around Cabo de Gata offer the most profuse underwater life. The Costa de la Luz also has some good spots, including watersport heaven, Tarifa.

Diving at Cabo de Gata

9 Football

A national obsession, football *(fútbol)* stirs up the deepest of passions here. In season, you'll encounter it in every bar, blaring out from the TV, along with animated locals.

10 Hot Air Ballooning

Glovento Sur: Cuesta de San Gregorio 25, Granada; 958 29 03 16; www.gloventosur.com

Soar in the peaceful morning skies aboard hot air balloons, enjoying views of the Andalucían countryside.

TOP 10 BIKE ROUTES

Bikers on a cycle path, Andalucía

1 Via Verde El Ronquillo, Sevilla
MAP B3
A pleasant 9-km (5.6-mile) route running along the Minilla reservoir.

2 Via Verde of Sierra Norte, Sevilla
MAP C3
Ride 15 km (9.3 miles) along the Ribera del Huéznar river to Cerro del Hierro.

3 Via Verde of Riotinto, Huelva
MAP B3–A4
A 35-km (21.7-mile) trail through hilly scrublands and Riotinto's Martian terrain.

4 Via Verde of Subbética, Córdoba
MAP E3
Starting from Luque, take in castles and caves in a 57-km (35.4-mile) trail.

5 Via Verde del Aceite, Jaén
MAP E3
Ride through rolling hills and olive groves on this 55-km (34.2-mile) route.

6 Via Verde Sierra de Baza, Granada
MAP G3
Pass meadows and the village of Baza on this 16-km (9.9-mile) ride to Caniles.

7 Via Verde of Entre Rios, Cádiz
MAP B4–5
Explore farmlands and dunes along the Atlantic coast in a 16-km (9.9-mile) ride.

8 Via the TransAndalus, Cádiz
MAP C6–B5
This 341 km (211.8 miles) route is best experienced on a mountain bike.

9 Via the TransAndalus, Málaga
MAP C5–E4
Climb through mountains and take in stunning gorges on this 214-km (132.9-mile) bike route.

10 Villanueva del Rosario, Málaga
MAP D4–E4
This is a 19-km (11.8-mile) child-friendly route from Camino de las Huertas.

🔟 Hikes and Drives

Walking through the verdant Sierra de Aracena natural park

1 Hike from Alájar to Linares de la Sierra
MAP B3

The Sierra de Aracena is defined by soaring cliffs, wooded valleys and whitewashed villages. A good 6-km (4-mile) hike along marked trails leads from Alájar to Linares, via the hamlet of Los Madroñeros. From Alájar's main square, it follows the old road, with only one steep section.

2 Hike around the Villages of the Southern Tahá
MAP F4

This hike descends south from Pitres to arrive first at Mecinilla, then along a ravine to Mecina-Fondales. From here, you take the short or long route to Ferreirola, climb up to Atalbéitar and then back to Pitres.

3 Hike from Rute to Iznájar
MAP E4

Leave Rute on the A331 south, veer left at the fork and then take the trail on the right about 500 m (550 yd) further on. This leads down to the reservoir; turn right and continue to a rocky promontory. Enjoy the views, then go up the hill and cross the bridge to the scenic village of Iznájar.

4 Serranía de Ronda Hike
MAP D5

An easy, picturesque hike connects the village of Benaoján Estación with Jimera de Líbar Estación. Begin at the Molino del Santo hotel, walk down the hill and left alongside the railway and then over it at the second crossing. Across the river is the path; when it divides, take the left fork and continue on Via Pecuaria to town.

5 Drive from Nerja to Almería
MAP E5 ■ **Rte N340**

This route takes you along some of the region's most panoramic coast-line. Nerja is built up on cliffs (see p33), and as you approach Almería the views are dramatic (see p119).

6 Río Borosa Hike
MAP G2

From the visitors' centre at the village of Torre del Vinagre, near Cazorla, this hike takes you along the narrow rock walls of the Cerrada de Elías gorge above the Río Borosa, criss-crossed by wooden bridges.

Cerrada de Elías gorge

7 Drive from Tarifa to Cádiz

MAP C6 ▪ Rte N340

With immense cliffs and mammoth sand dunes, this wild sweep of the Costa de la Luz *(see p106)* is the best of the Atlantic shore. The villages of Bolonia, with its ancient Roman sites, and Vejer de la Frontera, which is steeped in Moorish heritage, both make excellent side trips.

8 Drive from Ronda to Jerez

MAP D5 ▪ Rte N342

The attraction is the *pueblos blancos (see p105)*, in particular Grazalema, Zahara and Arcos de la Frontera, and the Roman ruins at Ronda la Vieja.

Puente Nuevo, Ronda

9 Drive from Guadalquivir Valley, Córdoba Province

MAP E2

Starting to the east of Córdoba, in the attractive hill town of Montoro, follow the river downstream. West of Córdoba, visit the once-fabulous Medina Azahara *(see p125)*, enjoy the view from Almodóvar del Río's castle walls and end at Palma del Río.

10 Drive in Las Alpujarras, Sierra Nevada

MAP F4

A region of villages and hamlets, many perched on the slopes of the Sierra Nevada. Begin at Lanjarón, then head for Órgiva market town. Continuing eastward, the landscape becomes more arid; eventually you will come to Yegen, made famous by Gerald Brenan's *South from Granada*.

TOP 10 TOWN AND CITY WALKS

Córdoba's Jewish quarter

1 Córdoba
Have a free-form wander around the ancient Jewish quarter and then make for the Puente Romano for sunset views *(see pp22–5)*.

2 Granada
Lose yourself in a maze of hilly streets in the Albaicín district *(see pp16–17)*.

3 Seville
Once you've done the main city-centre sights, head across the Puente de Isabel II and into the old gypsy quarter of Triana *(see p88)*.

4 Cádiz
Start at the northeast corner of Plaza de España and stroll around the city, taking in the seascapes and gardens *(see pp26–7)*.

5 Jerez de la Frontera
Stroll through the Barrio de Santiago, the town's gypsy quarter *(see p106)*.

6 Ronda
Cross the Puente Nuevo, turn left and follow the town clockwise, being sure to pass the main church *(see pp30–31)*.

7 Baeza
From charming Plaza del Pópulo most of the main sights are found within walking distance, in a counter-clockwise direction *(see pp34–5)*.

8 Úbeda
Take a westerly walk to the monumental Hospital de Santiago and the Plaza de Toros *(see pp34–5)*.

9 Málaga
Tour Málaga's historic sights north of the Paseo del Parque *(see p104)*.

10 Antequera
This ancient town's main attractions are at the foot of the Alcazaba, but enjoy the views from above *(see p104)*.

⓾ Children's Attractions

① Muelle de las Carabelas, La Rábida, Huelva

MAP A4 ■ **Paraje de La Rábida**
■ **959 53 05 97** ■ **Open mid-Jun–mid-Sep: 10:30am–8pm Tue–Sun; mid-Sep–mid-Jun: 9:30am–7:30pm Tue–Sun** ■ **Closed 1 Jan, 24, 25 & 31 Dec** ■ **Adm (under 5s free)** ■ **www.muelle delascarabelasentradas.com**

Down by the waterfront, the "Pier of the Caravels" is a great treat for kids (see p97). They'll love the chance to climb aboard full-size replica ships and imagine themselves setting sail to distant shores. There's also a small museum and a recreation of a 15th-century European village.

Replica ships, Muelle de las Carabelas

② Parque Zoológico, Jerez

Primarily, this is a care station for the rehabilitation of injured animals, in particular indigenous endangered species. Children will enjoy seeing the Iberian lynx, which is part of a breeding programme. There are also red pandas (see p58).

③ Isla Mágica, Seville

MAP K1 ■ **Pabellón España, Isla de Cartuja** ■ **954 48 70 30** ■ **Opening hours vary, check website for details** ■ **Adm** ■ **www.islamagica.es**

This amusement park recreates the exploits of the 16th-century explorers who set out on seafaring expeditions – rides have names such as Jaguar and Anaconda. There are also boat tours and a range of shows. To cool down, head to the adjoining water park, Aqua Mágica.

④ Carromato de Max, Mijas

MAP D5 ■ **Avda del Compás** ■ **662 18 12 56** ■ **Open Easter–Oct: 10am–8pm daily (Jul & Aug: to 10pm); Nov–Easter: 10am–6pm daily** ■ **Adm**

This oddball collection claims to be a compendium of the world's smallest curiosities. There's a fine copy of Da Vinci's *The Last Supper* executed on a grain of rice, fleas in suits and Churchill's head sculpted in chalk.

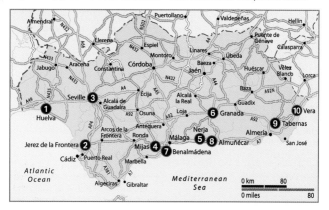

Impressive mineral formations in the Cuevas de Nerja

5 Cuevas de Nerja
MAP E5 ▪ Ctra Maro ▪ 952 52 95 20 ▪ Open 10am–5pm daily (Jul & Aug: to 7pm) ▪ Closed 1 Jan & 15 May ▪ Adm ▪ www.cuevadenerja.es

Discovered in 1959, these spectacular caves go back some five million years. The chambers will stimulate a child's imagination – with a little help from fanciful names and evocative lighting. The central column in Cataclysm Hall is the tallest in the world.

6 Parque de las Ciencias, Granada
MAP F4 ▪ Avenida de la Ciencia s/n ▪ 958 13 19 00 ▪ Open 10am–7pm Tue–Sat, 10am–3pm Sun & public hols ▪ Adm ▪ www.parqueciencias.com

This fascinating science centre and museum features a planetarium, a biodome holding more than 200 species of flora and fauna, inter-active exhibitions, mechanical games, workshops and optical effects sure to pique curious minds of all ages. There is also a café and restaurant.

7 Tívoli World, Benalmádena
MAP D5 ▪ Avda de Tívoli ▪ 952 57 70 16 ▪ Opening hours vary, check website for details ▪ Adm ▪ www.tivoli.net

Attractions at this theme park include a flamenco extravaganza and a Wild West show. With over 40 rides, Tívoli World is a great place for kids to have fun.

8 Aqua Tropic, Almuñécar
MAP F5 ▪ Playa de Velilla, Paseo Reina Sofia ▪ 958 63 20 81 ▪ Open mid-Jun–Sep: 11am–7pm daily ▪ Adm ▪ www.aqua-tropic.com

Hours of fun, with rides called Kamikazee, Wavebreaker, Ring Rapids, Blackhole Rapids, Soft Runs and a Children's Lake for little ones.

9 Mini Hollywood, Almería
The Wild West rides again at this old "spaghetti western" movie set. At show time, kids can see Jesse James in action *(see p118)*.

The streets of Mini Hollywood

10 Parque Acuático Vera
MAP H4 ▪ Ctra Vera/Garrucha-Villaricos ▪ 950 46 73 37 ▪ Open mid-May–Jun & Sep: noon–7pm daily; Jul & Aug: 11am–7:30pm daily ▪ Adm ▪ www.aquavera.com

This place will save the day when what your children need most is to cool off. There are five pools of various sizes, loads of undulating slides and tubes, as well as shaded areas.

≡10 Andalucían Dishes

1 Gazpacho

This signature Andalucían dish is a cold soup made of fresh tomatoes, green peppers, cucumber, garlic, olive oil, wine vinegar or lemon, breadcrumbs and salt. There are dozens of local variations of this nourishing refresher, which may involve almonds, grapes, melon, strawberries, red peppers and boiled egg or chopped ham garnishes. Perfect for a light lunch.

Battered *calamares* and prawns

Tortilla española

2 Tortilla Española and Patatas Bravas

Both of these dishes are ubiquitous not just in Andalucía but all over Spain. The first is a dense potato omelette with onions, fried into a savoury cake. It is served cold, by the slice, and is so filling it can make a full meal. The second consists of fried potato wedges served with a spicy tomato sauce and mayonnaise.

3 Fish Soups

The array of *sopas de mariscos* or *pescado* (shellfish or fish soups) seems to be limited only to the cook's imagination. Málaga favourites include *sopa viña*, a sherry-spiked version, and *cachoreñas*, with orange flavouring. Cádiz is known for its *guisos marineros* (seafood stews), made with the best seasonal fish of the region.

4 Calamares

All along the coast, you will encounter whole baby *calamares* (squids) served grilled – the essence of simplicity and delicious as long as they are fresh. A common alternative is to cut them into rings and batter-fry them – again, if they are fresh, they will taste sweet and tender. A complete *fritura de pescado* or *fritura mixta* (mixed fried fish) might add anchovies, prawns, chunks of cod or whatever is fresh that day.

5 Arroz a la Marinera

This is the Andalucían version of *paella*, an appellation that also appears on some menus. Saffron-flavoured rice is served with an assortment of fish and shellfish,

Arroz a la marinera

which can include prawns, clams and squid. Unlike the Valencia variety, it does not generally include sausage or chicken. The dish is also known as *arroz con mariscos*.

6 Monkfish
Monkfish *(rape)*, also called anglerfish, is one of the top choices for maritime eating in Andalucía. Only the tail of this unprepossessing looking fish is eaten, and it has a succulent quality similar to lobster tail or scallops. It is preferably served grilled, but can also be stewed in a rich sauce, usually tomato-based.

7 Tocino de Cielo
This rich egg custard pudding was traditionally made by nuns in Jerez de la Frontera.

Tocino de cielo, "heavenly custard"

8 Salads
Andalucían *ensaladas* (salads) are substantial and often include asparagus, boiled eggs, artichoke, carrots, olives, tuna and onions, in addition to lettuce and tomato.

9 Valle de los Pedroches
This soft sheep's cheese from Córdoba Province is typical of the regional type: strong in taste. The cheese is preserved in olive oil and enhanced with herbs.

10 Dessert Tarts
Cakes and sweet biscuits here typically involve Moorish ingredients such as anise, sesame, almonds and cinnamon. Most are sweetened with honey rather than sugar. Two common types are *alfajores*, with honey and almonds, and *piononos*, sometimes soaked in liqueur.

TOP 10 DRINKS

1 Mineral Water
Choose *sin gas* (still) or *con gas* (fizzy), the best being from Lanjarón, Granada.

2 Brandy
Brandy is distilled in Cádiz Province, Córdoba Province and Huelva Province.

3 Wine
Málaga's sweet wines come from Moscatel and Pedro Ximénez grapes, while fruity Condado wines are produced from Zalema grapes.

4 Beer
Cruzcampo is a local, Pilsner-type *cerveza* (beer) that is popular throughout the whole of Spain.

5 Liqueur
Aniseed-based liqueurs come primarily from Montilla in Córdoba Province. Other liqueurs include *aguardiente* from Huelva Province and *cazalla* from Sevilla Province.

6 Sangría
This classic red wine punch is world famous. The lighter *Tinto de Verano* is very popular in Andalucía.

7 Coffee
Opt for *café solo* (espresso) or *cortado* (espresso with very little milk). *Café con leche* (coffee with milk) is drunk by Spaniards for breakfast.

8 Mint Tea
Granada is particularly famous for its Moroccan-style tearooms *(see p122)*, and *teterías* serving mint tea are popping up more and more.

9 Soft Drinks
Refrescos include *batidos* (milkshakes), *granizados* (iced fruit crush) and *horchata* (a milky drink made from the tuber of the tigernut plant, or *chufa*).

10 Sherry
The region's most famous wine *(see pp76–7)* comes from Cádiz Province.

Sherry from the barrel

Tapas Dishes

1 Ensaladilla
"Russian salad" is sometimes an option for vegetarians – but not for vegans, as it usually consists of diced vegetables mixed in a thick mayonnaise. Watch out, however, as there are versions with cubes of ham mixed in as well. And make sure that this, and all mayonnaise-based dishes, are freshly prepared.

2 Chorizo al Vino
Chorizos are spicy, paprika- and garlic-flavoured red sausages that can be served grilled, sautéed with wine (*al vino*), or stewed with other ingredients. They are generally made of pork. *Morcilla* (blood sausage or black pudding) is a classic country delicacy.

Chorizo al vino

3 Mariscos
Berberechos (cockles), *almejas* (clams), *mejillones* (mussels), *pulpo* (octopus), *sepia* (cuttlefish) and *zamburiñas* (baby clams) are favourite seafood options everywhere in Spain. *Caracoles* (snails), simmered in a spicy broth, can be a rich but delicious treat.

4 Aceitunas
There are innumerable types of olives, from small to large, green to black, salty to sweet or whole to stuffed. The name of the dish can be confusing – although the Spanish

Aceitunas **from Andalucía**

name for the tree is the *olivo*, which comes from Latin, the word for the fruit comes from the Arabic *az-zait*, which means "juice of the olive".

5 Champiñones al Ajillo
Mushrooms sautéed with garlic are a regular on tapas menus. Other popular vegetable dishes include *judías* (green beans), often stewed with tomatoes and garlic, and *escalibadas* (roasted peppers) or *pisto*, the Spanish version of ratatouille.

6 Jamón Serrano
A complimentary slice of ham laid over the top of a *copa* (glass) is said to be how the custom of tapas (which literally means "lid") started. The finest regional type available is mountain-cured ham, but there is also *jamón york* (regular ham), as well as other cured pork products, including a local *tocino* (bacon) and *fiambres* (cold cuts). It's particularly fine when eaten with local cheese and bread, served as *tabla serrana* (plate of cured meat and cheese).

Tabla serrana

7 Albóndigas

"Meatballs" can be made from meat or fish and will most likely be stewed in a tomato sauce, together with garlic and spices. An alternative method of preparing chunks of meat, seafood or fish is by skewering them and grilling them as kebabs, either plain or spicy Moroccan-style.

8 Anchoas (Boquerones)

Anchovies and sardines are commonly served lightly fried in batter, but can just as likely be offered marinated and preserved in oil, or with a tomato sauce. You generally eat them minus the head but with all the bones.

Anchoas

9 Croquetas

Meat, fish or vegetables and mashed potatoes are mixed with béchamel and deep-fried to create these croquettes. A variation of this are *soldaditos* (fritters), which are made of vegetables, chicken or fish.

Croquetas

10 Alioli

This is mayonnaise laced with garlic and is served as a dish in its own right, for dipping bread into or as a condiment. Another popular relish is *pipirrana*, a compote made of tomato, onion and pepper.

TOP 10 TAPAS PREPARATION STYLES

A selection of tapas and bread

1 On Bread
Many tapas don't really come to life until applied to bread. Some are served already perched on a slice.

2 Marinated
Anchovies, sardines and seafood all come marinated. You'll see them sitting out on bars, possibly under glass, steeped in olive oil.

3 Cured
The hams of Andalucía are lightly salted – mountain-cured are the best.

4 With Mayonnaise
Any dish can be an excuse to slather on the *alioli*. Two dishes that often have mayonnaise are *patatas alioli* and *ensaladilla*.

5 Pickled
Mixed in with olives, you'll often find miniature gherkins, and possibly pearl onions, bits of garlic and hot peppers.

6 Egg-Based
Eggs are essential in *tortilla* (see p72) or come hard-boiled as a garnish.

7 Fried
Almost anything you can think of will turn up *frito* (batter-fried or sautéed), from fish to mushrooms.

8 Grilled or Roasted
If you want to ingest a little less oil, *a la plancha* (grilled) and *asado* (roasted) are the options to choose.

9 Stewed
Estofado variations include fish, meat, potato and vegetables, often cooked in tomato sauce.

10 A la Marinera
This technique, commonly used for fish and seafood, is similar to poaching and involves wine, garlic and parsley.

🔟 Bodegas and Wineries

Barrels of sherry fill the impressive Moorish cellars at Bodegas Fundador

1 Bodegas Fundador
MAP B5 ▪ Calle Puerta de Rota s/n, Jerez de la Frontera ▪ Enotourism Department: 956 15 15 52 ▪ Tour timings vary, check website for details ▪ Adm ▪ www.bodegasfundador.site

One of the most legendary of the names associated with sherry, this company was founded in 1730. A tour of the famous Moorish-style cellar "de la Ina" is *de rigueur* when in Jerez *(see p106)*.

Family-run González-Byass

2 González-Byass
MAP B5 ▪ C/Manuel María González 12, Jerez ▪ 956 35 70 16 ▪ Tour timings vary, check website for details ▪ Adm ▪ www.tiopepe.com

Although most of the main sherry producers are now largely owned by British multinationals, encouragingly, this *bodega* was bought back by the family. Founded in 1835, González-Byass's operation has two historic cellars, as well as the original tasting room.

3 Osborne Bodega
MAP B5 ▪ C/Los Moros, El Puerto de Santa María, Cadiz ▪ 956 86 91 00 ▪ Tours by appt ▪ Adm ▪ www.osborne.es

The black bull seen on Andalucían roadside hills is the symbol of this venerable sherry and brandy maker and a part of regional heritage.

4 Sandeman
MAP B5 ▪ C/Pizarro 10, Jerez de la Frontera ▪ 956 15 15 52 ▪ Tour and tasting timings vary, check website for details ▪ Adm ▪ www.sandeman.com

The distinctive silhouetted figure of The Don, in a black cape and wide-brimmed hat, dates from 1928 and is one of the first trademark images ever created. Sandeman was founded in London in 1790.

5 Bodegas Robles, Montilla
MAP D3 ▪ Ctra N331 Córdoba-Málaga km 47 ▪ 957 65 00 63 ▪ Tours by appt ▪ www.bodegasrobles.com

This organic wine producer employs an old system called *solera*, in which young wines are blended with older ones, until they mature.

6 Bodegas Alvear, Montilla
What distinguishes the wines here *(see p126)* is two-fold. Giant terracotta containers *(tinajas)* are sunk into the ground to keep the contents at a constant temperature, while the hot climate ripens the grapes for a stronger wine.

⑦ Bodegas Málaga Virgen

MAP D4 ■ A-92 km 132, Finca Vistahermosa, 29520 Fuente de Piedra, Málaga ■ 952 319 454 ■ Tours by appt ■ www.bodegasmalagavirgen.com

Producing traditional Málaga wines of the finest quality, this *bodega* has remained in the same family for four generations *(see p104)*.

⑧ Bodegas Antonio Barbadillo

MAP B5 ■ Calle Sevilla 6, Sanlúcar de Barrameda ■ 956 38 55 21 ■ Open 11am–3pm Tue–Sat by appt ■ Adm ■ www.barbadillo.com

A family-owned winery with 5 sq-km (2 sq-miles) of vineyards, the largest cellars in Sanlúcar and a museum on wine making. Barbadillo launched its first *manzanilla* in 1827 and now produces a range of wines, including one of Spain's best whites.

Bodegas Antonio Barbadillo

⑨ Bodegas Andrade

MAP B4 ■ Av de la Coronación 35, Bollullos Par del Condado, Huelva ■ 959 41 01 06 ■ Tours by appt ■ www.bodegasandrade.es

This *bodega* was one of the first to realize the potential of the Zalema grape for creating young wines.

⑩ Agroalimentaria Virgen del Rocío

MAP B4 ■ Av Cabezudos 3, Almonte, Huelva ■ 959 40 61 46 ■ Tours by appt ■ www.raigal.es

A series of fermenting vats form an underground cellar, where the Zalema grape is used to produce one of the region's few sparkling wines, Raigal.

TOP 10 SHERRIES AND WINES

Andalucían sherry

1 Fino
Clear, crisp and dry, with an aroma of almonds, *fino* sherry is served chilled as an aperitif.

2 Manzanilla
The *fino* sherry made in Sanlúcar de Barrameda, Cádiz Province. It is dry, pale and slightly salty.

3 Oloroso
The layer of flor yeast is thin, or absent, as a *fino* ages, allowing partial oxidation. *Oloroso* is a rich amber, with an aroma of hazelnuts.

4 Amontillado
Midway between a *fino* and an *oloroso*. The layer of flor yeast is allowed to die off, so it gets darker in colour.

5 Palo Cortado
This has an aroma reminiscent of an *amontillado*, while its colour is closer to *oloroso*.

6 Cream Sherry
This international favourite results when you take an *oloroso* and sweeten it by mixing in a measure of Pedro Ximénez wine.

7 Pedro Ximénez
This naturally sweet wine, when aged with care, is elegant and velvety.

8 Brandy de Jerez
Produced only in Jerez, it is sweeter and more caramelized than French brandy. It is made by ageing wine spirits in casks that have previously been used to age sherry.

9 Málaga
Málaga's famous sweet wines are made from the Moscatel and Pedro Ximénez grape varieties.

10 Raigal
One of Andalucía's few sparkling wines, this is refreshing on the palate.

Andalucía for Free

1 Archivo General de Indias, Seville

The UNESCO-listed archives building (see p88) was commissioned by Philip II in 1573 as a merchant's exchange and designed by architect Juan de Herrera (who worked on El Escorial). It contains more than 80 million documents, including letters sent by Columbus to his royal patrons, Ferdinand and Isabella.

2 Cathedral, Seville

Normally you pay to wander around the magnificent 15th-century cathedral (see pp18–9), set on the rectangular base of an Almohad mosque, but services here are free. There are choral masses at 8:30am daily from October to May.

3 El Mirador de San Nicolás, Granada

Go up to this high plaza to see a panoramic view of the Alhambra and surrounding districts and, on clear days, the peaks of the Sierra Nevada (see p17). It's a short walk up the hill from Plaza Nueva through the winding cobblestone alleys of the Albaicín area. There are hop-on, hop-off buses for those with limited mobility.

4 Patios, Córdoba

MAP D3

Since Roman and Moorish days, Córdoba citizens have

Torre del Oro, Seville

Pretty patio in Córdoba

used their inner courtyards to catch up or take in the air during summer. Many of the oldest are in the Alcázar Viejo district, between the Alcázar and San Basilio. There are more in Santa Marina, around the church of San Lorenzo and near la Magdalena, and in Judería. Guides take groups on tours but you may explore those open to the public for yourself. At the beginning of May, for 12 days, Córdoba celebrates the Fiesta of the Patios – an event included on UNESCO's Intangible Heritage list since 2012.

5 Torre del Oro, Seville

This 12-sided military watchtower built by the Almohad dynasty in the 13th century was used to control access to Seville via the Guadalquivir river and later became a prison (see p85). Its golden sheen comes from its building materials – mortar, lime and pressed hay – reflected in the river. Visitors can enter for free on Mondays.

6 Street Art, Granada

Far removed from the ancient artistic wonders of the Alhambra, Granada's side streets and walls provide rough canvases for designs by talented street artists. Some are inspired by abstract expressionist painter José Guerrero, and much of the work is witty as well as gritty.

7 Centro de Arte Contemporáneo, Málaga

MAP Q6 ■ C/Alemania ■ 952 20 85 00
■ www.cacmalaga.eu

The CAC has a permanent display of international artists including pieces by Louise Bourgeois, Olafur Eliasson, Thomas Hirschhorn and Damian Hirst, as well as post-1980s Spanish art, plus rotating temporary shows.

8 Fundación Picasso Casa Natal, Málaga

MAP R4 ■ Plaza de la Merced 15
■ 951 92 60 60 ■ www.fundacion
picasso.malaga.eu

The birthplace museum of Picasso, housing an array of his art, is free on Sundays between 4pm and 8pm.

Roman theatre, Ruinas de Acinipo

9 Ruinas de Acinipo, near Ronda

MAP D5 ■ Ctra Ronda-Sevilla km 22
■ 952 18 71 19

Founded in 45 BC to house retired soldiers from the Roman legions, the Acinipo ruins include a Roman theatre that is still in use today.

10 El Torcal de Antequera

Known for its striking limestone rock formations, El Torcal offers excellent hiking terrain (see p107). There are three marked routes taking from 30 minutes to three hours.

TOP 10 MONEY-SAVING TIPS

Tapas, free with a drink

1 In Granada – city and province – tapas still come free with a drink in most bars. The custom extends to some bars in Almería and Jaén province.

2 At lunch, ask for the "menú del día" (daily special). It is often as little as €7 and can be a two- or three-course meal.

3 Regional cuisine tends to be the best value, and you can easily fill up on a few tapas dishes.

4 Access free Wi-Fi at bars and cafés in most towns and in hotel lobbies.

5 Buy a tourist pass (bono turístico). The Granada Card, Málaga Card and Sevilla Card cover public transport and offer discounts or free entry to sights. Prices vary. Jaén, Úbeda, Baeza and Ronda also have discount bonos.

6 Be conscientious in Marbella; prices are much higher than elsewhere.

7 If you are a visitor from outside the EU and are leaving with purchased goods to the value of €90.15 or more, get a refund on Spain's 21 per cent sales tax (VAT, known here as IVA).

8 Avoid the tourist-heavy flamenco shows in Seville and aim instead for bars and clubs in Triana and places where talented singers perform for local people. Ask for recommendations at the tourist office or your hotel.

9 Don't go near any of the major cities around Easter Week (Semana Santa). Room rates can go through the roof, especially at the smarter hotels. August can also be an expensive month.

10 Consider camping, especially if walking in Grazalema, the Alpujarra or Sierra Nevada. The sites tend to be at a high altitude and so relatively cool and pleasant, even in summer. Prices start at €5 per night per tent.

Religious Festivals

1 Fiesta de los Reyes Magos
5 Jan

Traditionally, this evening commemorates the arrival of the Three Kings at the infant Jesus's manger crib. Parades across the region feature the trio, lavishly dressed, progressing through towns in small carriages drawn by tractors or horses. The next day, Epiphany, is the day that children receive gifts.

Revellers celebrating at Carnaval

2 Carnaval
Feb

Most Andalucían towns celebrate this Catholic festival (see p27), the most spectacular extravaganza being in Cádiz. Costumes and masked balls are the order of the day and night during these chaotic revels. The implicit anarchy invites every sort of political lampoon, which is why Franco tried to abolish these events.

3 Semana Santa
Easter week

Holy Week is observed in every town and village in the region, with dramatic and spectacular processions, especially in Seville (see p19). Effigies of Christ and the Virgin are carried through the streets on huge floats. Dressed in traditional outfits, people either maintain penitential silence or express commiseration with the suffering Lord and His mournful Mother.

4 Romerías
May–Oct

Taking part in one of these local festivals is an experience no visitor will forget – almost every community (see p19) has its own romería. Usually, the programme involves a colourful pilgrimage to a shrine outside of town, followed by days of merrymaking. The name may recall ancient pilgrimages, when devotees walked to Rome.

5 Corpus Christi
Dates vary

This festival celebrates the miracle of Transubstantiation, when the Host becomes the body of Christ and the wine, His blood. Granada's celebration is the most famous, with parades and partying, followed by bullfights and flamenco.

Corpus Christi procession

Fiesta de las Cruces
3 May

The Festival of the Crosses celebrates the discovery of the True Cross by St Helena in the 4th century. Modes of veneration vary widely in the region, but may include competitions for producing the most gorgeous flower-decked cross.

7 San Juan
23 & 24 Jun

This feast, in celebration of John the Baptist, is important in many parts of Andalucía. Midsummer fireworks and bonfires seem to be the order of the day in most communities.

8 Virgen del Carmen
15 & 16 Jul

The patron saint of sailors is all-important in coastal communities. Statues of the Virgin are put onboard a flower-adorned fishing boat and floated out to sea and back again, amid music, fireworks and cheering.

Virgen del Carmen festival

9 Assumption of the Virgin
15 Aug

At the height of the summer heat, the Virgin Mary's assumption into heaven is celebrated. There is much socializing, drinking and dancing. The day marks the beginning of the Feria de Málaga, a week-long party.

10 Fiesta de San Miguel
Last week Sep–first week Oct

This mix of bullfights, exhibitions and dancing is particularly note-worthy in Seville, Úbeda and the Albaicín quarter of Granada. In Torremolinos, it closes the summer season in festive style.

TOP 10 FERIAS AND OTHER FESTIVALS

Riders at Feria del Caballo

1 Flamenco Festivals
Summer months
These take place around the region.

2 Moros y Cristianos
Throughout the year
Festivals centre on re-enactments of Christian take-overs of various towns.

3 Feria de Abril
Apr/May
Held in Seville two weeks after Easter, this is the largest fair (see p86) in Spain.

4 Wine Festivals
Apr–Sep
Celebrations of the fruit of the vine with La Vendimia (grape harvest).

5 Feria del Caballo
May
This fair in Jerez de la Frontera centres on Andalucían horses.

6 Music and Dance Festivals
Jun–Jul
Granada hosts many such festivals.

7 Feria de Jamón
15 Aug
Witness traditional matanza (slaughter) of pigs and several celebrations of ham, notably in Trevélez.

8 Sherry Festivals
Sep–Oct
The towns of the "Sherry Triangle" (see p106) celebrate their fortified wines at various times, notably in Jerez.

9 Fiesta de la Aceituna
1st week Dec
The olive is celebrated in the Jaén Province town of Martos.

10 Fiesta de los Verdiales
28 Dec
In Málaga Province at Puerta de la Torre, this is a day for practical jokes and a chance to wear funny hats. It dates back to Moorish times.

Top 10 Andalucía and the Costa del Sol Area by Area

The Roman Bridge crossing the Río Guadalquivir in Córdoba

🔟 Seville

Andalucía's capital is an aristocratic yet relaxed city, with a fabulous cultural heritage that dates back beyond recorded history.

Mudéjar-style tiles at La Casa de Pilatos

Its fate has always been tied to the Río Guadalquivir ("the great river" in Arabic), and the trade it offered the city. Today, much of the riverfront is made up of an attractive promenade. There is a wealth of art and architecture to see in the historic centre of Seville as well as distinctive neighbourhoods, each with their own charm. But its highlights, including the splendid cathedral, Moorish and Renaissance palaces and fine museums, are within walking distance of each other.

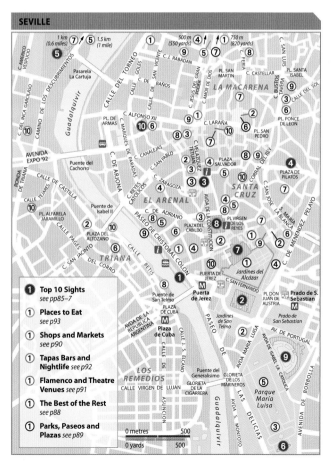

SEVILLE

1 Top 10 Sights
see pp85–7

1 Places to Eat
see p93

1 Shops and Markets
see p90

1 Tapas Bars and Nightlife *see p92*

1 Flamenco and Theatre Venues *see p91*

1 The Best of the Rest
see p88

1 Parks, Paseos and Plazas *see p89*

0 metres   500
0 yards   500

River view of the Torre del Oro

1 Torre del Oro and Torre de la Plata

MAP L4 ■ Torre del Oro: Paseo de Colón; 954 22 24 19; Open 9:30am–6:45pm Mon–Fri, 10:30am–6:45pm Sat–Sun; adm €3 (except Mon) ■ Torre de Plata: C/Santander 15 ■ Closed to public

Tradition states that the imposing 13th-century Moorish dodecahedral (12-sided) watchtower, the Torre del Oro (Tower of Gold), is named after the golden tiles that once adorned it. Others say its name derives from its use as a warehouse for the gold coming in from the Americas during Seville's heyday. It now houses a small maritime museum. Nearby stands the Torre de Plata (Tower of Silver), a more modest octagonal tower, which most likely gets its name as a complement to its neighbour. Both towers originally formed part of the city's defences.

2 Real Fábrica de Tabacos

MAP M5 ■ C/San Fernando 4 ■ 954 55 11 23 ■ Open 8am–8:30pm Mon–Fri

A part of Seville University, this stately 18th-century edifice is the second-largest building in Spain. Famous for its fun-loving workers, who at one time rolled three-quarters of Europe's cigars, the old factory has been immortalized by *Carmen*, the most popular opera in the world. The doomed heroine, a hot-blooded gypsy *cigarrera*, remains, for many, a symbol of Spanish passion.

3 Ayuntamiento

MAP L3 ■ Plaza Nueva 1 ■ 955 47 02 64 ■ Guided tours by appt: 5pm & 7:30pm Mon–Thu, 10am Sat; online reservations: oberonsaas.com/alcazarsevilla

This building has been the town hall since the 16th century. Inside, the rooms are decorated with historic paraphernalia of the city and the monarchy, in a blend of Gothic and Renaissance styles. Outside, the façades reflect the evolution of taste, from the original Renaissance Plateresque work with its finely carved stonework, to the 19th-century attempt to copy the style, seen from Plaza de San Francisco.

4 La Casa de Pilatos

MAP N3 ■ Plaza de Pilatos 1 ■ 954 22 52 98 ■ Open 9am–6pm daily (to 7pm Apr–Oct) ■ Adm ■ www.fundacionmedinaceli.org

Erroneously said to be based on the house of Pontius Pilate in Jerusalem, this 15th-century gem *(see p46)* is the most sumptuous of Seville's urban mansions. It is a blend of Mudéjar, Gothic and Renaissance styles, punctuated with Classical statuary and *azulejo* (Spanish painted ceramic tile) designs. Look for the carved head of the Greek boy, Antinous, who drowned and was deified by his grief-stricken lover, Emperor Hadrian.

Courtyard passage, La Casa de Pilatos

5 Monasterio de la Cartuja de Santa María de las Cuevas

MAP J1 ■ Centro Andaluz de Arte Contemporáneo: 955 03 70 70; open 11am–9pm Tue–Sat, 10am–3:30pm Sun; adm; www.caac.es

This 15th-century monastery has had its ups and downs over the centuries. During Spain's Golden Age, it was the favoured retreat of Christopher Columbus, whose remains were interred here for several decades. The monks went on to decorate their vast enclave with commissions from some of Seville's greatest artists – most of the works are now in the Museo de Bellas Artes (see p87). In 1841, it became a ceramics factory. Finally, the complex came to house a contemporary art museum, Centro Andaluz de Arte Contemporáneo.

Museo Arqueológico

6 Museo Arqueológico

MAP N6 ■ Plaza de America ■ 955 12 06 32 ■ Closed for renovations until 2025 ■ Adm

This Renaissance-style pavilion, designed by architect Anibal González, was also one of the fabulous structures created for the 1929 Exposition and now houses Andalucía's principal archaeological museum. The assemblage of artifacts ranges from Paleolithic finds, exhibited in the basement, to splendours of Roman and Moorish art displayed upstairs. The Carambolo treasures of Tartessian gold, also on display in the basement, and the Roman sculpture collection are outstanding.

Water tanks under the Real Alcázar

7 Real Alcázar

This lavish palace (see pp20–21) was primarily the brain-child of Pedro I, who had it built as a lavish love-nest for himself and his mistress, María de Padilla.

8 Seville Cathedral and La Giralda

Legend has it that when the *sevillanos* decided to build their cathedral in the 15th century, they intended to erect an edifice so huge that later generations would call them mad. They achieved their aim with the largest church (see pp18–19) (by volume) in Christendom.

FERIA DE ABRIL

The seven-day Spring Fair (**below**), about two weeks after Easter, is a riot of colour and high spirits. Andalucían horses strut on parade, ridden by *caballeros* in traditional leather chaps, waistcoats and wide-brimmed *sombreros cordobeses*, often with women in flamenco attire perched behind. The air is alive with music, the fairgrounds overflow with *casetas* (party marquees – most of them by invitation only), and partying continues until dawn. All festivities take place south of the river.

⑨ Plaza de España
MAP N6

This semicircular plaza was designed as the centrepiece for the Ibero-American Exposition of 1929. Almost completely covered with gorgeous glazed tiles, its surfaces depict historic moments and heraldic symbols of the 40 regions of Spain. A canal follows the arc of the structure, crossed by colourful footbridges. The site was used as a set in the film *Star Wars: Attack of the Clones*, for its other-worldly feel.

Gallery, Museo de Bellas Artes

⑩ Museo de Bellas Artes
MAP K2 ▪ Plaza del Museo 9 ▪ 955 54 29 42 ▪ Open Aug: 9am–3pm Tue–Sat; Sep–Jul: 9am–9pm Tue–Sat, 9am–3pm Sun ▪ Adm (free for EU members)

This museum *(see p52)*, second only to the Prado in Madrid, houses a range of great Spanish paintings. The collection is on display in a former 17th-century convent and focuses on the Seville School, led by Cano, Zurbarán, Valdés Leal and Murillo. Look out for Murillo's touching *Virgen de la Servilleta*. Don't miss El Greco's poignant portrait of his son and the polychrome terracotta of St Jerome by Florentine sculptor Pietro Torregiano, who was a colleague of Michelangelo.

A WALK AROUND THE BARRIO DE SANTA CRUZ

Cervecería Giralda — *Calle Mateos Gago* — *Casa Plácido* — *Calle Santa Teresa 8* — *Cathedral* — *Hospital de los Venerables* — *Plaza Santa Cruz* — *Real Alcázar* — *Arco de la Judería* — *Callejón del Agua* — *Jardines de Murillo*

▶ MORNING

Start at the exit to the **Real Alcázar** *(see pp20–21)* on Patio de las Banderas. Turn right to find the Arco de la Judería, a covered alleyway that leads to the Callejón del Agua, running along the old Jewish Quarter's southern wall. Peep into some of the famously lush patios of these perfectly whitewashed houses – the writer Washington Irving once stayed at No. 2. After the wall ends, find the **Jardines de Murillo** *(see p89)* on your right, and enjoy a tranquil stroll.

Turn back to find **Plaza Santa Cruz** *(see p89)*, where the church that gave the neighbourhood its name once stood, until it was burned down by the French in 1810. A 17th-century wrought-iron cross stands here now. Cross a couple of streets west to find the **Hospital de los Venerables** *(see p88)*. Take in its delightful central courtyard and important art gallery.

For lunch, try traditional tapas at the old **Casa Plácido** *(see p93)*.

AFTERNOON

From here, go east to Calle Santa Teresa 8, the former home of the great artist Bartolomé Murillo *(see p54)*, who died here in 1682 after a fall while painting frescoes in Cádiz.

Finally, work your way back towards the **cathedral** *(see pp18–19)* along Calle Mesón del Moro and then to Calle Mateos Gago. At No 1 you'll find the **Cervecería Giralda** *(954 22 82 50)*, excellent for a drink or food at any time of day.

See map on p84 ←

The Best of the Rest

Valdés Leal frescoes, Hospital de los Venerables

1 Hospital de los Venerables

MAP M4 ■ Plaza de los Venerables 8 ■ Opening hours vary, check website for details ■ Adm ■ www.fundacion focus.com

Founded in the 17th century as a home for the elderly, this is now a cultural centre. It features a *trompe-l'oeil* ceiling by Juan de Valdés Leal.

2 Archivo General de Indias

MAP M4 ■ Avda de la Constitución 3 ■ 954 50 05 28 ■ Open 9:30am–5pm Mon–Sat, 10am–2pm Sun

This is a storehouse for documents on the Spanish colonization of the Americas *(see p78)*.

3 Museo de Artes y Costumbres Populares

MAP N6 ■ Plaza de América 3 ■ 955 03 53 25 ■ Open 9am–9pm Tue–Sat (16 Jun–15 Sep: to 3pm), 9am–3pm Sun ■ Adm

Exhibits here include displays on flamenco and bullfighting.

4 Hospital de la Caridad

MAP L4 ■ C/Temprado 3 ■ Open 10am–7:30pm daily ■ Closed for Mass 12:30–2pm Sun ■ Adm (free 3:30–7:30pm Mon) ■ www.santa-caridad.es

A hospital founded by reformed rake Miguel de Mañara. The chapel contains artworks by Sevillian artists.

5 Real Maestranza

MAP L3 ■ Paseo de Cristóbal Colón 12 ■ 954 21 03 15 ■ Open 10am–6pm daily (Apr–Oct: to 9pm) ■ www.realmaestranza.es

The so-called "Cathedral of Bullfighting" becomes the focal point of Seville when the sporting season opens in April. It is closed from 3pm on fight days.

6 Barrio de Triana

MAP K4

This quarter, once home to Seville's gypsies, was known for producing bullfighters, flamenco artists and fine ceramics *(see p90)*.

7 Casa de la Condesa de Lebrija

MAP M2 ■ C/Cuna 8 ■ 954 22 78 02 ■ Open daily (Jul–Aug: Mon–Sat) ■ Adm

A 15th-century, typically Sevillian mansion, embellished with mosaics from Itálica *(see p97)*.

8 Museo de las Ilusione

MAP M1 ■ Calle San Eloy 28 ■ 955 66 98 39 ■ Open 10am–10pm daily ■ Adm ■ www.moisevilla.es

An infinity room, an anti-gravity room and a vortex tunnel are some of the highlights at this museum of illusions.

9 La Macarena

MAP N1

This district is home to the Rococo Iglesia de San Luis, the 15th-century Convento de Santa Paula, and Seville's adored religious icon, the Virgen de la Macarena. During Semana Santa *(see p80)* she is paraded on a float.

10 Museo del Baile Flamenco

MAP M3 ■ C/Manuel Rojas Marcos 3 ■ 954 34 03 11 ■ Open 10am–7pm daily ■ Adm ■ Daily shows from 7pm

Run by famous dancer Cristina Hoyos, this museum explores the wonderful world of flamenco dancing.

Parks, Paseos and Plazas

 1 Real Alcázar
These gardens are a blend of Moorish and Italian Renaissance styles *(see pp20–21)*.

 2 Plaza Santa Cruz
MAP N4
Created when Napoleon's soldiers destroyed a church that stood here, this square is now adorned by an iron cross, La Cruz de la Cerrajería.

 3 Plaza de San Francisco and Plaza Nueva
MAP L3 & M3
These squares represent the heart of the city. Plaza de San Francisco (also the Plaza Mayor, or main square) is Seville's oldest and hosts many public spectacles. Plaza Nueva is a pleasant park with a monument to King Fernando the Saint.

4 Jardines de Murillo
MAP N4
These formal gardens used to be the orchards and vegetable plots for the Alcázar. Donated to the city in 1911, they are named after Seville painter Bartolomé Murillo *(see p54)*. The Columbus monument features the bronze prows of the *Santa María*, the caravel that bore him to the Americas in 1492.

5 Parque de María Luísa
MAP M6
This park dominates the southern end of the city. Its present design, comprising the immense Plaza de España, was laid out for the 1929 Exposition *(see p59)*. Look for peacocks in the trees.

Parque de María Luísa

6 Plaza de la Encarnación
MAP M2
This square is dominated by the intriguing architecture of the Metropol Parasol complex, with its shops, bars, observation deck, market and subterranean museum.

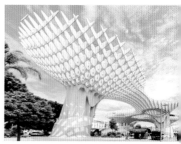
Plaza de la Encarnación

 7 Alameda de Hércules
MAP M1
Set off by pairs of columns at either end – the southern set are ancient Roman – this popular promenade is lined with trendy bars and restaurants, which draw a hip crowd.

8 Plaza de la Alfalfa
MAP M2
Once the location of the hay market, and later a Sunday morning pet market, the Alfalfa is now a good area for browsing. Visit clothing stores, flamenco boutiques, unique accessory shops and bars.

9 Paseo Alcalde Marqués de Contadero
MAP L4
With the Torre del Oro at one end *(see p85)*, this riverfront walkway makes for a pleasant stroll *(see p58)*.

10 Calle San Fernando and Avenida de la Constitución
MAP M5
These two streets form a pedestrian promenade through the heart of Seville, livened up by art exhibitions.

See map on p84

Shops and Markets

① El Corte Inglés
MAP L2 ▪ Plaza del Duque
de la Victoria 8

Although you're unlikely to find any bargains here, the range of merchandise is impressive. Spain's main department store chain carries not only clothes and accessories, but also perfume, housewares and sporting goods. There's also a gourmet food section and food hall, as well as a supermarket.

Pottery on sale at the Ceramica Triana

② Ceramica Triana
MAP J4 ▪ C/Callao 14
▪ 954 33 21 79

The place to buy the famous Triana pottery, this shop sells everything from replicas of 16th-century tiles to ashtrays. The old ceramics factory next door, a protected historical monument, is now a museum.

③ Xauen
MAP L2 ▪ C/O'Donnell 20;
Pasaje Comercial

For quality leather bags, wallets, jewellery and accessories, this is the place to go.

④ Desigual
MAP L2 ▪ Calle Sierpes 81

Spain's most unique and colourful fashions for men and women can be found at Desigual.

⑤ Aurora Gaviño
MAP M3 ▪ C/Álvarez Quintero
16 ▪ 628 24 56 26

This is a good spot to splurge on all the flouncy dresses, mantillas, shawls and so forth that are needed to participate in the various festivals (see pp80–81) that abound in the region.

⑥ Art Market
MAP K2 ▪ Plaza del Museo 9

On Sunday mornings from around 9am to 2pm, local artists display their works. Take home an original souvenir of Seville.

⑦ Botellas y Latas
MAP M1 ▪ C/Regina 14
▪ 954 29 31 22

This wine merchant and delicatessen has a large selection of excellent Spanish wines and gourmet regional produce. Carlos, the owner of this establishment, is very welcoming.

⑧ El Mercadillo
MAP M1 ▪ C/Feria 43
▪ Open 8am–3pm Thu

Just off the Alameda de Hércules (see p89), the eclectic Mercadillo El Jueves flea market is Seville's most famous second-hand market. It consists mostly of old junk, books and posters. Still, it's fun to look for the occasional treasure.

⑨ Hippy Market
MAP L2 ▪ Plaza del Duque
de la Victoria ▪ Open 9am–8:30pm
Wed–Sat

This is the place to find handmade jewellery, leather goods, unique clothes and other charming hand-crafted items.

⑩ Torre Sevilla Shopping Centre
MAP J2 ▪ C/Gonzalo Jiménez de Quesada 2

This open-air shopping centre offers an abundance of high-street shops and restaurants.

Flamenco and Theatre Venues

Performance, Teatro de la Maestranza

1 Teatro de la Maestranza

MAP L4 ▪ Paseo de Cristobal Colón 22 ▪ 954 22 33 44 ▪ www.teatrodelamaestranza.es

Built as part of Expo '92, Seville's main theatre serves primarily as the city's opera house, with productions of all the classics, particularly those set in Seville, including *Carmen*, *Don Juan*, *The Marriage of Figaro* and *The Barber of Seville*.

2 Teatro Lope de Vega

MAP M5 ▪ Avda de María Luísa ▪ 954 47 28 28 ▪ www.teatrolopedevega.org

This Neo-Baroque theatre, named after the "Spanish Shakespeare", was built in 1929 as a casino and theatre for the Ibero-American Exposition. Modern and classical works are performed here.

Flamenco dancers at El Patio Sevillano

3 Sala Cero

MAP N2 ▪ Calle Sol 5 ▪ 954 22 51 65 ▪ www.salacero.com

This venue showcases regional music and theatre productions.

4 Teatro Alameda

C/Crédito 11 ▪ 955 47 44 94 ▪ www.teatroalamedasevilla.org

Contemporary Andalucían drama and flamenco feature strongly at this popular, modest theatre.

5 Teatro Central

MAP J1 ▪ C/José de Gálvez 6, Isla de Cartuja ▪ 955 54 21 55 ▪ Closed Jul–Sep

In season, this theatre highlights the *Flamenco Viene del Sur* series, alongside all sorts of theatre, dance and classical music. It's a starkly modern facility right on the river.

6 El Arenal

This venue has hosted flamenco performances for more than four decades. Visitors can enjoy tapas, drinks or a full meal while watching the performers. See the first show and the second is free.

7 La Carbonería

MAP N3 ▪ C/Céspedes 21A ▪ 954 22 99 45 ▪ Shows Mon & Thu

A relaxed, authentic Flamenco bar with a good atmosphere.

8 El Patio Sevillano

MAP L4 ▪ Paseo de Cristobal Colón 11A ▪ 954 21 41 20 ▪ Open 7pm & 9:30pm daily ▪ www.elpatiosevillano.com

Rousing flamenco shows to please the throngs of tourists.

9 Los Gallos

MAP N4 ▪ Plaza de Santa Cruz 11 ▪ 954 21 69 81 ▪ Open 8pm & 10pm daily ▪ www.tablaolosgallos.com

Excellent flamenco artists impress at the oldest *tablao* in Seville.

10 Casa de la Memoria de al-Andalus

MAP M2 ▪ C/Cuna 6 ▪ 954 56 06 70 ▪ Open 7:30pm & 9pm daily ▪ www.casadelamemoria.es

Dedicated to flamenco, this cultural centre hosts exhibitions, concerts and dance performances.

See map on p84

Tapas Bars and Nightlife

El Rinconcillo, arguably the most authentic tapas bar in Spain

1 Sala Malandar
MAP K1 ▪ C/Torneo 43 ▪ 690 95 39 12 ▪ www.salamalandar.com

Come to this laid back club for an eclectic array of music – from funk to reggae and ska via soul, folk and indie pop – by live bands and DJs.

2 Malavida
MAP M2 ▪ Plaza de la Encarnacion ▪ 954 22 77 63

Situated under the Metropol Parasol, this cheery bar has traditional and innovative tapas as well as a good selection of wine.

3 Casa Morales
MAP L3 ▪ C/García de Vinuesa 11 ▪ 954 22 12 42

Reputedly the second-oldest bar in town (1850), and it doesn't seem to have changed much. Drinks are still poured from old casks. Simple tapas.

4 Antigüedades
MAP M3 ▪ C/Argote de Molina 40 ▪ 954 56 51 27

The eccentric decor of this bar, which changes regularly, features Roman and Arab elements. Traditional cuisine and reasonably priced drinks attract locals and tourists alike.

5 Pura Vida Terraza
MAP M3 ▪ Hotel Fontecruz, Calle Segovias 6 ▪ 667 71 74 44

At this lively rooftop pool and bar, you are invited to chill out, sip a cocktail and enjoy stunning views of the city. Beer and wine are also served.

6 El Rinconcillo
MAP M2 ▪ C/Gerona 40 ▪ 954 22 31 83

The city's oldest *taberna* dates from 1670 and is an essential stop on your Seville itinerary. Extensive choice of traditional Moorish-Andalucían food.

7 Antique Theatro
C/Matemáticos Rey Pastor y Castro, La Cartuja ▪ 666 55 05 50 ▪ Closed Mon–Wed

Dress to impress at Seville's most upscale club, and you might just get past the doormen. In summer, the terrace Rosso hosts live events.

8 La Terraza de EME
MAP M3 ▪ C/Alemanes 27, 4th Floor of EME Catedral Hotel ▪ 954 56 00 00

Enjoy the spectacular views of the cathedral and the Giralda while sipping a cocktail on the terrace bar of the upmarket Eme hotel.

9 Bar El Garlochi
MAP M2 ▪ C/Boteros 26 ▪ 666 66 66 66

A Seville institution with a religious decor. Expect Baroque exuberance and lively locals. Try the signature cocktail *Sangre de Cristo*.

10 Puratasca
MAP J3 ▪ C/Numancia 5 ▪ 954 33 16 21

Discover delicious twists on the classics at this fusion tapas bar, where the menu changes with the seasons.

Places to Eat

① Kiosco Restaurante Torre de los Perdigones

MAP L1 ■ C/Resolana 41 ■ 954 90 93 53 ■ Closed Mon & Tue ■ €€

Located in a city park, this restaurant serves a modern take on classic Spanish dishes. The alfresco terrace is a great place to enjoy an aperitif in the evenings.

② Lobo Lopez

MAP L3 ■ Calle de Rosario 15 ■ 854 70 58 34 ■ €

Tucked away on a side street, this smart restaurant offers a fusion of international cuisine. Try the scallop risotto with shrimp tartare.

③ Casa La Viuda

MAP L3 ■ C/Albareda 2 ■ 954 21 54 20 ■ €

Choose from a wide variety of classic dishes and tapas at this Michelin-starred Sevillan bodega. Don't miss their famous cod.

Taberna del Alabardero

④ Taberna del Alabardero

MAP L3 ■ C/Zaragoza 20 ■ 954 50 27 21 ■ €€€

This superb restaurant has earned itself a Michelin star. The setting is sumptuous, while the menu excels in meat dishes and local seafood.

PRICE CATEGORIES

For a three-course meal for one with half a bottle of wine (or equivalent meal), taxes and extra charges

€ under 30   €€ €30–€50   €€€ over 50

---

⑤ El Disparate

MAP M1 ■ Alameda de Hercules 31 ■ 680 12 74 13 ■ €€

Set on the ground level of a stylish hotel, this innovative restaurant has earned a Michelin star. Expect fresh Mediterranean cuisine made using local and seasonal ingredients.

⑥ Modesto

MAP N4 ■ C/Cano y Cueta 5 ■ 954 41 68 11 ■ €

Enjoy garlic shrimp and excellent homemade paella at great value.

⑦ Casa Plácido

MAP M3 ■ C/Mesón del Moro 11 ■ 954 56 39 71 ■ €

Convenient for all the major sights, this venerable bar has hams dangling, barrels of sherry, old posters and traditional tapas.

⑧ Abades Triana

MAP L5 ■ C/Betis 69 ■ 954 28 64 59 ■ €€€

This modern restaurant has a commanding location on the river. Diners can book a spot in El Cubo, a private area with a "floating" glass floor. There are tapas, tasting and gourmet tasting menus on offer.

⑨ Eslava

MAP L1 ■ C/Eslava 3–5 ■ 954 90 65 68 ■ €

This tapas bar and restaurant adds a dash of innovation to traditional cuisine using fresh, seasonal produce.

⑩ Mariatrifulca

MAP K4 ■ Puente de Isabel II ■ 954 33 03 47 ■ €€

Enjoy a contemporary twist to classic Sevillian food while admiring stunning views of the city and the Guadalquivir.

See map on p84

ᵀᴼᴾ**10** Sevilla and Huelva Provinces

Leaving behind the magnetic allure of glorious Seville, the rest of Sevilla Province and neighbouring Huelva Province are among the least visited areas of Andalucía. Consequently, much of the zone has remained a rural hinterland, where time moves slowly and the old customs prevail. Some of the finest nature preserves are here, too, including Parque Nacional de Doñana, mountainous reaches and pristine beaches, generally frequented by Spaniards rather than tourists. Culturally rich as well, each town and village shelters surprising art treasures and ancient marvels, where you may find yourself the only visitor – a welcome relief after the throngs encountered elsewhere in Andalucía.

Bell tower, Écija

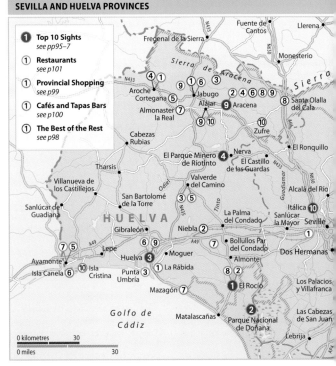

SEVILLA AND HUELVA PROVINCES

① **Top 10 Sights**
see pp95–7

① **Restaurants**
see p101

① **Provincial Shopping**
see p99

① **Cafés and Tapas Bars**
see p100

① **The Best of the Rest**
see p98

Fuente de Cantos
Llerena
Fregenal de la Sierra
Monesterio
Sierra de Aracena
Sierra
N433
④① ⑨①⑥③ ②④⑥⑧⑨
Aroche
Cortegana ⑤ Jabugo ⑧ Santa Olalla del Cala
Alájar ⑨ Aracena
Almonaster ⑦
la Real
⑨⑩ ⑩
Zufre
Cabezas Rubias
Nerva El Ronquillo
El Parque Minero ④ El Castillo de las Guardas
de Ríotinto
Tharsis
Valverde del Camino
Villanueva de los Castillejos
Odiel
San Bartolomé ③⑤
de la Torre
Alcalá del Río
Sanlúcar de Guadiana
HUELVA
La Palma del Condado
Itálica ⑩
Sanlúcar la Mayor Seville
Gibraleón
Niebla ②
④①
Lepe
⑦⑤ ⑥⑨
Bollullos Par del Condado
Dos Hermanas
Ayamonte
Huelva ③ Moguer
Almonte
⑦
Isla Canela ⑥ Isla
Cristina Punta ③ ① La Rábida
Umbría
⑧②
Mazagón ⑦
Los Palacios y Villafranca
① El Rocío
Matalascañas
② Parque Nacional de Doñana
Las Cabezas de San Juan
Golfo de Cádiz
Lebrija

0 kilometres   30
0 miles   30

The Hermitage of El Rocío

1 El Rocío
MAP B4

The fact that this town resembles an Old West frontier outpost is no accident. The Spaniards who settled what are now the states of Texas, New Mexico and Arizona mostly came from this part of Spain and took their architectural style with

them. Horseback is still a normal way to get around here. The place bursts into life during the annual Romería (see p36), one of Spain's biggest festivals.

2 Parque Nacional de Doñana

Europe's largest nature reserve (see pp36–7) has important wetlands and shifting dunes that are gradually moving inland. The fragile area can only be visited on guided tours.

3 Huelva
MAP A4 ■ Museo de Huelva: Alameda Sundheim 13; 959 65 04 24; open Sep–Jun: 9am–9pm Tue–Sat, 9am–3pm Sun; adm (free to EU members)

Founded by the Phoenicians, Huelva was at its peak under the Romans – Huelva's provincial museum holds remarkable archaeological finds. The city's other claim to fame is as the starting point of Columbus's seafaring expedition (see p43). Huelva was the first port for Americas trade, before Seville took over.

El Parque Minero de Ríotinto

4 El Parque Minero de Ríotinto
MAP B3 ■ Museo Minero: Plaza Ernest Lluch; 959 59 00 25; open 10:30am–3pm & 4–6pm daily; adm ■ www.parquemineroderiotinto.es

The Ríotinto (Red River) mines, the world's oldest, have been exploited for minerals for some 5,000 years, and the gradual stripping away of the rich ore has left a weird moonscape shot through with coloured fissures. A museum details the mines' history.

Carmona and its castle tower

5 Carmona

MAP C3 ▪ Necrópolis: Avda Jorge Bonsor 9; 600 14 36 32; opening hours vary, call ahead for details; closed Mon

The closest major town east of Seville, Carmona has been continuously inhabited for more than 5,000 years. Its Roman remains are exceptional, especially the huge necropolis. The view from the originally Roman Puerta de Córdoba (Córdoba Gate) out over the sweeping plains shouldn't be missed. Fine churches, palaces and *alcázares* adorn the site – one of the ancient castles is now a spectacular parador *(see p141)*.

6 Cazalla de la Sierra

MAP C3 ▪ La Cartuja de Cazalla arts centre; 951 19 34 46; open 11am–3pm Sat, Sun & public hols; adm; www.la cartujadecazalla.com

The main town in the Sierra Norte is a steep cluster of whitewashed houses. It's a popular place for weekend getaways by *sevillanos* and particularly known for producing some of the area's famous anise-based tipples. Just 3 km (2 miles) outside of town is a former Carthusian monastery, restored as part hotel, part arts centre.

7 Écija

MAP D3 ▪ Museo Histórico Municipal: Palacio de Benamejí, C/Cánovas del Castillo 4; 955 90 29 19; opening hours vary, call ahead for details; closed Mon; museo.ecija.es

Two nicknames for this town east of Seville give an idea of its chief glory and its biggest challenge. "The Town of Towers" refers to its 11 Baroque bell towers, all adorned with glazed tiles. "The Frying-Pan of Andalucía" alludes to its searing summer temperatures, due to the fact that it's one of the few towns not on a hill. Écija's archaeological museum is worth a visit.

8 Osuna

MAP D4 ▪ Museo de Osuna: C/Sevilla 37; 954 81 57 32; open 10am–2pm & 5–8pm Tue–Sun (summer hours vary, call ahead for details)

Exhibit in the Osuna museum

This ancient Roman enclave has of many fine examples of Roman and pre-Roman architecture. The city of Osuna was an important hub of Renaissance Spain, which has resulted in some exceptional architecture such as the church, the Colegiata and the University. The Osuna Museum is home to, among a number of important artworks, a permanent exhibition dedicated to the popular TV series *Game of Thrones*, which was filmed here.

SOCIALISM VERSUS FEUDALISM

The fertile Campiña valley has been owned by a few noble families since the Catholic Monarchs handed out tracts as fiefdoms. The people who worked the land were little more than serfs, a situation that still accounts for local poverty. The mayor of Marinaleda, however, has created an island of social idealism, and has wrestled plots of property away from landlords to be communally owned by the workers.

⑨ Gruta de las Maravillas

MAP B3 ■ C/Pozo de la Nieve, Aracena ■ 663 93 78 76 ■ Open 10am–1:30pm & 3–6pm daily ■ Adm

A guided tour of these marvellous caves will wind through beautiful chambers with naturally coloured formations and names such as the Hut, Organ, Cathedral, Quail and Twins. The last room is a notorious crowd-pleaser – the *Sala de los Culos* (Chamber of the Buttocks). There are 12 caverns and six underground lakes. The "Great Lake" lies under a vaulted ceiling, 70 m (230 ft) high.

Inside the Gruta de las Maravillas

⑩ Itálica

MAP B3 ■ Avda de Extremadura 2, Santiponce ■ 600 141 767 ■ Jan–Mar & mid-Sep–Dec: 9am–6pm Tue–Sat, 9am–3pm Sun; Apr–Jun: 9am–8pm Tue–Sat, 8am–3pm Sun; Jul–mid-Sep: 9am–3pm Tue–Sat ■ Adm (free for EU members)

These wind-blown ruins were once the third-largest city in the Roman empire, founded in 206 BC and home to half a million people during the reign of Emperor Hadrian in the 2nd century. He was following in the glorious footsteps of his predecessor Trajan, another Itálica native. There's an amphitheatre and some mosaics amid the crumbling walls. Most of the wonders are still buried, or have been moved to the Archaeological Museum in Seville (see p86).

HALF A DAY IN SANTIPONCE

▶ MORNING

Venture 7 km (4 miles) north of Seville to Santiponce, a town famous for being the home of the ruins of the Roman city Itálica. Make your way to the **Monastery of San Isidoro del Campo** (*Avenida de San Isidoro del Campo 18*), founded in 1301 by Alonso Pérez de Guzmán. This vast complex is home to two churches, and is a juxtaposition of Gothic, Baroque, Languedoc and Mudejar design.

From the monastery, take a 20 minute walk north to the **Cotidiana Vitae** (*Plaza de la Constitución*), close to the **Teatro Romano de Italica** (*currently open only for concerts or plays*). This cultural centre recreates the daily life of the Romans of the 2nd century, both in their homes and in the street.

Leaving the centre, head north on Avenida de Extremadura and turn right on Avda Rocio Vega to reach **La Caseta De Antonio** (*Avda Rocío Vega 10; 955 99 63 06*) for lunch. Try one of its delectable rice dishes.

AFTERNOON

After lunch, head to **Itálica**, the first Roman city on the Iberian peninsula. Stroll through the grounds of the ancient settlement, passing some astonishing mosaics, a temple, the remains of thermal baths and the 2,500-seat amphitheatre.

Round off the afternoon with a cup of coffee from your pick of one of the Spanish restaurants near the ruins.

See map on pp94–5

The Best of the Rest

 Jabugo
MAP B3

The "home of ham" produces Spain's most famous, known as *jamón ibérico* (cured Iberian ham), *jamón serrano* (mountain-cured ham) and *pata negra*, named after the black pigs that forage in the Sierra de Aracena.

 Niebla
MAP B4

Massive ramparts, built by the Moors in the 12th century, attest to the central role this town played in defending the land. The walls stretch for about 2.5 km (1.5 miles).

3 Sierra de Aracena y Picos de Aroche Park
MAP B2

This wild area *(see p60)* provides plenty of inspiring views and fauna.

 Aroche
MAP A2 ▪ Museo del Santo Rosario: Calle Fray Juan Bross ▪ 678 03 03 86 ▪ Open mid-May–Sep: 11am–3pm Thu–Sun & public hols; Oct–mid-May: 10am–2pm & 3–5pm Fri–Sun & public hols

This well-preserved village contains a wonderful oddity, the Museo del Santo Rosario, packed with rosaries that have belonged to Mother Teresa, John F Kennedy and General Franco.

5 Cortegana
MAP B3

A 13th-century castle dominates one of the largest towns in the area.

The town of Cortegana

 Aracena
MAP B3

Capital of the sierra, this is a lovely little town. The crumbling castle offers views of the surrounding hills.

 **Almonaster la Real**
MAP B3

A 10th-century mosque *(see p44)* and castle, as well as a bullring, are clustered on a citadel overlooking the village *(see p56)*.

The Mezquita at Almonaster la Real

 Santa Olalla del Cala
MAP B3

In the heart of the ham-curing area, this village has a 13th-century castle and a 15th-century Baroque church.

 Alájar
MAP B3

A small town *(see p56)* of cobbled streets and white-washed buildings.

 Zufre
MAP B3

This cliff-top community is like a mini-Ronda *(see pp30–31)*. The Paseo de los Alcaldes has rose and lime trees and views across the plain.

Provincial Shopping

 Aroche Markets
Thursday is the day the market stalls arrive in this Huelvan town. The market in Plaza de Abastos features a traditional produce spread, including the strong-flavoured goat's cheese favoured by the locals.

2 Souvenirs
In Aracena, head for the Calle Pozo de la Nieve, a cobbled street lined with souvenir shops. In El Rocío *(see p95)*, souvenir stalls flank the church, hawking paraphernalia associated with the famous Romería pilgrimage *(see p36)*.

3 Crafts
In addition to leather, Valverde del Camino is known for furniture and fine wooden boxes. Embroidery work from Aracena and Bollullos del Condado is worth seeking out, as well as linen tablecloths from Cortegana and Moguer. Wickerwork is widely sold around Huelva, while nearer the coast it is also common to see Moroccan goods for sale.

4 Pottery
In this area, pottery has traditional patterns influenced by Moorish art. Look for water jugs, plates and jars, decorated in blue, green and white glazes.

5 Leather
The most notable leather goods come from Valverde del Camino. Choose *botos camperos* (cowboy boots) or the longer *botos rocieros* (Spanish riding boots). Many shops produce footwear, and a number of craftsmen make boots to order, taking three to four days to make a pair. There are workshops devoted to making saddles and bridles.

Jamón ibérico **from Jabugo**

6 Ham
The Mesón Sánchez Romero Carvajal in Jabugo is one of the top producers of the local *jamón ibérico*.

7 El Condado Wine District
The name refers to an area noted for its reliable white wine. Local *finos* include Condado Pálido and Condado Viejo.

8 Anise Liqueur
The liqueur of choice throughout the region is anise-based. One of the best is Anis Cazalla from the eponymous town *(see p96)*.

Local pottery

9 Huelva
The provincial capital *(see p95)* has its own El Corte Inglés department store on Plaza de España, while the area around it and just off Plaza 12 de Octobre constitutes the main shopping district. The Mercadillo (open-air market) is held every Friday on the Recinto Colombino.

10 Cured Fish
Considered a great delicacy and priced accordingly, raw wind-cured tuna *(mojama)* is an acquired taste. Isla Cristina is the main centre of production, but you can buy it in the Mercado del Carmen in Huelva, and other food markets.

See map on pp94–5

Cafés and Tapas Bars

An appetizing tapas platter

1 Bar Plus Ultra, La Rábida
MAP A4 ■ Avenida de America 34 ■ 959 53 00 34 ■ Closed Mon

Close to the Monasterio de Santa María de la Rábida, this traditional, family-friendly restaurant serves fabulous tapas.

2 Bar Goya, Carmona
MAP C3 ■ C/Prim 2 ■ 954 14 30 60 ■ Closed Wed

This restaurant is set in a 15th-century, Moorish-style building in the heart of Carmona. Andalucían home cooking with a modern twist is the speciality here.

3 El Martinete, Cazalla
MAP C3 ■ Ctra Estación de Cazalla km 12 ■ 955 88 65 33 (information) ■ Closed Mon–Wed

Enjoy good-value tapas and seasonal, local produce in a beautiful setting sorrounded by woods and waterfalls.

4 Bar La Reja, Ecija
MAP D3 ■ C/Cintería 16 ■ 954 83 30 12 ■ Closed Sun & Mon

This local favourite offers a wide choice of tapas and *raciones* and the leisurely atmosphere invites lingering.

5 La Puerta Ancha, Ayamonte
MAP A4 ■ Plaza de la Laguna 14 ■ 959 32 06 66 ■ Closed Mon

A sociable place that purports to be the original town bar. There are tables on the square and good prices, too, for their line of drinks, tapas and other snacks.

6 Espuma del Mar, Isla Canela
MAP A4 ■ Paseo de los Gavilanes 28 ■ 959 47 72 85

This beachside establishment has alfresco tables and tasty tapas. The speciality is, of course, fresh fish and seafood. Try *raya* (skate) in one of its various manifestations.

7 El Refugio, Mazagón
MAP B4 ■ C/Santa Clara 43 ■ 610 74 53 31 ■ Closed Mon–Wed

A laid-back, popular haunt in this surfer's paradise. Located a short stroll from the beach, El Refugio is renowned for its fresh fish dishes.

8 Mesón La Reja, Aracena
MAP B3 ■ Ctra N433 km 87 ■ 959 12 76 70

This tapas bar specializes in regional food including wild mushrooms, local cheeses and snails.

9 Café Bar Manzano, Aracena
MAP B3 ■ Plaza del Marqués de Aracena 22 ■ 959 12 81 23 ■ Closed Tue

On the south side of the town square this traditional bar is a classic Sierra place for coffee and a pastry.

10 Casa Curro, Osuna
MAP D4 ■ Plazuela Salitre 5 ■ 955 82 07 58

A few blocks from the main square, this is a premier tapas bar. Worth seeking out for the quality.

Patatas bravas

Restaurants

1 La Choza de Manuela, Bormujos

MAP B4 ▪ C/Menendez Pidal 2 ▪ 649 44 56 16 ▪ €

Popular with locals, this restaurant specializes in a variety of succulent, grilled meats, served by friendly staff. Go early to avoid the long queues.

2 Meson Rey Arturo, Osuna

MAP D4 ▪ C/Sor Angela 3 ▪ 662 13 22 21 ▪ Closed Mon–Wed, Sun D ▪ No credit cards ▪ €

The medieval decor in "The inn of King Arthur" does not disappoint. Feast on grilled meats and modern interpretations of regional classics.

3 Restaurante Miramar, Punta Umbría

MAP A4 ▪ C/Miramar 1 ▪ 959 31 12 43 ▪ €

Fresh fish from the Atlantic is paired with rice dishes.

4 Restaurante Montecruz, Aracena

MAP B3 ▪ Plaza de San Pedro 36 ▪ 959 12 60 13 ▪ €€

Local, organic produce is key, with game, ham, chestnuts and wild mushrooms when in season. Exceptional food in both the restaurant and tapas bar.

5 Cambio de Tercio, Constantina

MAP C3 ▪ C/Virgen del Robledo 53 bajo, Constantina ▪ 955 88 10 80 ▪ Closed Tue ▪ €

This place is popular with devotees of rural cookery. Specialities include Iberian pork loin in wild mushroom sauce and for dessert *tarta de castañas* (chestnut tart).

6 Restaurante Azabache, Huelva

MAP A4 ▪ C/Vázquez López 22 ▪ 959 25 75 28 ▪ Closed Sat D, Sun ▪ €€€

A smart traditional restaurant that's popular with locals (later in the evening) and is known for its *raciones*, or large servings of tapas.

PRICE CATEGORIES

For a three-course meal for one with half a bottle of wine (or equivalent meal), taxes and extra charges.

€ under €30   €€ €30–€50   €€€ over €50

7 Casa Luciano, Ayamonte

MAP A4 ▪ C/Palma del Condado 1 ▪ 959 47 10 71 ▪ Closed Sun D, Mon ▪ €€

The place for fresh, tempting seafood and fish stews. Try the delicious *coquinas* (steamed baby clams) or the appetizing grilled calamari.

Choza-style façade of Aires de Doñana

8 Aires de Doñana, El Rocío

MAP B4 ▪ Avda La Canaliega 1 ▪ 959 44 22 89 ▪ Closed Mon, 20 days in July ▪ €€

French windows provide panoramic views of the marshes here. The "shack" specializes in local dishes. Sample the goose liver pâté, beef burger and the blueberry cheesecake.

9 Posada de Cortegana, Cortegana

MAP A2 ▪ Ctra El Repilado – La Corte km 2.5 ▪ 959 50 33 17 ▪ €€

A wide variety of meat, such as Iberian pork, venison and game, is on offer at this lovely grillhouse.

10 Casa El Padrino, Alájar

MAP B3 ▪ Plaza Miguel Moya 2 ▪ 959 12 56 01 ▪ Closed Mon–Thu ▪ €

This rustic favourite is known for its tasty regional cuisine.

See map on pp94–5

TOP10 Málaga and Cádiz Provinces

These two Andalucían provinces are a heady mix of cultural and recreational riches. Europe's oldest city, Cádiz, is found here, but the presence of history is balanced by the hedonistic delights of the Costa del Sol and its fine beaches. Some of the region's most dramatic

landscapes lure nature-lovers, while others are drawn by the charms of the famed *pueblos blancos* (white villages), the most renowned being Ronda, birthplace of that strongest of Spanish traditions, the bullfight. This is also the area that produces the world-famous fortified wines known as *Jerez* (sherry), as well as the celebrated sweet wines of Málaga. Finally, Europe's southernmost point is located here, Tarifa, with views of North Africa, and a stone's throw away, the Rock of Gibraltar.

Statue outside Ronda's bullring

MÁLAGA AND CÁDIZ PROVINCES

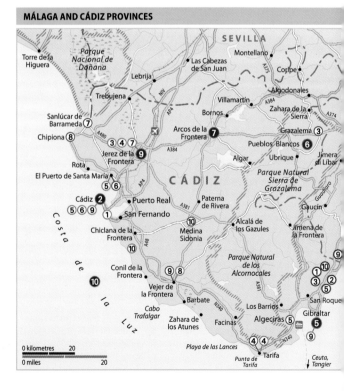

Puento Nuevo, Ronda

1 Ronda

To many visitors over the centuries, this town evokes the "real" Andalucía, wild and spectacular. This mountain rock eyrie is breathtaking, being dramatically sliced down the middle by El Tajo, a fantastically deep and narrow limestone ravine, formed over thousands of years by the Río Guadalevín. Thus Ronda is a town of two halves – the ancient half is steeped

in rich Moorish history, with cobbled streets, while the more modern part is on the north side *(see pp30–31)*.

2 Cádiz

At the apex of the Atlantic's untamed Costa de la Luz *(see p106)*, ancient Cádiz floats on what was originally its own island. It is possibly Europe's oldest city, thought to have been founded by the Phoenicians in around 1104 BC. Much of what can be seen today, however, dates from the 18th century – the city was destroyed by an Anglo-Dutch raid in 1596. Catedral Nueva (1722) is one of Spain's largest churches, and many Baroque edifices enhance this unpretentiously beautiful provincial capital. Apart from two weeks in February when Cádiz stages Spain's most celebrated Carnaval *(see p80)*, it remains under-visited *(see pp26–7)*.

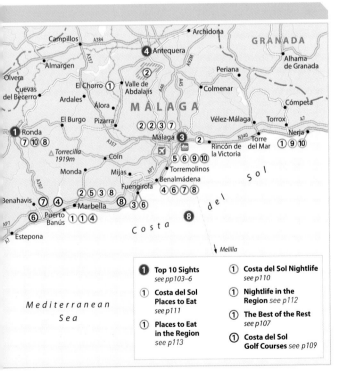

Roman amphitheatre, Málaga

③ Málaga

MAP E5 ▪ Museo Picasso: C/San Agustín 8 ▪ 952 12 76 00 ▪ Opening hours vary, check website for details ▪ Adm ▪ www.museopicassomalaga.org

Despite being home to the main airport bringing holidaymakers to the Costa del Sol, this provincial capital has been bypassed by the brunt of "sun coast" development and has managed to hold onto its Spanish-ness quite admirably. It has a thriving arts scene and attracts foodies to its many restaurants. The modern waterfront complex has bars, shops, the Centre Pompidou Málaga museum (see p52), a promenade and space for plush yachts. Important as a trading port since ancient times, it was the favourite city of poet García Lorca (see p55), who loved its rawness. But its even greater claim to artistic fame is that it was the birthplace of Pablo Picasso, whose creative genius is celebrated in the Picasso museum (see p52). Málaga's alcázar, built between the 8th and 11th centuries, includes a Roman amphitheatre.

④ Antequera

MAP D4 ▪ Museo Municipal: Palacio Nájera, Plaza del Coso Viejo ▪ 952 70 83 00 ▪ Open Tue–Sun ▪ Adm

So ancient that even the Romans called it Antiquaria, this market town presents a wonderfully condensed architectural history of the entire area, beginning with Neolithic dolmens dating from between 4500 and 2500 BC. In addition, there are significant Roman ruins, including villas with outstanding mosaics, a Moorish Alcazaba, the 16th-century Arco de los Gigantes and fine Renaissance palaces and churches to explore. Many treasures originally found in the town – including the exquisite Ephebe of Antequera, a rare, life-size Roman bronze statue of a young boy – are displayed in the Municipal Museum, housed in an 18th-century palace.

⑤ Gibraltar

MAP C6

This gargantuan chunk of limestone rising up from the Mediterranean was one of the mythic Pillars of Hercules. Yet, despite being nick-named "The Rock", as a worldwide symbol of stability and security, this fortress is the subject of contention between Spain and Great Britain.

The Rock of Gibraltar

Nonetheless, many people cross the border to visit this slice of England today. The town centre is home to museums, restaurants and shops, and from here visitors can take a cable car to the Upper Rock. Here, several interesting attractions can be found, including St. Michael's Cave, the tunnels from the Great Siege of 1779–83 and tunnels from World War II. The Skywalk lookout, perched at 340 m (1,115 ft) above sea level, and the Windsor Suspension Bridge offer incredible views. Don't miss the Apes' Den, which houses one of Gibraltar's most iconic residents: the Barbary Macaques (tailless monkeys).

Casares, a pretty *pueblo blanco*

6 Pueblos Blancos
MAP C5

The term "white villages" refers to the profusion of whitewashed hillside hamlets in the Serranía de Ronda, the mountainous territory around Ronda. Many are truly beautiful and it's well worth spending several days driving from one to the other, and then striking out on foot to take in some of the views (see p69). Towns not to miss include Gaucín, Casares, Grazalema, Setenil, Zahara de la Sierra (see p57), Jimena de Libár and Manilva. Villagers, who originally settled here to protect themselves from bandits in the lowlands, retain a centuries-old way of life and strong agricultural tradition. Between Grazalema and Zahara, you'll go through Andalucía's highest mountain pass, the breathtaking Puerto de las Palomas (The Pass of the Doves).

A MORNING WALK IN JEREZ DE LA FRONTERA

Church of San Mateo
Barrio de Santiago
Museo Arqueológico
Church of San Dionisio
Tabanco Plateros
Bodegas Fundador
Cathedral
Alcázar
González-Byass bodega

▶ MORNING

Begin your tour at the impressive Alcázar, with its many Moorish remains, including restored gardens, a mosque and a *hammam* (baths), and a *camera obscura* providing views of the city and beyond. Beside it is the stunningly decorated cathedral, extravagantly rich inside and out. Note the fine painting of *The Sleeping Girl* by Zurbarán in the sacristy.

Next take the tour – with tastings – of the **González-Byass bodega** (see p76), possibly the oldest cellars in Jerez, including one designed by Gustave Eiffel. Don't miss the many signatures of famous people on the barrels (called "butts"), including Queen Victoria, Cole Porter, Martin Luther King and General Franco, among others.

Continuing on north, the **Bodegas Fundador** (see p76) also offers tours and is distinctively Moorish in style. A block further north, pass the Gothic style Church of San Mateo, then pop into the **Museo Arqueológico** to see the prized Greek bronze helmet from the 7th century BC, and then enter the **Barrio de Santiago**. This gently dilapidated neighbourhood of maze-like alleyways is home to a sizeable gypsy community and numerous flamenco venues.

To cap off your walk, continue southeast out of the *barrio*, past the **Church of San Dionisio**, then turn back to **Tabanco Plateros** (C/Algarve 35; 956 10 44 58), for some light tapas and a great selection of wine and cheese.

See map on pp102–3 ←

7 Arcos de la Frontera

MAP C5 ■ Galería de Arte Arx-Arcis: C/Marqués de Torresoto 11 ■ 956 70 39 51 ■ Open 10:30am–8:30pm daily

Another town built atop a sheer cliff, this is probably the most dazzling of the *pueblos blancos* and the one situated furthest west. Little remains of the period before the *reconquista*, when it received its "de la Frontera" appellation, as a bastion "on the frontier" between Christian and Moorish Spain. The Galería de Arte Arx-Arcis crafts museum and shop displays local carpets, blankets, baskets and pottery.

8 The Costa del Sol

This string of former Mediterranean fishing villages still lives up to its reputation as one of the world centres for sun, surf and fun. But beyond the bustling tourist enclaves there is still much authentic charm on offer and even places that invite tranquility – especially in the towns of Estepona, Nerja, Mijas and ultra-classy Marbella *(see p65)*. Year-round golf makes the whole area a great attraction for international fans of the sport *(see p109)* and, in high

Nerja beach, The Costa del Sol

season in particular, Torremolinos *(see p33)* is the place to find some of Spain's liveliest nightlife.

9 Jerez de la Frontera

MAP B5 ■ Alcázar de Jerez: C/Alameda Vieja ■ 650 80 01 00 ■ Open Jul–Sep: 9:30am–6pm; Oct–Jun: 9:30am–3pm daily; seasonal hours vary, call ahead to check ■ Adm

The largest city in Cádiz Province is synonymous with "sherry", which is a corruption of "Jerez" – itself a corruption of the Phoenician name of Xeres *(see pp76–7)*. Before that, it was part of the fabled Tartessian civilization (8th century BC). Sights include Jerez's Moorish fortress, once part of a 4-km (2.5-mile) wall *(see p105)*. A well-preserved mosque, now the Santa María La Real chapel, features an octagonal cupola over the *mihrab* (prayer niche). Jerez is renowned for equestrian art, Andalucían style, as well as for flamenco *(see pp50–51)*.

10 The Costa de la Luz

MAP B5–C6

Named for its shimmering sunlight *(luz)*, the stretch of coast from Huelva down to Tarifa is opposite to the Costa del Sol; its low-key resorts attract mainly Spanish visitors and watersports lovers – the latter drawn by the strong ocean breezes. But there are plenty of pretty beaches, many backed by shady pine forests, and the combination of Arabic forts, Moorish castles, medieval churches, sherry and old-school charm makes the Costa de la Luz a great choice for adventurous holidaymakers.

THE SHERRY TRIANGLE

Jerez, Sanlúcar de Barrameda and El Puerto de Santa María mark the famed "Sherry Triangle". Production of the fortified wine (**above**) was started by the Phoenicians using vines they imported some 3,000 years ago. In Roman times it was exported all over the empire, and it has been popular in England since the Elizabethan age. Sherry varies in degrees of dryness or sweetness. The *fino* and *manzanilla* are dry and light, while the *amontillado* and *oloroso* are more robust *(see p77)*.

The Best of the Rest

El Torcal de Antequera
MAP D4

This mountain nature reserve *(see p60)* is great for hiking. The odd limestone rock formations are a big draw.

El Chorro
MAP D4

A geographical wonder, the Chorro Gorge's immense chasm, 180-m (590-ft) high, was created by the Río Guadalorce slashing through the limestone mountain. A 7.7-km- (4.7-mile-) long path, the El Caminito del Rey, runs along the gorge.

El Caminito del Rey

Grazalema
MAP C5

Nestled in the foothills of the Sierra del Pinar, Grazalema is a charming village – Spain's rainiest, according to some – and the main access point for the Sierra de Grazalema Natural Park, one of the best hiking areas in Andalucía *(see p60)*. Known for its local cheeses, stews and honey, it's also a great place to plan a picnic.

4 Tarifa
MAP C6

One of Andalucía's hippest coastal towns *(see p64)*, Tarifa features a sizable windsurfing and kitesurfing *(see p66)* contingent and various Moroccan touches.

5 Algeciras
MAP C6

Although the town of Algeciras is industrial and polluted, its port is the best in Spain; from here you can catch the ferry to Morocco. Peruse the Moorish bazaars while waiting for the boat to take you across.

6 El Puerto de Santa María
MAP B5

One of the Sherry Triangle towns, several *bodegas (see p76)* can be visited here for tours and tastings.

7 Sanlúcar de Barrameda
MAP B5

Famed for its *manzanilla* sherry and superb seafood, the town also offers beautiful churches, palaces and tours of the *bodegas*.

8 Chipiona
MAP B5

This pretty resort town is crowded with Spanish beach enthusiasts in high season. The pace of life here is leisurely, consisting of enjoying the surf and miles of golden sand during the day, then strolls and ice cream until late in the evening.

9 Vejer de la Frontera
MAP C6

Of all the *pueblos blancos (see p105)*, this one has kept its Moorish roots most intact. Its original four Moorish gates still stand and its streets have barely changed in 1,000 years.

10 Medina Sidonia
MAP C5 ▪ Iglesia de Santa María la Coronada: Plaza Iglesia Mayor; 956 41 03 29; opening hours vary, call ahead for details; adm

The most important edifice here is the 15th-century church of Santa María la Coronada, built over an earlier mosque. The interior features a 15-m (50-ft) high *retablo*.

See map on pp102–3

Provincial Shopping

1 Málaga Wines
MAP Q5 ■ El Templo del Vino:
C/de Sebastián Souvirón 11, Málaga
■ 952 21 75 03

The region is famed for its sweet wines (see p77), and Málaga has plenty of establishments where they can be sampled and purchased. El Templo del Vino is particularly well stocked with local tipples and also with wines from all over Spain.

Delicacies in a Málaga grocer

2 Chocolates Artesanales Frigiliana
MAP E5 ■ C/Real 27, Frigiliana
■ 669 20 90 56

Set in a picturesque village, Chocolates Artesanales Frigiliana sells over 15 unique chocolate flavours and a range of cosmetics, all made with a natural chocolate base.

3 Alegrías de Cádiz, Cádiz
MAP B5 ■ Fabio Rufino 5
■ 956 06 87 09

This gourmet shop sells an array of wine, cheese, ham, olive oil, sweets and other delicacies of the region.

4 Xauen, Conil de la Frontera
MAP B5 ■ C/San Sebastián 18, Conil de la Frontera ■ 661 27 14 30

A specialist in expertly crafted leather goods, this shop offers wallets, bags and bracelets.

5 Flamenco Costumes
MAP B5 ■ Tamara Flamenco:
C/Santa Maria 5, Jerez ■ 956 34 74 89

Jerez is one of the very best places to find genuine flamenco gear.

6 Equestrian Equipment
MAP B5 ■ Hipisur: C/Circo 1,
Jerez ■ 956 32 42 09 ■ www.hipi sur.com

Jerez has to be one of the best places in the world to find refined horse-riding gear. Hipisur has an extensive range of clothing and kit.

7 Sherry
Jerez de la Frontera is, of course, also the prime spot to savour the finer points of a *fino*, a *manzanilla*, an *amontillado* or an *oloroso*. Tasting tours are available at most *bodegas* (see pp76–7).

8 Traditional Textiles
The villages of Grazalema and Arcos de la Frontera (see pp106) are known for their blankets, ponchos, rugs and other woven textiles.

9 Shopping in Gibraltar
MAP C6

The shopping draw here is twofold: there's no sales tax and it's mostly duty-free. Several UK high-street names are represented, such as The Body Shop and Marks & Spencer.

10 Leather
In the shops of Ronda (see pp30–31) you'll find some of the best prices on leather goods of anywhere in Spain. Many of the items have well-known labels, since fashion houses often have contracts with leather factories in this area.

Shopping in Ronda

Costa del Sol Golf Courses

Lush greens on the Valderrama course

designed by Robert Trent Jones. The grounds have raised greens, sand traps and water features. Opened in 1968, it has hosted the World Cup twice and the Spanish Open three times.

1 Valderrama
MAP C6 ■ Avda los Cortijos s/n San Roque ■ 956 79 12 00 ■ www.valderrama.com

The most famous golf club along the Costa, the Valderrama has hosted the Ryder Cup and is a Robert Trent Jones masterpiece.

2 Real Club de Golf Sotogrande
MAP D6 ■ Paseo del Parque, Sotogrande ■ 956 78 50 14 ■ www.golfsotogrande.com

Royal Sotogrande opened in 1964 and remains one of Europe's top 10 courses. Green-fee-paying visitors are welcome if they book in advance. The Robert Trent Jones design features mature trees and water obstacles.

3 San Roque
MAP C6 ■ N340 km 126.5, San Roque ■ 956 61 30 30 ■ www.sanroqueclub.com

Opened in 1990, San Roque is a Dave Thomas design and has been planned so that the holes are in the same direction as the prevailing wind.

4 Real Club Las Brisas
MAP D5 ■ Urbanización Nueva Calle Londres 1 (Andalucía), above Puerto Banús, Marbella ■ 952 81 08 75 ■ www.realclubdegolflasbrisas.com

Recognized as one of the finest courses in Europe, this was also

5 Alcaidesa Links
MAP C6 ■ Avda del Golf, San Roque ■ 956 79 10 40 ■ www.alcaidesagolf.com

The only links course in Spain, Alcaidesa opened in 1992, designed by Peter Alliss and Clive Clark.

6 Golf El Paraíso
MAP D5 ■ Ctra de Cádiz km 167, Estepona ■ 952 88 38 35 ■ www.elparaisogolf.com

This British-style golf venue was designed by Gary Player.

7 Los Arqueros
MAP D5 ■ Ctra de Ronda A397 km 44.5, Benahavis ■ 952 78 46 00 ■ www.losarquerosgolf.com

The Costa's first course to be designed by Seve Ballesteros is a tough test.

8 Miraflores
MAP D5 ■ Urbanización Riviera del Sol, Ctra de Cádiz km 198, Calle Severiano Ballesteros ■ 952 93 19 60 ■ www.miraflores-golf.com

Folco Nardi's design has many challenging holes.

9 La Duquesa
MAP D5 ■ Urbanización El Hacho, N340 km 143, Manilva ■ 952 89 07 25 ■ www.golfladuquesa.com

A Trent Jones design, the front nine holes begin in a westerly direction then finish with a long par five.

10 La Cañada
MAP C6 ■ Ctra Guadiaro km 1, Guadiaro, San Roque ■ 956 79 41 00 ■ www.lacanadagolf.com

The long 1st hole sets the tone for a tough round – the 4th offers no view of the green until the third shot.

See map on pp102–3 ←

Costa del Sol Nightlife

① Ocean Club, Marbella
MAP D5 ■ Avda Lola Flores
■ 952 90 81 37

A chic club featuring a saltwater swimming pool and a VIP area with huge round beds.

② La Suite, Marbella
MAP D5 ■ Puente Romano Hotel, Bulevar Príncipe Alfonso von Hohenlohe, Ctra de Cádiz km 177 ■ 952 89 09 00

Live it up at this club with fire-eaters, belly dancers and jugglers. In the summer, the club becomes Suite del Mar and moves beachside.

③ Club de Jazz y Cócteles Speakeasy, Fuengirola
MAP D5 ■ Centro Comercial Las Rampas 10, 29640 Fuengirola ■ 656 48 79 19

Styled after the speakeasies of the 1920s, this bar has live jazz music at weekends and great cocktails.

④ Seven, Puerto Banus
MAP D5 ■ Avda Ribera, Puerto Banus 29660 Marbella ■ 646 60 88 24

Typical of Marbella, this is an elegant club to enjoy cocktails and dance the night away.

⑤ Olivia Valère, Marbella
MAP D5 ■ Ctra de Istán km 0.8
■ 952 82 88 61

This exclusive club is a Costa hot spot. Designed by the same creative genius who did Paris's famous Buddha Bar, it attracts a well-heeled crowd.

Diners at Olivia Valère

⑥ Puerto Marina, Benalmádena
MAP D5 ■ Puerto Marina

A large complex with a variety of bars, nightclubs, shops and restaurants.

⑦ Mango, Benalmádena
MAP D5 ■ Plaza Solymar
■ 952 56 27 00

Popular with the younger crowds, this club has an electric atmosphere.

Dancing crowds at Mango

⑧ Casino Torrequebrada, Benalmádena
MAP D5 ■ Avda del Sol ■ 952 57 73 00
■ www.casinotorrequebrada.com

Located in the Hotel Torrequebrada, the casino has tables for blackjack, chemin de fer, punto y banco and roulette. Dress smart.

⑨ La Taberna de Pepe Lopez, Torremolinos
MAP E5 ■ Plaza de la Gamba Alegre
■ 952 38 12 84 ■ Closed Sun

This flamenco venue is highly touristy, but fun. Shows take place here between 10pm and midnight.

⑩ Torremolinos for LGBTQ+ Nightlife
MAP E5

Torremolinos has the best LGBTQ+ nightlife on the Costa del Sol. Start at terrace bar El Gato (Paseo Marítimo Antonio Machado 1), then try Parthenon (Calle Nogalera) or AQUA Club (Calle Nogalera). Centuryon (Calle Casablanca 15) is the biggest LGBTQ+ club outside Madrid or Barcelona.

Costa del Sol Places to Eat

PRICE CATEGORIES

For a three-course meal for one with half a bottle of wine (or equivalent meal), taxes and extra charges.

€ under €30   €€ €30–€50   €€€ over €50

1 La Pappardella, Marbella

MAP D5 ▪ Muelle Benabola, Casa A, local 4, Puerto Banus ▪ 952 81 50 89 ▪ €€

Enjoy true Neapolitan cuisine at this family-orientated restaurant with a wide range of pasta, pizza and seafood.

2 El Tintero II, Málaga

MAP E5 ▪ Avda Salvador Allende 340 ▪ 952 20 68 26 ▪ €

An open-air fish restaurant on the beach. There's no menu – the waiter will tell you what's on offer.

3 El Estrecho, Marbella

MAP D5 ▪ C/San Lázaro 12 ▪ 952 77 00 04 ▪ Closed Sun ▪ €

Another winning tapas bar and local favourite. There's a terrace, seafood treats and nice *fino*. Try the *boquerones al limón* (anchovies in lemon).

4 La Sirena, Benalmádena

MAP D5 ▪ Paseo Maritimo ▪ 952 56 02 39 ▪ €

On the beachfront, and the paella is one of the best in the area.

5 Bodegas Quitapenas, Torremolinos

MAP E5 ▪ C/Cuesta del Tajo 3 ▪ 952 38 62 44 ▪ €

An excellent tapas bar with Spanish seafood, including *pulpo* (octopus).

6 Restaurante La Escalera, Torremolinos

MAP E5 ▪ C/Cuesta del Tajo 12 ▪ 952 05 80 24 ▪ Closed Sun ▪ €

A great little choice with dreamy terrace views. The international menu includes curry soup with peas.

7 Tapeo de Cervantes, Málaga

MAP E5 ▪ C/Cárcer 8 ▪ 952 60 94 58 ▪ Closed Mon ▪ www.eltapeo decervantes.com ▪ €€

This charming, rustic *bodega* serves hearty regional food with some novel touches. Try the *estofado de cordero* (lamb stew with mint and couscous).

8 Bar Altamirano, Marbella

MAP D5 ▪ Plaza Altamirano 3 ▪ 952 82 49 32 ▪ €

Despite Marbella's glitzy image there are affordable, traditional tapas bars. This is one of them, just southeast of Plaza Naranjos; seafood specialities are listed on ceramic menus.

Alfresco dining at Bar Altamirano

9 Restaurante 34, Nerja

MAP E5 ▪ Calle Hernando de Carabeo 34 ▪ 952 52 54 44 ▪ €€€

Cut into the cliff, the café gives views of the sea while you are protected under palm frond umbrellas.

10 Lan Sang, Nerja

MAP E5 ▪ C/Malaga 12 ▪ 952 52 80 53 ▪ Closed Sun L, Mon ▪ €€

For a change of cuisine, try this Thai/Laotian restaurant. The modern, elegant decor is matched by the sophisticated flavours and beautiful presentation of the food.

See map on pp102–3 ←

Nightlife in the Region

An evening out in Nerja

① Nerja by Night
MAP E5 ▪ Seven: Plaza Tutti Frutti ▪ Sala Rockerfeller: C/Chaparil 7

If you're looking for nightlife in Nerja, head to Plaza Tutti Frutti where there are around 25 bars and nightspots offering everything from cocktails to karaoke. Two of the best-known clubs here are Seven and the nearby Sala Rockerfeller.

② Barsovia, Málaga
MAP R4 ▪ C/Mendez Nuñez 3

This old-town disco attracts people of all ages. The music is a mix of 1980s feel-good, with some current hits thrown in.

③ ZZ Pub, Málaga
MAP Q4 ▪ C/Tejón y Rodríguez 6

Mostly students come to this modest establishment in the old town to hear the bands that play here on weekdays. A DJ fills in the quiet moments every night.

④ Tarifa
MAP C6 ▪ Almedina Tarifa: C/Almedina ▪ Café del Mar: Paseo Marítimo

Almedina Tarifa is one of the oldest and most beautiful bars in town, with flamenco on Thursday nights. Nightclub Café del Mar has three floors including a roof terrace.

⑤ Cádiz
MAP B5 ▪ Momart Theatre: Paseo Pascual Pery Junquera ▪ 660 58 04 86 ▪ Open Fri & Sat ▪ Adm

The zone around the harbour is loaded with venues and Momart Theatre is one of the best.

⑥ Flamenco in Cádiz
MAP B5 ▪ Peña La Perla: C/Carlos Ollero ▪ Peña Enrique el Mellizo: Punta San Felipe, C/Nuevo Mundo 1

The flamenco clubs burst with life in Cádiz. Good bets include Peña La Perla and Peña Enrique el Mellizo.

⑦ Flamenco in Jerez
MAP B5

Here you will find genuine flamenco at its impassioned best. The gypsy quarter of Santiago is the place to make for, where you will find a number of *peñas* (clubs), but don't expect much before 10pm.

⑧ Ronda
MAP D5 ▪ Café Las Bridas: C/Virgen de los Remedios 18 ▪ Café Pub Dulcinea: C/Rios Rosas 3

Café Las Bridas offers imported brews, with live music on weekends from midnight. Dance to Spanish electro-pop at Café Pub Dulcinea.

⑨ Gibraltar
MAP C6

There are more than 360 pubs in Gibraltar. If you enjoy late nights you should visit Queensway Quay, Marina Bay and Casemates Square, which have a wide selection of bars.

⑩ Bars in Sancti Petri
MAP C6

Sip a cocktail and watch the sunset at one of the popular beach bars along the Costa de la Luz.

Places to Eat in the Region

PRICE CATEGORIES

For a three-course meal for one with half a bottle of wine (or equivalent meal), taxes and extra charges.

€ under €30   €€ €30–€50   €€€ over €50

1 Ventorrillo del Chato, Cádiz

MAP B5 ■ Ctra Cádiz-San Fernando km 2 (Via Augusta Julia) ■ 956 25 00 25 ■ €€€

The oldest restaurant in Cádiz (1780) is also one of the best. Try *salmorejo*, a thick tomato soup served as a dip or side dish, and *dorada a la sal*, a local fish baked in a salt crust.

2 Antigua Casa de Guardia, Málaga

MAP Q5 ■ Alameda Principal 18 ■ 952 21 46 80 ■ Closed Sun ■ €

The city's oldest *taberna*, dating from 1840, has barrels of local wine in the bar. The steamed mussels are great.

Wine in Antigua Casa de Guardia

3 Rigodón, Jerez

MAP B5 ■ C/Torneria 3 ■ 856 10 03 30 ■ €€

This small, trendy restaurant is sure to please with influences from Brazil, Italy, Greece and India.

4 Bar Juanito, Jerez

MAP B5 ■ C/Pescadería Vieja 8 & 10 ■ 956 33 48 38 ■ Closed Wed ■ €

Famous for the best tapas in town. It closes during the Feria in May.

5 Restaurante Los Portales, El Puerto de Santa María

MAP B5 ■ C/Ribera del Marisco 7 ■ €€

Savour traditional Cádiz delicacies in a renovated winery. Fish and seafood are the speciality here.

6 Sollo, Fuengirola

MAP D5 ■ Avenida del Higuerón 48 ■ 951 38 56 22 ■ Closed L ■ €€€

Caviar at Sollo

Chef Diego Gallegos serves up unusual tapas-style dishes using snail caviar, eels, trout ceviche and ox-steak – all beautifully presented.

7 Tragatá, Ronda

MAP D5 ■ C/Nueva 4 ■ 952 87 72 09 ■ €€

Former El Bulli chef Benito Gómez creates some of the best tapas in Andalucía. Stocks local Schatz organic wines.

8 Jardin del Califa, Vejer de la Frontera

MAP C6 ■ Plaza de España 16 ■ 956 45 17 06 ■ €€€

Truly exquisite North African and Middle Eastern cuisine is served in an enchanting complex of medieval buildings. Dine in the shady garden or a stone vaulted cellar.

9 Balandro, Cádiz

MAP B5 ■ Alameda Apodaca 22 ■ 956 22 09 92 ■ €€

In an 18th-century mansion overlooking the bay, Balandro serves superb fried and grilled fish.

10 Restaurante Tropicana

MAP D5 ■ Calle Virgen de los Dolores 11 ■ 952 87 89 85 ■ Closed Sun–Thu D ■ €€

Stylish restaurant with innovative international fusion dishes.

See map on pp102–3

TOP 10 Granada and Almería Provinces

Seduced by the photogenic fantasy that is the Alhambra, tourists often forget to make time to see the area's other attractions. Besides Granada's many religious and cultural landmarks, the entire region is worth exploring. Hikers will enjoy the mountain trails of the Sierra Nevada, beach-lovers will discover still unspoiled coastal areas and fans of Spaghetti Westerns will marvel at desert locations and movie film sets.

Urn, Cueva-Museo, Guadix

1 Guadix

MAP F4 ■ Cueva-Museo: Plaza Padre Poveda; 958 66 55 67; open 10am–2pm & 4–6pm Mon–Fri (Jul & Aug: 5–7pm), 10am–2pm Sat; adm; www.mcicuevasdeguadix. blogspot.com

This ancient town is famous for its cave dwellings, inhabited for centuries. They were developed after the *reconquista* by local Moors who had been cast out of society by the Christians. The Barrio de las Cuevas is a surreal zone of brown hills with rounded whitewashed chimneys. To learn more, visit the Cueva-Museo or stay in a cave hotel *(see p146)*.

2 Capilla Real and Catedral, Granada

MAP Q2 ■ Catedral: C/Gran Via de Colón 5; open 10am–2pm & 3–7pm Mon–Sat; adm ■ Capilla Real: C/Oficios 3; 958 22 78 48; open Jun–Sep: 10am–2pm & 3–7pm daily; Oct–May: 10:15am–6:30pm Mon–Sat, 11am–6pm Sun; adm; www.capillarealgranada.com

To establish Christian rule, these triumphalist structures were built by some of the greatest architects of the age. The interior of Granada's cathedral is one of the most stunning achievements, while Alonso Cano's façade echoes the ancient triple arch favoured by Roman emperors. The

GRANADA AND ALMERÍA PROVINCES

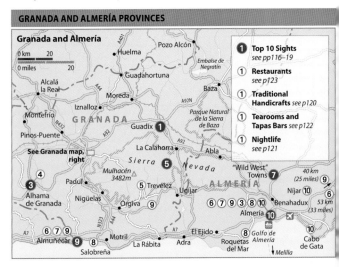

Granada and Almería

- ① Top 10 Sights see pp116–19
- ① Restaurants see p123
- ① Traditional Handicrafts see p120
- ① Tearooms and Tapas Bars see p122
- ① Nightlife see p121

Capilla Real (Royal Chapel) is Granada's finest Christian building (*see p45*) and a repository of rare treasures, including a *reja* (gilded grille) by Bartolomé de Jaén, priceless jewels and paintings by Roger van der Weyden and Sandro Botticelli.

③ Alhama de Granada
MAP E4

Clinging precariously to the edge of a breathtaking gorge, this whitewashed village was known in Moorish times for its beauty and natural thermal waters (*al-hamma* means "hot spring" in Arabic). Hotel Balneario preserves an 11th-century *aljibe* (cistern), graced by Caliphal arches. In the 16th-century Iglesia de la Encarnación, some of the vestments are said to have been embroidered by Queen Isabel the Catholic.

④ Moorish Granada
MAP Q2 ▪ **Museo**

CajaGRANADA: Memoria de Andalucía, Avda de la Ciencia 2; 958 22 22 57; open Sep–Jun: 9:30am–2pm Tue–Sat (also 4–7pm Thu–Sat), 11am–3pm Sun & hols; Jul: 10:30am–2:30pm Mon–Sat, 11am–3pm Sun & hols; closing hours vary, check website for details; adm; www.memoriadeandalucia.com

The fairy-tale palace of the Alhambra (*see pp12–13*) draws millions of visitors each year. In the city below, the ancient Albaicín (*see pp16–17*) district embodies a microcosm of a North African village, a "Little Morocco", with colourful market streets and tearooms. Behind the area stands Sacromonte, the traditional home of cave-dwelling gypsies. Also worth a visit is the Museo CajaGRANADA, devoted to Andalucían culture.

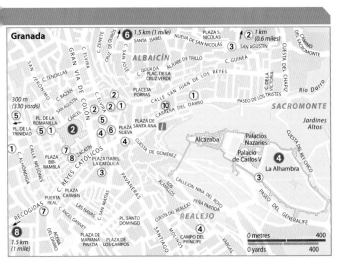

The magnificent Alhambra overlooking Granada

Late-winter skiing in the Sierra Nevada mountains

⑤ Sierra Nevada

Spain's tallest peaks – and, after the Alps, Europe's second-loftiest chain – make Andalucía home to some excellent winter sports and robust trekking in spring and summer, as well as abundant wild flowers and wildlife. Stop in the historic villages of the Alpujarras, on the southern slopes, where time seems to have stood still, and see local artisans at work (see pp38–9).

Monasterio de la Cartuja, Granada

⑥ Monasterio de la Cartuja, Granada

MAP F4 ■ Paseo de la Cartuja ■ 958 16 19 32 ■ Open summer: 10am–1pm & 4–8pm daily ■ Adm

Founded in 1516, this Carthusian monastery has a deceptively austere exterior considering the flamboyant Spanish Baroque detailing that can be found inside its church and sacristy. The busy flourishes and arabesques of polychromed and gilded stucco almost swallow up the architectural lines. The dazzling cupola by Antonio Palomino is a particular highlight.

⑦ "Wild West" Towns

MAP G4 ■ Fort Bravo: Ctra N340 km 468, Paraje de Unihay s/n, Tabernas; 902 07 08 14; open 9am–7:30pm daily; adm; www.fortbravo.org ■ Mini Hollywood: Ctra N340 km 464, Tabernas; 950 36 52 36; open summer: 10am–7:30pm Tue–Sun; winter: 10am–6pm Sat–Sun; adm; www.oasys parquetematico.com ■ Western Leone: Ctra A92 km 378, Tabernas; 950 16 54 05; open 10am–8pm daily; www.western-leone.es

The interior of Almería Province resembles the deserts and canyons of the American Southwest: it was the perfect spot for filming the Wild West epics known as "Spaghetti Westerns" of the 1960s and 1970s. Three of the sets are now theme parks: Mini Hollywood (see p71), Fort Bravo and Western Leone offer stunt shows and memorabilia.

⑧ Museo Parque de las Ciencias

MAP F4 ■ Avda de la Ciencia, Granada ■ 958 13 19 00 ■ Open 10am–7pm Tue–Sat, 10am–3pm Sun & hols ■ Adm ■ www.parqueciencias.com

This exciting complex (see p53), dedicated to science and exploration, is made up of numerous interactive areas, such as Journey Through the Human Body, Perception, Eureka and Biosphere. There's an Observation Tower, a Planetarium and the Sala Explora, exclusively for children aged 3–7, where they can conduct their first experiments. There are temporary exhibitions too.

PLASTICULTURA

If you approach the coastal area of these provinces from the west, you will notice the extent of plastic tenting, a phenomenon that reaches a peak before Almería. This agricultural technique is known as *plasticultura* and squeezes out every drop of moisture from these desert lands in order to produce crops. The process is anything but organic, but this huge agribusiness provides jobs and year-round produce.

⑨ Almuñécar and Around

MAP F5 ■ Museo Arqueológico Cueva de Siete Palacios: Barrio de San Miguel; 607 86 54 66; opening hours vary, call ahead for details; adm

The Costa Tropical is a spectacular coast with towering mountains rising from the shore. Almuñécar is the chief town on this stretch and it is almost entirely devoted to resort life. Yet it has an ancient heritage, dating back to the Phoenicians, and was an important port under the Moors. The intriguing archaeological museum has a unique Egyptian vase dating from the 7th century BC.

Alcazaba, Almería

⑩ Almería and Around

MAP G4 ■ Alcazaba: C/Almanzor; 950 80 10 08; open Tue–Sun; call ahead for opening hours; adm (free for EU members)

Almería, the "mirror of the sea", has lost much of its shine due to modern development. Still, its 10th-century Alcazaba is one of the most impressive surviving Moorish forts, and there are many spots with North African influences in the old quarter.

A MORNING IN GRANADA

▶ MORNING

Begin your walk at Plaza Bib-Rambla, enhanced with flower stalls and the Neptune fountain. Fronting the western side of the square is the warren of ancient shopping streets called **La Alcaicería** *(see p120)*. Don't miss the 14th-century Moorish Corral del Carbón, which now houses a cultural centre.

Once the **cathedral** *(see pp116–17)* opens, it's time for a visit. Be sure to see the main chapel, a masterpiece by Siloé, and the ornaments and priceless treasures in the Chapter Room. The next stop is the **Capilla Real** *(see pp116–17)*; you should visit the crypt under the ostentatious marble sarcophagi of the kings and queens, where their bodies repose in plain lead boxes. On the carved Renaissance sepulchres, note the split pomegranate, symbol of a defeated Moorish Granada.

Continue on across the busy thoroughfares until you get to the river and the long expanse of **Plaza Nueva** *(see p59)*. Choose an outside table (the cafés here are all similar), order a drink and take in the street life.

It's time to enter the labyrinth of the **Albaicín** *(see pp16–17)*. Take Calle Elvira up to Calle Calderería Vieja for the vibrant bazaar of the Moorish Quarter. Following the old steep streets, keep going until you reach the fanciful **La Tetería del Bañuelo** *(see p122)*, an inviting place to sip some mint tea and sample Moroccan sweets.

See map on pp116–17 ←

Traditional Handicrafts

 Albaicín, Granada
The authentic Moroccan shops in this ancient quarter *(see pp16–17)* are all concentrated on two sloping streets off Calle Elvira – Calderería Vieja and Calderería Nueva.

2 Capricho del Artesano (Hermanos Fabres), Granada
MAP Q2 ▪ Plaza Pescadería 10 ▪ 958 28 81 92

This traditional ceramics store sells the typical style of the region: blue patterns on white tiles, often with a pomegranate motif.

3 Taracea Laguna, Granada
MAP S2 ▪ Real de la Alhambra 30 ▪ 958 22 90 19

Opposite the entrance to the Alhambra, you can see how *taracea* (Moorish marquetry, often inlaid with bone, mother of pearl or silver) is made, and take home a souvenir unique to this area.

4 Munira Mendonca, Granada
MAP Q2 ▪ Plaza Nueva 15 ▪ 958 22 19 39 ▪ www.munira.net

Exquisitely hand-tooled leather goods, including bags and belts, can be found in this family-run shop.

5 El Rocío, Granada
MAP Q2 ▪ C/Capuchinas 8 ▪ 958 26 58 23

The complete outfitter for *romería* and festival-going gear. All the frills, polka dots and bright colours will dazzle your eye, and it all comes in every size, so even babies can have a flounce or two.

6 Bazar el Valenciano, Almería
MAP G4 ▪ C/Las Tiendas 34 ▪ 950 23 45 93

This is the oldest store in town. Look for "El Indalo" souvenirs, which are items bearing the symbol of Almería for good luck.

7 Carrera de la Virgen, Granada
MAP F4 ▪ Ibérica: Carrera de la Virgen 44 ▪ Abuela Ili: Carrera de la Virgen 51

This street has some great gourmet shops. Ibérica, a deli specializing in local fare, is a must-try, while Abuela Ili is a specialist chocolate shop best suited to those with a sweet tooth.

8 La Alcaicería, Granada
MAP Q2

In Moorish times this was the silk market, although the horseshoe arches and stucco are a modern re-creation. The narrow alleyways are bursting with colourful wares such as silver jewellery, embroidered silk shawls and ceramics.

Narrow alleys of La Alcaicería

9 Alpujarras Crafts
MAP F4–G4

The hill towns of this zone are rich in traditional crafts, including ceramics and weaving. Local *jarapas* (rugs), bags, ponchos and blankets are hand-loomed in age-old patterns. They're sold at local weekly markets.

10 Níjar, Almería Province
MAP H4

This coastal town is known for its distinctive pottery and *jarapas*. Head for Calle Las Eras, in the Barrio Alfarero, to find the genuine article.

Nightlife

1 La Canastera, Almería

Enjoy Flamenco performances at this venue in the Pescadería neighbourhood of Almería *(see p51)*. Entrance fee is generally around €10, which includes one drink from the bar.

2 Boom Boom Room

MAP Q2 ▪ C/Carcél Baja 10 ▪ 608 66 66 10 ▪ www. boomboomroom.es

Outdoor seating at El Camborio

An opulent nightclub set in a 1930s theatre with a preserved decor. You can dance under crystal chandeliers, Neo-Classical-style plasterwork and plush private boxes. The latest dance hits attract people of all ages.

3 TragoFino-San Matias 30, Granada

MAP Q2 ▪ Plaza de las Descalzas 3 ▪ 665 40 93 12

This trendy bar, located in the heart of Granada, is a popular spot with the locals. It serves a variety of reasonably priced, delicious cocktails. The service is friendly and attentive.

4 Sala Prince, Granada

MAP R3 ▪ Campo del Príncipe 7 ▪ 696 29 00 35

This two-storey disco hosts live music by emerging artists as well as popular bands. The venue is styled after the Nasrid palaces on the hill above.

5 Planta Baja, Granada

MAP F4 ▪ C/Horno de Abad 11 ▪ www.plantabaja.club

A two-storey venue: the upper floor is a quiet bar; downstairs, the DJs play chart hits and everyone dances. There is live music on the weekends.

6 Abanicos, Almería

MAP G5 ▪ C/Goya 2, 04648 Pulpí ▪ www.abanicosterreros.com

This summer-only bar specializes in cocktails served with a tropical flair.

7 El Camborio, Granada

MAP S1 ▪ Camino del Sacromonte 47 ▪ 958 22 12 15

This is a popular night venue in the caves of Sacromonte *(see p17)*. Music echoes from four dance floors to the rooftop terraces, offering a striking view of the Alhambra at sunrise. The venue is open from Tuesday to Saturday.

8 Chaplin's Pub, Almería

MAP G5 ▪ Calle Sierra Nevada 27, Roquetas de Mar ▪ 618 82 43 68 ▪ Closed Mon & Tue ▪ www.chaplinspub.business.site

Watch sporting events, play bar games and enjoy a pint of beer at this classic British pub.

9 Maui Beach, Almería

MAP H4 ▪ Paseo del Mediterráneo 40, Mojácar Beach ▪ 950 47 87 22

This charming *chiringuito* (beach bar) offers a variety of zones, each with a great ambience. At night, Maui Beach transforms from a bar-cum-restaurant into a lively club.

10 Le Chien Andalou, Granada

MAP R2 ▪ Carrera del Darro 7 ▪ 617 10 66 23

Dine while watching an enchanting flamenco show in a cosy cave setting at the Le Chien Adalou. Reservations recommended.

See map on pp116–17

Tearooms and Tapas Bars

① La Tetería del Bañuelo, Granada

MAP R2 ▪ C/Bañuelo 5

A more relaxed and inviting place is hard to imagine. The little rooms and intimate niches are suffused with a gentle light, the air with the aromas of tea and flowers and the sound of songbirds. Try sweets and fragrant brews, and enjoy unsurpassed views.

② Kasbah, Granada

MAP Q2 ▪ C/Calderería Nueva 4

Relax amid the comforts of this candlelit café. Silky pillows and romantic nooks abound. You can taste Arab pastries and a selection of Moroccan teas.

Casa Puga, a traditional tapas bar

③ Casa Puga, Almería

MAP G4 ▪ C/Jovellanos 7
▪ Closed Sun

One of the city's best tapas bars. The wine list is exhaustive, as you might guess from the wine racks on view.

④ Bar La Buena Vida, Granada

MAP Q2 ▪ C/Almiceros 12

A welcoming tapas bar with a good variety of wines and beers. There's free tapas with each drink, so you can sample a wide variety of treats without breaking the bank.

⑤ La Riviera, Granada

MAP Q2 ▪ C/Cetti Meriem 7

Located in the heart of the city, La Riviera offers a good variety of beer and tapas.

⑥ Antigua Bodega Castañeda, Granada

MAP Q2 ▪ C/Elvira 5

Antique wine barrels and hanging hams give a rustic feel. The cheese boards are a good bet, as are the *montaditos* (small sandwiches).

⑦ Casa Enrique, Granada

MAP Q3 ▪ C/Acero de Darro 8
▪ Closed Sun

Another wonderfully old-fashioned hole-in-the-wall lined with antique barrels. Try the *montaditos de lomo* (small sandwiches with pork fillet) and *torta del casar* (sheep's-milk cheese).

⑧ Tetería Al Hammam Almeraya, Almería

MAP G4 ▪ C/Perea 9 ▪ Closed
Mon–Wed

Escape from the crowds and head for the tranquil tearoom of Almería's Arab baths, where you can enjoy Moorish-inspired teas and snacks.

⑨ Bodega Francisco, Almuñécar

MAP F5 ▪ C/Real 11

A forest of ham shanks hanging from the ceiling greets the eye, along with barrels of *fino* in this traditional tapas bar. The attached restaurant next door, Francisco II, serves full meals.

⑩ El Quinto Toro, Almería

MAP G4 ▪ Juan Leal 6 ▪ Closed
Sat D, Sun

The name derives from the tradition that the best bull of a *corrida* is chosen to fight in the fifth *(quinto)* confrontation of the day. This tapas bar is favoured by local aficionados of the bullfight.

Restaurants

1 Cunini, Granada
MAP F4 ▪ Plaza Pescadería
14 ▪ 958 25 07 77 ▪ Closed Sun D,
Mon ▪ €€

The fresh seafood, brought in daily
from Motril, is highly recommended,
and is a big hit with the food critics.

Arrayanes Moroccan restaurant

2 Arrayanes, Granada
MAP Q2 ▪ Cuesta Marañas 4
▪ 958 22 84 01 ▪ Closed Tue ▪ €

A sophisticated and authentic North
African restaurant in the Moroccan
quarter. Halal meat and no alcohol.

3 Carmen Mirador de Aixa, Granada
MAP R2 ▪ Carril de San Agustín 2 ▪ 958
22 36 16 ▪ Closed Sun L, Mon ▪ €€

Enjoy excellent interpretations of
regional dishes such as *habas con
jamón* (broad beans with ham). Views
of the Alhambra from the terrace.

4 Restaurante El Ventorro, Alhama de Granada
MAP E4 ▪ Ctra de Jatar km 2
▪ 958 35 04 38 ▪ Closed Mon ▪ €€

In this lovely rural restaurant you
can try Grandma Currilla's potato
stew, as well as sumptuous
casseroles and grilled meat.

5 Restaurante González, Trevélez
MAP F4 ▪ Plaza Francisco Abellán
▪ 958 85 85 33 ▪ €

Perfect spot to try the flavourful
ham that the region is known for,
while taking in the scenic views.

6 El Chaleco, Almuñécar
MAP F5 ▪ Avda Costa del Sol
37 ▪ 958 63 24 02 ▪ Closed Sun D,
Mon (except Jul & Aug) ▪ €€

French cuisine, lovingly prepared
with attention to detail, is served
in a romantic, intimate setting.

7 Restaurante Mar De Plata, Almuñécar
MAP F5 ▪ Avenida Mar de Plata 3
▪ 958 63 30 79 ▪ €

At this Mediterranean restaurant
choose from a wide selection of
dishes, particularly focused on fresh
fish and seafood. Do not miss *arroz
con bogavante* (rice with lobster).

8 Pesetas, Salobreña
MAP F5 ▪ C/Bóveda 11
▪ 958 61 01 82 ▪ Closed Mon ▪ €

Absorb the ambience of the old
quarters of Salobreña and the
excellent views of the coast
while dining here. The *choco a la
marinera* (squid in tomato sauce)
is a speciality. Good salads, too.

9 Restaurante Valentín, Almería
MAP G4 ▪ C/Tenor Iribarne 19 ▪ 950
26 44 75 ▪ Closed Mon, Sep ▪ €€

Specialities at Restaurante Valentín
include highly delectable *arroz negro*
(rice in squid ink) and *pescado en
adobo* (marinated fish).

10 La Goleta, San Miguel del Cabo de Gata
MAP H5 ▪ Paseo Marítimo Cabo de
Gata ▪ 950 37 02 15 ▪ Closed Mon,
first 2 weeks in Nov ▪ €€

All the seafood is at its freshest
here, of course, since this village
is located right in the middle of
Andalucía's most unspoiled coast.

See map on pp116–17

TOP 10 Córdoba and Jaén Provinces

These two provinces are an attractive blend of exquisite urban architecture, famed agricultural zones and great wildlife reserves within rugged mountain ranges. The ancient treasure-trove of Córdoba is the star, but the Renaissance towns of Baeza and Úbeda are among the region's most beautiful. For lovers of delicious wine, ham and olive oil, the areas around Montilla, Valle de los Pedroches and Baena should not be missed. Meanwhile, nature lovers can hike for days amid the wilds of the Parque Natural de la Sierra de Cardeña y Montoro in Córdoba and the Sierra de Cazorla in Jaén.

Iberian art, Museo Provincial de Jaén

Alcázar, Córdoba

1 Córdoba

This town *(see pp22–5)*, wonderfully rich in history and cultural importance, is also small enough to cover easily and enjoyably on foot. It has a delightfully contrasting mix of sights, from the architectural splendour of the great mosque – with a Christian church oddly sprouting out of its centre – to the whitewashed glories of the old Jewish quarter, the splendid Alcázar and the Zoco

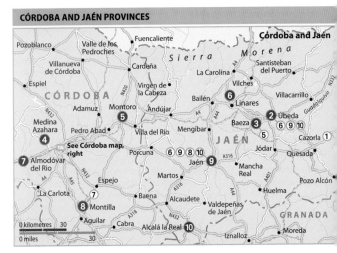

CÓRDOBA AND JAÉN PROVINCES

Municipal with its diverse selection of goods made by local artists. There are engaging museums as well, featuring works of art by Old Masters and local artists, and ancient artifacts evoking the area's influential past.

2 Úbeda

Ignore the downtrodden outskirts as you approach this town (see p35) – once you get to the historic centre you will realize that it is one of Andalucía's most remarkable splendours. The keynote here is architecture – an entire district of Renaissance edifices built for local nobility in the 16th century. One of Andalucía's greatest architects, Andrés de Vandelvira, was the genius who gave most of these structures their harmonious forms.

3 Baeza

Like nearby Úbeda, this smaller town (see p34) is also a jewel of Renaissance glory, but includes earlier remains dating back to the Moors and, before them, the Romans. The town radiates a sense of tranquillity as you walk from one cluster of lovely buildings to another. Again, much of the beauty owes its existence to the architect Andrés de Vandelvira.

Ruins of Medina Azahara palace

4 Medina Azahara

MAP D3 ■ Ctra Palma del Río km 5.5, W of Córdoba ■ 957 10 49 33 ■ Opening hours vary, check website for details ■ Adm (free for EU members) ■ www.medinaazahara.org

The building of the first palace here dates from AD 936, commissioned by Caliph Abd ar-Rahman III, Emir of Córdoba and the man who brought the city to glory. He named it after his favourite wife, Az-Zahra (the Radiant). Though it is little more than a ruin now, at one time it held a zoo, ponds and gardens, baths, houses, barracks, markets, mosques, a harem of 6,000 women and accommodation for 4,000 enslaved people. Nighttime visits are available in the spring and summer months, providing a magical experience.

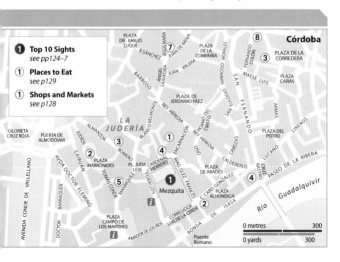

Top 10 Sights
see pp124–7

Places to Eat
see p129

Shops and Markets
see p128

5 Montoro

MAP E2 ▪ Museo Arqueológico: Plaza de Santa María de la Mota; 957 16 23 00; open May–Sep: 9:30am–1:30pm daily; Oct–Apr: 10am–2pm daily ▪ Casa de las Conchas: C/Criado 17; 957 16 00 89 (tourist office); adm

Laid out on an undulating series of five hills at a bend in the river, this ancient town sports a Baroque tower and a handsome 15th-century bridge. Other sights include a good Museo Arqueológico Municipal and the eccentrically kitsch Casa de las Conchas, a shell-encrusted folly; contact the tourist office for a tour.

6 Cástulo

MAP F2 ▪ Ctra Linares-Torrreblascopedro (JV-3003) km 3.3 ▪ 953 106 074 ▪ Opening hours vary, check website for details ▪ Adm (free for EU members) ▪ Monographic Museum of Cástulo: Calle General Echagüe 2, 23700 Linares; 953 60 93 89; opening hours vary, check website for details; www.museosdeandalucia.es

The ruins of this ancient city are situated in a strategic position in the Guadalquivir Valley. Cástulo is open to the public and is home to some immaculately preserved mosaics. The Monographic Museum of Cástulo, dedicated to this city and its history, is located 7 km away in Linares.

7 Castillo de Almodóvar

MAP D3 ▪ Almodóvar del Río 25 km (16 miles) W of Córdoba ▪ 957 63 40 55 ▪ Open 11am–2:30pm Mon–Fri, 11am–7pm Sat–Sun & public hols (Apr–Sep: to 8pm) ▪ www.castillodealmodovar.com ▪ Adm

Originally the site of a Roman, then a Moorish, fortification, the present castle goes back to the 1300s, when it was embellished in Gothic style. Legend holds that ghosts of those who died while imprisoned here haunt the eight monolithic towers.

8 Montilla

MAP D3 ▪ Bodegas Alvear: Avda de María Auxiliadora 1; 957 65 01 00; open daily for tours in English, by appt; adm; www.alvear.es

The centre of Córdoba's wine-making region, this town gave *amontillado* sherry its name (it means "in the style of Montilla"). The wine here is like sherry, but nuttier and more toasted. Since the region is hotter than around Jerez, the grapes ripen more intensely and the wines need no fortifying. You can taste the difference at Bodegas Alvear *(see p76)*, founded in 1729.

BAENA OLIVE OIL

This Córdoba Province town is famed for its olive oil, and you can catch its unmistakable fragrance as you enter the district. The Museo del Olivar y el Aceite *(C/Cañada 7; 957 69 16 41; open Tue–Sun)* is well worth a visit **(above)**. It shows how each organically grown olive is carefully kept from bruising and the paste is extracted by the process of stone crushing.

Castillo de Almodóvar

⑨ Jaén

MAP E3 ■ Cathedral: Plaza Santa María; open 10am–2pm & 4–8pm Mon–Fri, 10am–2pm & 4–7pm Sat, 10am–noon & 4–7pm Sun; adm ■ Museo Provincial de Jaén: Paseo de la Estación 29; open Jul–Aug: 9am–3pm Tue–Sun; mid-Sep–Jun: 9am–9pm Tue–Sat, 10am–3pm Sun; adm (free for EU members)

This modern provincial capital is set off by the dramatically placed ramparts of the mighty Castillo de Santa Catalina (see p47) and the immensity of its double-towered cathedral by Vandelvira (see p45). You can experience the castle and its spectacular views of the city and surrounding olive groves, as it now houses a parador. The Museo Provincial de Jaén houses the country's finest collection of 5th-century BC Iberian sculpture.

Castillo de Santa Catalina, Jaén

⑩ Alcalá La Real

MAP E3 ■ Fortress: 953 10 27 17 ■ Open Apr–mid-Oct: 10:30am–7:30pm daily; mid-Oct–Mar: 10am–6pm daily ■ Adm

The 12th-century Fortaleza de la Mota (see p46) dominates this once strategic town and is unique in Jaén Province in that its original Moorish castle was built by Badis Aben Habuz, the ruler of Granada. Mostly in ruins, it still preserves the original seven gates. Inside, built on the remains of a mosque, is the Gothic-Mudéjar church of Santo Domingo, which uses the former minaret as a bell tower.

A MORNING WALK THROUGH BAEZA

▶ MORNING

Your tour of this Renaissance town starts at the lovely **Plaza del Pópulo** (see p34). The tourist office is inside a fine Plateresque palace, the Casa del Pópulo. Next to it are the arches of the **Puerta de Jaén** (see p34) and the Arco de Villalar, and in the centre is the Fuente de los Leones. The ruined lions and their eroded mistress, said to be a statue of Hannibal's wife, still manage to convey an undeniable elegance.

Exiting the square to the left of the tourist office, continue southeast to the **Plaza Santa María** (see p34) and the **cathedral**. Inside the cathedral, don't miss the extravagant choir screen by Bartolomé de Jaén.

Next stop, to the north, is the **Palacio de Jabalquinto** (see p34), with one of the most eccentric façades in the region, an example of Isabelline Plateresque style. It is now a university but you can still go and visit its inner patio, then that of the Antigua Universidad next door. Opposite the palace, admire the **Iglesia de Santa Cruz** (see p26), a well-preserved church from the 13th century.

Down the street, you can see the 1,000-year-old Moorish Torre de los Aliatares and around the corner, facing **Paseo de la Constitución** (see p34), La Alhóndiga, the old corn exchange, with its triple-tiered façade.

🍴 Have lunch at traditional **Taberna El Pájaro** (Portales Tundidores 5; 953 74 43 48; closed Mon), with its rustic stone walls, local fare and extensive wine list.

See map on pp124–5 ⬅

Shops and Markets

Meryan leather workshop

1 Meryan, Córdoba
MAP D3 ▪ Calleja de las Flores 2
▪ 957 47 59 02

Specialists in hand-tooled leather goods; pick up a souvenir from your visit – from handbags, accessories and frames to furniture.

2 Zoco Municipal, Córdoba
MAP D3 ▪ C/Judios s/n
▪ 957 20 40 33

This historic house and patio has been converted into a co-op for local artists working in ceramics, leather, metalworks and woodwork.

3 Kuvo Plata, Córdoba
MAP D3 ▪ C/Rodríguez Marín 18 ▪ 957 485 552 ▪ www. kuvoplata.com

Located in the heart of Córdoba, close to the Templo Romano, this shop sells traditional silver jewellery inspired by Córdoba's history and culture.

4 Bodegas Mezquita, Córdoba
MAP D3 ▪ Calle Cardenal Herrero 8
▪ 957 10 06 06 ▪ www. bodegasmezquita.com

This is an excellent place for local foodstuffs: slow-cured hams, fine wines, olive oils and many other delectables. It also has a tapas bar around the corner.

5 Baraka, Córdoba
MAP D3 ▪ C/Manríquez
▪ 957 48 83 27

This is a good spot for quality souvenirs. Choose from ceramics, leather goods, glassware and other accessories, all handmade.

6 Ubedíes Artesanía con Esparto, Úbeda
MAP F2 ▪ C/Real 45–7 ▪ 639 56 37 88
▪ www.artesaniaconesparto.com

Here you'll find an innovative selection of items made with esparto grass, ranging from shoes to decorative items.

7 Monsieur Bourguignon, Córdoba
MAP D3 ▪ C/Jesús María 11
▪ 605 98 75 84

A decadent shop offering an assortment of chocolates, biscuits and handmade sweets, which are almost too pretty to eat.

8 Galería de Vinos Caldos, Jaén
MAP E3 ▪ C/Ceron 12 ▪ 953 23 59 99

One of the area's best, this wine shop stocks regional wines, including those from Montilla (see p126).

9 Pottery Quarter, Úbeda
MAP F2 ▪ C/Valencia

Úbeda is famous for its dark green pottery, fired in wood kilns over olive stones. Its intricate, pierced designs are Moorish-inspired and the workmanship superb.

Intricate green Úbeda pottery

10 Flea Market, Jaén
MAP E3 ▪ Recinto Ferial, Avda de Granada

Thursday mornings see this street come to life with a catch-all market that can net you anything from pure junk to a rare treasure.

Places to Eat

PRICE CATEGORIES

For a three-course meal for one with half a bottle of wine (or equivalent meal), taxes and extra charges.

€ under €30 €€ €30–€50 €€€ over €50

1 Restaurante & Bistró Casa Alfonso, Cazorla

MAP G3 ■ Placeta Consuelo Mendieta 2 ■ 953 72 14 63 ■ Closed Tue ■ €€

Expertly prepared dishes and attentive service are on offer at this restaurant with an elegant setting. Try one of the taster menus *(menu de degustación)*.

2 Horno San Luis, Córdoba

MAP D3 ■ C/Cardenal Gonzalez 73 ■ 957 47 45 29 ■ €€

Housed in a historic *panaderia* (bread bakery), this stylish restaurant serves a varied cuisine.

3 El Churrasco, Córdoba

MAP D3 ■ C/Romero 16 ■ 957 29 08 19 ■ Closed Aug ■ €€€

One of the city's smartest, this restaurant serves sumptuous traditional fare. Sample the eponymous *churrasco* (grilled pork loin with spicy red pepper sauce).

4 Almudaina, Córdoba

MAP D3 ■ Plaza Campo Santo de los Martires 1 ■ 957 47 43 42 ■ Closed Sun D ■ €€

Set in a 16th-century mansion, this is another great place to try traditional dishes, such as *pechuga de perniz en salsa* (partridge breasts in sauce).

5 Xavi Taberna, Baeza

MAP F2 ■ Portales Tundidores 8 ■ 953 82 33 39 ■ Closed Wed ■ €€

An excellent choice of seafood, plus a number of vegetarian dishes, are available at this centrally located restaurant. There is also an extensive and reasonably priced wine list. The service is friendly and attentive.

6 Casa Rubio, Córdoba

MAP E3 ■ Calle Melchor Cobo Medina 7 ■ 953 00 64 54 ■ Closed Sun D ■ €€

This Michelin-star restaurant serves a combination of nouvelle cuisine with the traditional flavours of the region.

7 Las Camachas, Montilla

MAP D3 ■ Ctra Madrid-Málaga, Avda de Europa 3 ■ 957 65 00 04 ■ €€

Fish dishes are a speciality; opt for the hake loin with clams and prawns, paired with the delightful local wine.

The popular Taberna Salinas

8 Taberna Salinas, Córdoba

MAP D3 ■ C/Tundidores 3 ■ 957 48 29 50 ■ Closed Sun, Aug ■ €

A bustling place, with dining rooms around a patio. Try the *naranjas picás con aceite y bacalao* (cod with orange and olive oil).

9 Panaceite, Jaén

MAP E3 ■ Calle Bernabe Soriano 1 ■ 953 24 06 30 ■ €

If you're looking for a good selection of local specialities, head to Panaceite. Try the pork loin with onion marmalade.

10 Mesón Navarro, Úbeda

MAP F2 ■ Plaza Ayuntamiento 2 ■ 610 78 53 21 ■ €

Try the *pinchitos* (kebabs) and *ochios* (rolls) at this local institution.

See map on pp124–5

Streetsmart

**Horse riders take part in the Feria
in Jerez de la Frontera**

Getting Around

Arriving by Air

Andalucía is served by **airports** in Málaga, Almería, Granada-Jaén, Jerez and Seville.

Málaga–Costa del Sol Airport (AGP) is Spain's fourth busiest, with frequent scheduled and charter connections to many European cities and seasonal services to Canada and the US. Buses run from the airport to Marbella (45 minutes, €6.15). Trains depart every 20 minutes on Line C1 for the María Zambrano station in Málaga, which is 14 km (8.6 miles) away; a one-way ticket costs €1.80 and the journey takes 8 minutes. In the opposite direction, the C1 stops at Torremolinos, Benalmádena and Fuengirola.

The much smaller Almería (LEI), Federico García Lorca Granada-Jaén (GRX), Jerez de Frontera (XRY) and Seville (SVQ) airports are served by domestic as well as European airlines, with chartered services increasing in the summer months. There are excellent public transport links from the airports to their nearest cities.

Gibraltar (GIB) airport operates flights to UK airports and to Morocco.

International Train Travel

Spain's international and domestic rail services are operated by state-run Red Nacional de Ferrocarriles Españoles (**Renfe**).

Safety and hygiene measures, timetables, ticket information, transport maps, and more can be obtained from the Renfe website. For international train trips, it is advisable to purchase your ticket well in advance. **Eurail** and **Interrail** sell passes (to European non-residents and residents respectively), which are valid on Renfe trains.

International train services terminate in either Barcelona or Madrid, from where you can catch a domestic service to Andalucía. Trains from London, Brussels, Amsterdam, Geneva, Paris, Zürich and Milan reach Barcelona via Cerbère. At Cerbère, you can connect to the Tren Articulado Ligero Goicoechea Oriol (TALGO), a high-speed luxury train service (operated by Renfe).

There are two main rail routes from Portugal to Spain. The Sud Express departs daily from Lisbon and terminates in the French town of Hendaye, from where you can catch one of the regular services to Madrid. Alternatively, Lusitania is a sleeper train from Lisbon, which will take you to Madrid in around nine hours.

Regional and Local Trains

Renfe, along with some regional companies, operates a good train service throughout Andalucía. You can buy tickets online on the individual operators' websites or at stations. The fastest intercity services are the TALGO and AVE (operated by Renfe), which link Madrid with Seville in two and a half hours. AVE routes also link Barcelona with Seville and Málaga – both trips take five and a half hours. As a guide, a one-way *turista* (second-class) ticket from Madrid to Málaga starts at €48.

The *largo recorrido* (long-distance) trains are much cheaper than the high-speed trains, but they are so slow that you usually need to travel overnight. Book at least a month in advance. *Regionales y cercanías* (the regional and local services) are frequent and cheap.

Long-Distance Bus Travel

Often the cheapest and easiest way to reach and travel around Andalucía is by coach. Coaches run frequently between major cities and towns in Andalucía, and connect the region to the rest of Spain. The major coach stations in Andalucía are in Seville, Córdoba, Granada, Málaga and Almería. **Eurolines** links Andalucía to Portugal and there are also international links to France, the Netherlands, Belgium, Switzerland and Austria.

Spain has no national coach company, but private regional companies operate routes around the country. The largest of these is **Alsa**. Other companies operate in particular regions – Alsina Graells, for instance, covers most of the south and east of Spain. The modern buses are comfortable, clean, air-conditioned and also tend to offer WI-FI.

For short journeys, tickets can be bought from the driver when boarding the bus. For medium- to long-distance travel, you can make reservations at bus stations, or online via **Movelia**, as well as from individual bus companies. Note that it is not always possible to book tickets for long-distance travel in advance.

Public Transport

Sightseeing and getting around Andalucía is best done on foot and by public transport. In most towns and cities, bus services suffice as the sole means of public transport; Seville, Málaga and Granada also have tram and metro systems. Jaén

has the infrastructure for a tram system, but it is currently out of use. Municipal or tourism websites in **Córdoba**, **Seville**, **Granada**, **Málaga**, **Almería** and **Cádiz** offer up-to-date information about their public transport options.

Tickets

The best place to purchase public transport tickets is at stations themselves, either from windows or automatic machines. They are also available at newsagents. They come either in the form of a physical ticket or as a smart card which can either hold a season ticket or be topped up with cash and used pay-as-you-go.

Metro

The **Metro de Sevilla** was designed to aid transport between the outer areas of Seville and the city centre. The system will eventually consist of four metro lines, which will provide easy access to

bus and train stations and include a line to the airport (Line 4).

The **Metro de Málaga** has two lines, which connect the outer suburbs to El Perchel station in the city centre.

The **Metropolitano de Granada** connects central Granada with the towns Armilla, Albolote and Maracena.

Trams

Seville's city centre operates a tram system called the MetroCentro. It provides air-conditioned, rapid transport between San Bernardo station and Plaza Nueva in an otherwise pedestrian-only zone. Other lines are in the works, which will extend the network to Puerta Osario and Santa Justa train station.

Pay at the machine at tram stops (or pass your smart card over the reader on board) and press the green button to open the door. MetroCentro trams run every 3 to 5 minutes and stop briefly at all stops.

DIRECTORY

ARRIVING BY AIR

Airports
☎ 91 321 10 00
w aena.es (which operates all Spain's main airports)

INTERNATIONAL TRAIN TRAVEL

Eurail
w eurail.com

Interrail
w interrail.eu

Renfe
w renfe.com

LONG-DISTANCE BUS TRAVEL

Alsa
w alsa.es

Eurolines
w eurolines.com

Movelia
w movelia.es

PUBLIC TRANSPORT

Almería
w almeriaciudad.es

Cádiz
w cadizturismo.com

Córdoba
w cordoba.es

Granada
w granada.org

Málaga
w malaga.eu

Seville
w visitasevilla.es

METRO

Metropolitano de Granada
w metropolitano granada.es

Metro de Málaga
w metromalaga.es

Metro de Sevilla
w metro-sevilla.es

Bus

Buses remain the most common mode of public transport throughout Andalucía, and are the easiest and cheapest way to get around Seville's main sights. However, they can sometimes follow an erratic timetable and many services do not run after 10pm.

Bus routes can be found on the **TUSSAM** website but, generally speaking, the most useful lines for visitors are the circulares, numbered C1 to C6, which run around the city centre. In Granada, C30, C32 and C35 run from the centre to the Albaicín, Alhambra and Sacramonte.

Taxis

Throughout Andalucía, particularly in cities and towns, taxis are a reasonably priced way to get around if public transport isn't an option. Generally speaking, the journey starts with a flat fee and then increases depending on the distance travelled. Fares tend to be higher at night and also during the weekend and public holidays. Surcharges usually apply for trips to airports, and bus and train stations.

For a more affordable option, visitors can use ridesharing services, such as **BlaBlaCar**, to travel between cities.

Málaga is famous for its Bike Taxis or Trixis. Passengers sit in a pod-like carriage, towed along behind a bicycle. You are completely covered, so it can be an all-weather travel option.

Driving

If you drive to Spain in your own car, you must carry the vehicle's registration document, a valid insurance certificate, a passport or a national identity card, and your driving licence at all times. You must also display a sticker on the back of the car showing its country of registration. Note that you risk on-the-spot fines if you do not carry a red warning triangle and a reflective jacket with you at all times.

Spain has two different types of motorway: *autopistas*, which are toll roads, and *autovías*, which are toll-free. You can establish whether a motorway is toll-free by the letters that prefix the number of the road: A = free; AP = toll motorway.

Carreteras nacionales, Spain's main roads, have black-and-white signs and are designated by the letter N (Nacional) plus a number. Those with Roman numerals start at the Puerta del Sol in Madrid, and those with ordinary numbers have kilometre markers giving the distance from the provincial capital.

Carreteras comarcales, secondary roads, have a number preceded by the letter C. Other minor roads have numbers preceded by letters representing the name of the province, such as the LE1313 in Lleida.

Parking can be difficult, especially in the *pueblos blancos* where the roads are narrow and there is limited availability. Instead, park outside the old town areas and walk in.

Car Hire

With its sleepy villages, national and natural parks, dramatic mountain roads and excellent coastal highways, Andalucía lends itself to car hire. All airports have several providers and there are many more smaller companies operating in the city centres. To hire a car you'll need a valid full driving licence, passport and credit card; some agencies will only accept customers over 21 or even 25 years.

The most popular car-hire companies in Spain are **Europcar**, **Avis** and **Hertz**. All have offices at airports and major train stations, as well as in the larger cities. Fly-drive, an option for two or more travellers where car hire is included in the cost of your airfare, can be arranged by travel agents and tour operators. If you wish to hire a car locally for around a week or less, you will be able to arrange it with a local travel agent. A car for hire is called a *coche de alquiler*.

Rules of the Road

When using a car in Spain, drive on the right and use the left lane only for passing other vehicles.

If you have taken the wrong road, and it has a solid white line, turn round as indicated by a *cambio de sentido* sign. At crossings, give way to all on-coming traffic, unless a sign indicates otherwise.

The speed limit is 120 km/h (74 mph) on motor-ways/highways and dual carriageways, 100 km/h (62 mph) on roads with more than one lane in each direction and 90 km/h (55 mph) on all other ordinary roads, unless otherwise indicated. In urban areas, the speed can be as low as 20 km/h (12 mph).

The blood-alcohol concentration (BAC) limit for drivers of private vehicles and cyclists is 0.5 mg/ml and is strictly enforced. After a traffic accident, all those involved have to undergo a breath test. The **RAC** has further information for driving in Spain.

Boats and Ferries

Ferries connect the Spanish mainland to the Balearic and Canary Islands, and to North Africa, Italy and the UK. All the important routes are served by car ferries. **Acciona Trasmediterránea** operates a weekly service from Cádiz to the main ports of the Canary Islands. Always make an advance booking, especially in summer.

Cycling

There are cycle lanes in most Andalucían cities. Seville has pedestrianized a main thoroughfare in the centre, creating a wide promenade, which allows for bikes. Rural Andalucía is bicycle-friendly, with an extensive network of back roads, though steep inclines can be testing for inexperienced cyclists.

For easier cycling, try the **Via Verde** – "Greenway" – established throughout Spain by converting

unused railway lines into recreational areas for leisure cycling, walking and horse riding. There are routes through each province in Andalucía. Bike hire is available in all the main towns and cities.

SEVICI is a self-service bike rental programme in Seville, with 2,500 bikes available 24 hours a day. Bikes can be hired free for 30 minutes and are charged per hour after that. A €150 credit card deposit is paid and refunded upon return of the bike.

Motorists tend to treat cyclists as a nuisance and city traffic can be dangerous for cyclists. Helmets are highly recommended.

Walking

All of Andalucía's towns and cities are highly walkable, and many areas are pedestrianized. On foot, you can take in the architectural details, absorb street life and peek into any church, shop or bar that catches your interest. Be aware that pavements can be narrow and uneven in historic centres. On hot days, try to keep to the shade and carry water with you at all times.

There are long-distance trails criss-crossing Andalucía for the more intrepid. One of the most established is the **GR7**, which starts at Tarifa and runs through Málaga and Granada, connecting the region with northern Spain, Andorra and France before linking, in Alsace, to the E5 path. In Granada's wild interior, the GR7 hops from village

to village. There is also a (chargeable) luggage transfer service which will pick up or drop off bags from the start or end of your planned walk.

The Camino Mozárabe is a waymarked route which serves as a conduit for pilgrims from southeastern Spain as it is part of the famous St James Way network (known as the Camino de Santiago). The Andalucían section runs for 396 km (246 miles) from Granada to Córdoba and then to Mérida where it picks up the route north to Santiago de Compostela.

Practical Information

Passports and Visas

For entry requirements, including visas, consult your nearest Spanish embassy or check the **Exteriores** website. Visitors from outside the European Economic Area (EEA), European Union (EU) and Switzerland need a valid passport to enter Spain. EEA, EU and Swiss nationals can use identity cards instead.

Citizens of the UK, Canada, the US, Australia and New Zealand can visit Spain for up to 90 days without a visa as long as their passport is valid for 6 months beyond the date of entry. For longer stays, a visa is necessary. Most other non-EU nationals need a visa, and should consult the Exteriores website or the Spanish Embassy in their country for details. Schengen visas are valid for Spain.

A number of countries, including the UK, US, Canada and Ireland, have consulates in Andalucía and can provide consular assistance to nationals.

Government Advice

Now more than ever, it is important to consult both your and the Spanish government's advice before travelling. The **UK Foreign and Commonwealth Office**, the **US Department of State**, the **Australian Department of Foreign Affairs and Trade** and the Spanish Exteriores website offer the latest information on security, health and local regulations.

Customs Information

You can find information on the laws relating to goods and currency taken in or out of Andalucía and the Costa del Sol on the **Turespaña** (Spain's national tourist board) website.

For EU citizens there are no limits on most goods carried in or out of Spain as long as they are for personal use. There are, however, exceptions that include firearms and weapons, some types of food and plants and endangered species.

Non-EU citizens are allowed to import 200 cigarettes and a litre of spirits per adult, and can get a refund on Spain's 21 per cent sales tax (VAT, known here as IVA) on purchases over €90.15 – do this at the airport when leaving.

Insurance

We recommend that you take out a comprehensive insurance policy covering theft, loss of belongings, medical care, cancellations and delays, and read the small print carefully.

UK citizens are eligible for free emergency medical care in Spain provided they have a valid European Health Insurance Card (**EHIC**) or UK Global Health Insurance Card (**GHIC**).

Spain has a reciprocal health agreement with other EU countries, and EU citizens receive emergency treatment under the public healthcare system if also carrying a valid EHIC. Prescriptions have to be paid for up-front. Non-EU visitors should check (with their embassy) to see if there are reciprocal arrangements with Spain.

Health

Spain has a world-class healthcare system. Emergency medical care in Spain is free for all UK and EU citizens. If you have an EHIC or GHIC, be sure to present this as soon as possible. You may have to pay after treatment and reclaim the money later.

For visitors coming from outside the UK or EU, payment of medical expenses is the patient's responsibility, so it is important to arrange comprehensive insurance before travelling.

Seek medicinal supplies and advice for minor ailments from a pharmacy (farmacia), identifiable by a green or red cross. Each pharmacy displays a card in the window showing the address of the nearest all-night pharmacy, or call **Pharmacy on Duty** (or look online for Farmácias de Guardia) to locate the nearest one. Emergency contraception is available on prescription.

The cities and coastal areas of Andalucía have good hospitals and clinics. In an accident, or for urgent medical help, call the emergency services or the **Cruz Roja** (Red Cross), who will send an ambulance and paramedics. There are also dedicated lines for emergency dentists, narcotics or poisoning. If you are able to get to hospital, use the entrance marked *Urgencias* (Accident and Emergency). For less serious cases, visit one of the many private walk-in clinics. Consulates can provide a list of English-speaking physicians. Those covered by private health insurance can contact **Doctors on Call**.

For information regarding COVID-19 vaccination requirements, consult government advice. No other vaccinations are required to enter Spain, but routine vaccines should be kept up-to-date.

Smoking, Alcohol and Drugs

Smoking is banned in enclosed public spaces and is a fineable offence, although you can still smoke on the terraces of bars and restaurants. Spain has a relaxed attitude towards alcohol consumption, but it is frowned upon to be visibly drunk.

The drink-drive limit is strictly enforced *(see p135)*. Recreational drugs are illegal, and possession of even a very small quantity can lead to an extremely hefty fine. Amounts that suggest an intent to supply drugs to other people can lead to custodial sentences.

ID

By law you must carry identification with you at all times in Spain. A photocopy of your passport should suffice, but you may be asked to report to a police station with the original document. Keep your original passport safely stored in your hotel.

Personal Security

Andalucía is a safe region to visit but petty crime does take place. Pickpockets work known tourist areas, stations and busy streets. Use your common sense and be alert to your surroundings, and you should enjoy a stress-free trip.

If you do have anything stolen, report the crime within 24 hours to the nearest police station and take ID with you. Get a copy of the crime report *(denuncia)* to make an insurance claim. Contact your embassy if you have your passport stolen, or in the event of a serious crime.

As a rule, Andalucíans are very accepting of all people, regardless of their race, gender or sexuality. Homosexuality was legalized in Spain in 1979 and in 2007, the government recognized same-sex marriage and adoption rights for same-sex couples. That being said, the Catholic church still holds a lot of sway here and some conservative attitudes prevail, especially outside of urban areas. If you do feel unsafe, head for the nearest police station.

Torremolinos is a major centre for gay nightlife *(see p110)*. Seville, Granada and Cádiz also have thriving LGBTQ+ scenes.

Should you need them, Spain's **ambulance**, **police**, **fire services** and **municipal police** can be called for free from any landline, mobile or phone booth during a crisis.

Travellers with Specific Requirements

Spain is well-equipped when it comes to accessibility, but it is still advisable to call hotels and restaurants ahead of time and ask about the specific amenities available. The Confederación Española de Personas con Discapacidad Física y Orgánica (**COCEMFE**) and **Accessible Spain** provide information and tailored itineraries for those with reduced mobility, sight and hearing.

Spain's public transport system generally caters for all passengers, providing wheelchairs, adapted toilets and ramps. All public transport in Seville can accommodate wheelchair users. Airports offer reserved car parking, as well as other facilities. Metro maps are in Braille are available from the Organización Nacional de Ciegos (**ONCE**).

Time Zone

Spain is on Central European Time (CET), an hour ahead of Greenwich Mean Time, 6 hours ahead of US Eastern Standard Time and 11 hours behind Australian Eastern Standard Time. The clock moves forward 1 hour during daylight saving time from the last Sunday in March until the last Sunday in October.

Money

Spain uses the euro (€). Most establishments accept major credit, debit and prepaid currency cards. Contactless payments are common in cities, but it's always a good idea to carry cash for smaller items and to buy transport tickets. ATMs are widely available throughout Andalucía, although many charge for cash withdrawals.

Spain does not have a big tipping culture, but it's appreciated and common to round-up the bill.

Electrical Appliances

Power sockets are type F and C, fitting a two-prong, round-pin plug. Standard voltage is 230 volts.

Mobile Phones and Wi-Fi

Cities and towns across Andalucía are provided with plenty of wireless internet hotspots . Visit the **WiFi Map** website to find free hotspots near you.

Visitors with EU tariffs can use their devices without being affected by roaming charges. Some UK networks have reintroduced roaming charges; check with your provider before travelling.

Postal Services

Spanish mail is efficient, reliable and fast. **Correos**, is the national mail service; note that opening hours vary. Buy stamps from the post office or vending machines.

Weather

The mild, Mediterranean climate in Andalucía is the envy of much of Europe. The year-round average temperature is 18–20° C (64–68° F) with 320 sunny days. Coastal areas have highs fluctuating between 15° C (59° F) and 30° C (86° F). Inland, average city highs vary from 12° C (54° F) in January to 36° C (97° F) in August.

Along the Costa del Sol it is mild and dry from April to September, very hot in July and August, and cool and wet in winter. Inland the temperature climbs where the wind is absent and falls where the land rises significantly, as in the Sierra Nevada and Alpujarra.

Every season offers its reasons to come here: summer for nightlife, spring and autumn for nature, winter for skiing. But autumn is arguably the best time – the weather and water are still warm, the crowds have gone, prices are lower and there are lots of local festivals.

Opening Hours

Typical business hours are Monday–Saturday, 9:30am–1:30pm and 4:30–8pm. Major shopping centres and department stores are open all day 10am–9pm. In the high season in coastal areas many stay open until after 10pm. Smaller stores usually close by 3pm on Saturday.

COVID-19 Increased rates of infection may result in temporary opening hours and/or closures. Always check ahead before visiting museums, attractions and hospitality venues.

Visitor Information

There are official tourist information booths at the airport and in cities and bigger towns. Here you can get maps and city passes that allow discounts on sights, arrange hop on/hop off bus tours, or find out what's on locally. The official websites for the **Andalucía** and **España** tourism boards offer further information.

Some cities offer a visitor's pass or discount card that can be used for free or reduced-price entry to events and museums, and even discounts at participating restaurants. Passes are not free, so consider carefully how many of the offers you are likely to take advantage of before purchasing one of them.

Local Customs

A famous Spanish tradition is the siesta, when many shops close between 1pm and 5pm.

Spain retains a strong Catholic identity, and most churches and cathedrals will not permit visitors during Sunday Mass. When visiting religious buildings ensure that you are dressed modestly, with knees and shoulders covered.

Bullfighting

Corridas (bullfights) are widely held in Andalucía. Supporters argue that the bulls are bred for the industry and would be killed as calves were it not for bullfighting, while organizations such as the Asociación Defensa Derechos Animal (**ADDA**) say that it's cruel and organize protests throughout the country. If you do decide to attend a *corrida*, bear in mind that it's better to see a big-name matador because they are more likely to make a clean and quick kill. The audience will make their disapproval evident if they don't.

Language

Castellano (Castilian) is Spain's primary language and is spoken in Andalucía. English is widely spoken in the cities and other tourist spots, but the same cannot always be said for rural areas. Mastering a few phrases in *Castellano* will go down well with locals.

Taxes and Refunds

IVA (value added tax) in mainland Spain tends to be 21 per cent, but with lower rates for certain goods and services.

Under certain conditions, non-EU citizens can claim a rebate of these taxes. Retailers can give you a form to fill out, which you can then present to a customs officer at your point of departure. If the shop offers IVA, you can fill that form out instead and validate it at one of the self-service machines found at Spain's main ports and airports.

Accommodation

Andalucía offers everything from boutique villas to campsites. Throughout peak season (June to August) and during major fiestas, room rates are high and hotels are soon fully booked, so reserve in advance where possible. Most hotels quote their prices without including tax, which is 10 per cent.

Sites such as **Trivago**, **Laterooms** and **Booking. com** can help you explore the range of options, while **Airbnb** is good for private villas and rooms.

DIRECTORY

TRAVELLERS WITH SPECIFIC REQUIREMENTS

Accessible Spain
w accessiblespain travel.com

COCEMFE
w cocemfe.es

ONCE
w once.es

MOBILE PHONES AND WI-FI

WiFi Map
w wifimap.io

POSTAL SERVICES

Correos
w correos.es

VISITOR INFORMATION

Andalucía
w andalucía.org

España
w spain.info

BULLFIGHTING

ADDA
w addaong.org

ACCOMMODATION

Airbnb
w airbnb.com

Booking.com
w booking.com

Laterooms
w laterooms.com

Trivago
w trivago.com

Places to Stay

PRICE CATEGORIES
For a standard, double room per night (with breakfast if included), taxes and extra charges.

€ under €100   €€ €100–€200   €€€ over €200

Seville Stays

Hotel Un Patio al Sur
MAP L2 ■ C/Fernán Caballero 7 ■ 954 22 10 35 ■ www.patioalsur.es ■ €
Housed in an 18th-century Andalucían mansion, this eco-friendly boutique hotel is conveniently located near the Museo de Bellas Artes. The rooftop terrace offers wonderful city views. Free Wi-Fi.

Oasis Backpackers' Palace
MAP L2 ■ C/Almirante Ulloa 1 ■ 955 22 82 87 ■ www.oasisseville. com ■ €
Once a grand palace, this hostel has spacious dorms and double rooms with en-suite bathrooms. There's free Wi-Fi, a shared kitchen, lounge and rooftop pool.

Alcoba del Rey
MAP N1 ■ C/Becquer 9 ■ 954 91 58 00 ■ www. alcobadelrey.com ■ €€
This boutique hotel features Indian- and Moroccan-style decor and king-size canopy beds. Great views from the rooftop terrace. Free Wi-Fi.

H10 Corregidor Boutique Hotel
MAP M1 ■ C/Morgado 17 ■ 954 38 51 11 ■ www. h10hotels.com ■ €€
Just around the corner from the lively Alameda de Hercules, in a trendy part of town, this hotel is clean and comfortable. It also provides free access to a gym across the street. Free Wi-Fi.

Murillo Apartamentos
MAP M4 ■ Lope de Rueda 16 ■ 954 21 60 95 ■ www.hotelmurillo. com ■ €€
These lovely apartments are named after the Baroque painter who hailed from the flower-decked old quarter, where they are located. The terrace offers great city views. Free Wi-Fi.

EME Catedral Hotel
MAP M3 ■ C/Alemanes 27 ■ 954 56 00 00 ■ www. emecatedralhotel.com ■ €€€
Opposite the cathedral, this hotel has a trendy ambience. Highlights include a spa, a gym, an excellent Italian restaurant, a Mediterranean-fusion bistro and a rooftop lounge with unparalleled views.

Eurostars Sevilla Boutique
MAP M2 ■ C/Abades 41 ■ 954 97 90 09 ■ www. eurostarshotels.com ■ €€€
In the heart of Barrio de Santa Cruz, with excellent views of the Giralda and the cathedral from its roof terrace, expect minimalist luxury in contrast to the classic façade. There's an outdoor pool.

Hotel Alfonso XIII
MAP M4 ■ C/San Fernando 2 ■ 954 91 70 00 ■ www.mariott.com ■ €€€
This historic palace, now a five-star hotel, was erected by the eponymous king to house royals and other dignitaries during the 1929 Exposition. Rooms are luxuriously decorated, and the hotel has an outdoor swimming pool with alfresco dining alongside.

Hotel Taberna del Alabardero
MAP L3 ■ C/Zaragoza 20 ■ 954 50 27 21 ■ €€€
Seven elegant rooms are gathered around a central patio filled with greenery at this restored mansion. The hotel also offers a Michelin-starred restaurant that adds a touch of innovation to traditional cuisine. Free Wi-Fi.

Las Casas del Rey de Baeza
MAP N2 ■ Plaza Jesús de la Redención 2 ■ 954 56 14 96 ■ www.hospes.es ■ €€€
Close to La Casa de Pilatos, this chic hotel is located in a beautiful setting, which fuses historic traditional architecture with modern style. Shaded walkways and stone flooring echo the natural tones in the courtyards. The rooftop pool is a bonus.

Melía Colón Hotel
MAP L2 ■ C/Canalejas 1 ■ 954 50 55 99 ■ www. melia.com ■ €€€
This grand five-star hotel combines Andalucían elegance and maximum

comfort. Enjoy fabulous views from the solarium, cool off in the pool or relax in the spa. The cocktail bar hosts live music.

Granada Stays

Hotel Rosa D'Oro
MAP R2 ▪ Carrera del Darro 23 ▪ 656 82 88 54 ▪ www.hotelrosadeoro.es ▪ €
A former Franciscan convent, this 16th-century palace overlooking the Darro River has been restored in its original style. Some of the rooms have spectacular views and there is also an elegant central courtyard. Free Wi-Fi.

Hotel Sacromonte
MAP F4 ▪ Plaza del Lino 1 ▪ 958 26 64 11 ▪ www. hotelsacromonte.es ▪ €
This modern, three-star hotel in the centre of Granada has beautifully appointed rooms, a well-equipped gym and a swimming pool for relaxing. Free WiFi.

Hotelito Boutique Suecia
MAP R3 ▪ C/Molinos (Huerta de los Angeles) 8 ▪ 958 22 50 44 ▪ €
In a leafy cul-de-sac, this traditional Andalucían house has arched windows, terracotta tiles and a patio. The rooftop terrace is perfect for admiring the nearby Alhambra. Free Wi-Fi.

Oasis Backpackers' Hostel
MAP Q2 ▪ Placeta Correo Viejo 3 ▪ 958 21 58 48 ▪ www.oasisgranada. com/granada-hostel ▪ €
Set in a historic building, this hostel has a rooftop

terrace with great views, an interior patio, a bar, a kitchen and free Wi-Fi. All rooms are en-suite. The hostel also organises activities for its guests to explore the city.

Posada Pilar del Toro
MAP Q2 ▪ C/Elvira 25 ▪ 958 22 73 33 ▪ www. posadadeltoro.com ▪ €
In the heart of the Albaicín, this *posada* features traditional wooden beams and ceramic tiles, creating a rustic ambience with modern comforts.

Santa Ana Apartamentos Turísticos
MAP F4 ▪ Puente Cabrera 9 ▪ 958 22 81 30 ▪ www. apartamentos-santaana. com ▪ €
Situated just above the river, these apartments come with views of the Albaicín quarter. Each apartment has large, stylish rooms. Minimum two-night stay. Free Wi-Fi.

El Ladrón de Agua
MAP R2 ▪ Carrera del Darro 13 ▪ 958 21 50 40 ▪ www.ladrondeagua. com ▪ €€
This superbly located boutique hotel is set in a 16th-century mansion. Eight of the beautifully decorated rooms have views of the Alhambra. Guests can enjoy complimentary appetizers and regional wines every evening.

Hotel Reina Cristina
MAP F4 ▪ C/Tablas 4 ▪ 958 25 32 11 ▪ www.hotel reinacristina.com ▪ €€
Everything has been kept more or less the same as when the poet García Lorca was forced to hide

out here – this is the last place the poet stayed, before his untimely end *(see p55)*. Each room has a unique style and there are patios and fountains in the public areas.

Room Mate Leo
MAP Q3 ▪ C/Mesones 15 ▪ 958 53 55 79 ▪ www. room-matehotels.com ▪ €€
This trendy hotel is located on a pedestrianised street within walking distance of most sights. There are stunning views of the Alhambra and the city from the top floor terrace and some rooms, which are modern, with a creative mix of colour and decor. There's a breakfast buffet available until noon.

Alhambra Palace
MAP R3 ▪ Plaza Arquitecto García de Paredes 1 ▪ 958 22 14 68 ▪ www.h-alhambra palace.es ▪ €€€
The style of this *belle époque* extravaganza is Neo-Moorish. The public rooms are palatial. Just steps away from the Nasrid palace, it has great views from every room, terrace and balcony.

Paradors

Parador Alcázar del Rey, Carmona
MAP C3 ▪ Alcázar s/n ▪ 954 14 10 10 ▪ €€
One of the most impressive of all the paradors, this 14th-century Moorish fortress-palace overlooks the Río Corbones. Rooms are large and decorated in classic Andalucían style, set off by antiques. Cool off in the garden pool or on the expansive terrace.

Parador Arcos de la Frontera

MAP C5 ▪ Plaza del Cabildo ▪ 956 70 05 00 ▪ €€

Right on the banks of the Río Guadalete, this has an impressive view of the fertile plain of the river and of the old part of town. An ideal starting point for the *pueblos blancos* routes, as well as Jerez de la Frontera. The courtyard is graced with traditional latticework and ceramic tiles.

Parador Condestable Dávalos, Úbeda

MAP F2 ▪ Plaza de Vázquez Molina ▪ 953 75 03 45 ▪ €€

Live like 16th-century nobility in a Renaissance palace in the heart of one of Spain's best preserved historic centres. Rooms reflect the noble tone, with high ceilings and antique furnishings.

Parador de Antequera

MAP D4 ▪ Paseo García del Olmo 2 ▪ 952 84 02 61 ▪ €€

This quiet parador, surrounded by gardens and a swimming pool, is near the spectacular El Torcal *(see p61)*. The rooms offer scenic views of the Andalucían landscape.

Parador de Ayamonte

MAP A4 ▪ Avda de la Constitucíon ▪ 959 32 07 00 ▪ €€

A modern facility with sunlit rooms and a perfect position for exploring the area where Huelva Province meets Portugal. Most rooms afford panoramic views of the Atlantic from the high point of town.

Parador de Cazorla

MAP G3 ▪ 953 72 70 75 ▪ Sierra de Cazorla s/n ▪ Closed Jan–Feb ▪ €€

In a remote location in the heart of the Parque Natural Sierra de Cazorla, with stunning views, this graceful country house lets you relax in comfort. The restaurant offers regional fare and game in season.

Parador de Ronda

MAP D5 ▪ Plaza de España ▪ 952 87 75 00 ▪ €€

Set in the former town hall, views from the rooms are amazing, while the decor reflects the colours of the area.

Parador del Gilbralfaro, Málaga

MAP S4 ▪ Castillo de Gibralfaro ▪ 952 22 19 02 ▪ €€€

Facing the Alcázaba this parador stands surrounded by pine trees. It's handy for golf courses and tennis nearby.

Parador de Mazagón

MAP B4 ▪ Ctra San Juan del Puerto-Matalascañas km 31 ▪ 959 53 63 00 ▪ €€€

Unspoiled beauty on the shores of the sea is what this modern property is all about. It's ideal for those who want to commune with nature, especially with the wonders of the Coto Doñana nearby. Facilities include gardens, pools and a sauna – all facing Mazagón beach.

Parador de Mójacar

MAP H4 ▪ Paseo del Mediterraneo 339 ▪ 950 47 82 50 ▪ €€€

This beachside parador, 1.5 km (1 mile) from the village of Mójacar and 3 km (just under 2 miles) from a golf course, has an inviting atmosphere with spectacular views from the bedroom terraces and the upstairs dining room. Ultra-modern, clean and child-friendly.

Parador de San Francisco, Granada

MAP S3 ▪ C/Real de la Alhambra ▪ 958 22 14 40 ▪ €€€

You'll need to book about a year in advance to lodge here, but it's the premier stay in town. Housed in a restored 15th-century monastery, with a wisteria-covered patio, it is truly beautiful. For the best experience, get a room with a view out over the Albaicín on one side and the cloister on the other.

Luxury Hotels

Casa Vesta, Zufre

MAP B3 ▪ C/Santa Zita, Zufre ▪ 647 72 38 08 ▪ www.casa-vesta.com ▪ €€

Located in the countryside of Huelva, this charming boutique hotel has world-class service and boasts a billiards room, library, outdoor swimming pool and free Wi-Fi. No under-16s.

Hotel Infanta Cristina, Jaen

MAP E3 ▪ Avenida de Madrid 1 ▪ 953 26 30 40 ▪ www.hotelinfanta cristina.com ▪ €€

Located in the heart of Jaen, this contemporary hotel offers tastefully decorated rooms and suites. The restaurant offers traditional delicacies. There is an outdoor pool and a solarium.

Hotel Jerez & Spa, Jerez

MAP B5 ▪ Avda Álvaro Domecq 35 ▪ 956 30 06 00 ▪ www.hace.es ▪ €€
Rooms here have been decorated in a warm style and overlook the gardens. All have satellite TV and Internet; many also have a Jacuzzi. There's a delightful spa.

Hotel Montelirio, Ronda

MAP D5 ▪ C/Tenorio 8 ▪ 952 87 38 55 ▪ www.hotelmontelirio.com ▪ €€
A beautifully restored 17th-century palace offering every comfort. Perched on the edge of Ronda's famous gorge, it has stunning views. There's an outdoor pool and a Turkish bath.

Club Marítimo de Sotogrande

MAP C6 ▪ Puerto Deportivo, Sotogrande ▪ 956 79 02 00 ▪ www.clubmaritimodesoto grande.com ▪ €€€
Luxurious and tastefully decorated in neutral tones, this hotel affords amazing views from every room – sometimes from the bathtub. Free bike use and discounts for golfing.

El Fuerte, Marbella

MAP D5 ▪ Avda El Fuerte ▪ 952 86 15 00 ▪ www.fuertehoteles.com ▪ €€€
In the centre of Marbella, this hotel is next to the sea and surrounded by subtropical gardens. It is within easy walking distance of the historic quarter too, so you can discover the "real" Marbella, as well as soak up the glamour. Minimum two- or three-night stay during peak seasons.

Hospes Palacio del Bailío, Córdoba

MAP D3 ▪ Ramírez de las Casas Deza 10–12 ▪ 957 49 89 93 ▪ www.hospes. es ▪ €€€
Dating back to the 16th century, Hospes Palacio del Bailío is a complex of former granaries, coach houses and stables surrounded by beautiful gardens and patios.

Hotel Barrosa Palace, Chiclana de la Frontera

MAP B5 ▪ Novo Sancti Petri ▪ 956 49 22 00 ▪ www.hipotels.com/hotel-barrosa-palace-en-cadiz.htm ▪ €€€
A spa-resort right on the beach, just south of Cádiz. It has three restaurants, a fitness centre, indoor and outdoor pools and a range of beauty treatments. Minimum two- or three-night stay during high seasons.

Vincci Selección Aleysa, Benalmádena

MAP D5 ▪ Avda Antonio Machado 57 ▪ 952 56 65 66 ▪ www.vinccihoteles.com ▪ €€€
This boutique hotel on the beachfront has great sea views. There's a wellness spa and healthy activities including free yoga and pilates in the garden.

Resorts

Barceló Jerez, Montecastillo

MAP B5 ▪ Ctra Jerez-Arcos km 6 ▪ 956 15 12 040 ▪ www.hotelbarcelo montecastillo.com ▪ €€
Towering like a castle of pale yellow stucco beside one of Europe's top golf courses, the hotel gives lots of activity, eating and drinking options.

Hotel Paraíso del Mar, Nerja

MAP E5 ▪ C/Prolongación de Carabeo 22 ▪ 952 52 16 21 ▪ www.hotel paraisodelmar.es ▪ €€
All rooms at this converted villa have a Jacuzzi and a terrace with views of either the beach, the mountains or the hotel's gardens. Guests have private access to the Burriana beach.

Hotel Playa de la Luz, Rota

MAP B5 ▪ Avda de la Diputación ▪ 956 81 05 00 ▪ www.hace.es/en/hotelplayadelaluz ▪ €€
Most rooms have a terrace or balcony at this hotel, nestled by an unspoiled beach. Minimum two- or three-night stay during peak seasons.

Hotel Vincci Rumaykiyya, Sierra Nevada, Monachil

MAP F4 ▪ Urb. Sol y Nieve s/n ▪ 958 48 25 08 ▪ www.vinccihoteles.com ▪ Closed mid-Apr–Dec ▪ €€
With an alpine-style decor, Hotel Vincci Rumaykiyya is at the heart of the ski resort. The terrace offers great views of the surrounding. There's a chair lift service at its door.

Isla Cristina Palace & Spa, Isla Cristina

MAP A4 ▪ Avda del Parque s/n ▪ 959 34 44 99 ▪ www.sensimarisla cristinapalace.com ▪ €€
Enjoy beachfront access and a range of massages, Turkish baths and saunas. All rooms have balconies.

For a key to hotel price categories see p140

Barceló la Bobadilla, Loja (Granada)

MAP E4 ▪ Ctra Salinas-Villanueva de Tapia (A333) km 65.5 ▪ 958 32 18 61 ▪ www.barcelo.com ▪ €€€

Fabulous and reminiscent of a tiny Moorish village with its own chapel, Barceló la Bobadilla features beautiful gardens and charming patios.

Hotel Fuerte Conil, Conil de la Frontera

MAP B5 ▪ Playa de la Fontanilla ▪ 956 44 33 44 ▪ www.fuerte-hoteles.com ▪ Closed Nov–Feb ▪ €€€

An award-winner for its environmentally friendly practices, this Neo-Moorish-style resort is not far from the fishing village of Conil. There's a choice of restaurants, a pool, spa and sports facilities.

Hotel La Fuente de la Higuera, Ronda

MAP D5 ▪ Partido de los Frontones ▪ 952 16 56 08 ▪ www.hotel-lafuente.com ▪ €€€

Set in a renovated olive oil mill where Spanish architecture meets Post-Modern design. Rooms have individually designed interiors and a garden area or terrace. There's also an outdoor pool.

Kempinski Resort Hotel, Estepona

MAP D5 ▪ Ctra de Cádiz km 159 ▪ 952 80 95 00 ▪ www.kempinski.com/es/marbella ▪ €€€

A magnificent resort with a whimsical take on Moorish and regional architecture that suits the seaside setting perfectly.

Marriott Marbella Beach Resort

MAP D5 ▪ Marbella del Este, Ctra de Cádiz km 193 ▪ 952 76 96 00 ▪ www.marriott.com ▪ €€€

Surrounded by lush gardens with multiple pools, a great gym, sauna and plenty of activities to keep children amused.

Historic Finds

Hotel La Casa del Califa, Vejer de la Frontera

MAP C6 ▪ Plaza de España 16 ▪ 956 44 77 30 ▪ www.califavejer.com ▪ €

A sojourn at this hotel, created out of eight different houses including the 17th-century Casa del Juzgado, is like staying in a private house. Excellent views and service and a recommended restaurant.

Palacio de la Rambla, Úbeda

MAP F2 ▪ Plaza del Marqués 1 ▪ 953 75 01 96 ▪ www.palaciodelarambla.com ▪ €

This 16th-century palace offers eight rooms for guests to experience the refined atmosphere. The patio is said to have been designed by the architect Andrés de Vandelvira.

Amanhavis Hotel, Benahavis, Málaga

MAP D5 ▪ C/Pilar 3 ▪ 952 85 60 26 ▪ www.amanhavis.com ▪ Closed mid-Jan–mid-Feb ▪ €€

This place is like an Andalucían theme park, albeit very tasteful. Rooms are linked to an episode in Spanish history, such as Boabdil or Christopher Columbus, and styled accordingly. Free Wi-Fi.

Hacienda de Orán, Utrera

MAP C4 ▪ Ctra A8029 km 7 ▪ 955 81 59 94 ▪ www.haciendadeoran.com ▪ €€

This stately 17th-century Andalucían manor is decorated with antiques and rich textiles. There are bougainvillea-covered porches, horse stables, a carriage museum, a pool and even a small airstrip.

Hotel Convento Aracena

MAP B3 ▪ C/Jesus y Maria 19 ▪ 959 12 68 99 ▪ www.hotelconvento aracena.es ▪ €€

Housed in a 17th-century convent, this hotel has an outdoor pool as well as a spa and wellness centre. Buffet breakfast. Bike hire available at the reception.

Hotel Hacienda Posada de Vallina, Córdoba

MAP D3 ▪ C/Corregidor Luis de la Cerda 83 ▪ 957 49 87 50 ▪ www.hhposadadevallina.es ▪ €€

In the heart of Córdoba's Jewish Quarter, this charming, historic hotel retains original features, including beamed ceilings and exposed stone walls.

Hotel Monasterio San Miguel, El Puerto de Santa María

MAP B5 ▪ C/Virgen de los Milagros 27 ▪ 956 54 04 40 ▪ www.monasteriosanmiguelhotel.com ▪ €€

This former monastery, with Baroque architecture and art, is equipped with modern luxuries including an excellent restaurant, a pool and a solarium.

Hotel Puerta de la Luna, Baeza

MAP F2 ▪ Canónigo Melgares Raya s/n ▪ 953 74 70 19 ▪ €€
Set in a 16th-century building, Hotel Puerta de la Luna is in the heart of old Baeza. Rooms are each uniquely furnished. Free Wi-Fi and an outdoor pool.

Soho Boutique Palacio San Gabriel, Ronda

MAP D5 ▪ C/Marqués de Moctezuma 19 ▪ 952 19 03 92 ▪ www.en.sohohoteles.com ▪ Closed 1–9 Jan, 19–31 Jul & 21–31 Dec ▪ €€
Built in 1736, this converted mansion, with its original coat of arms and handsome façade, offers sumptuous rooms for the price.

NH Amistad Córdoba

MAP D3 ▪ Plaza de Maimónides 3 ▪ 957 42 03 35 ▪ www.nh-hotels.com ▪ €€€
Just a few minutes from La Mezquita and built into the old city walls. The large patio-cloisters are lovely, and there's also a plunge pool and sun terrace. Free Wi-Fi.

Budget Charmers

Hosteria Lineros 38, Córdoba

MAP D3 ▪ C/Lineros 38 ▪ 957 48 25 17 ▪ www.hosterialineros38.com ▪ €
With its striking Mudéjar-style architecture, Hosteria Lineros 38 is a pleasing building that epitomizes the city's cross-cultural charm. It's a great choice in the old quarter. Free Wi-Fi.

Hotel Doña Blanca, Jerez de la Frontera

MAP B5 ▪ C/Bodegas 11 ▪ 956 34 87 61 ▪ www.hoteldonablanca.com ▪ €
This place provides all the services you'd expect of more high-end properties. The rooms are maintained well, and there's parking and free Wi-Fi.

Hotel Embarcadero de Calahonda de Granada

MAP F5 ▪ C/Biznaga 14 ▪ 958 62 30 11 ▪ www.embarcaderodecalahonda.com ▪ €
Set right on the beach, this hotel has stylish, well-equipped rooms overlooking the sea. Excellent restaurant on site. Free Wi-Fi.

Hotel González, Córdoba

MAP D3 ▪ C/Manríquez 3 ▪ 957 47 98 19 ▪ www.hotel-gonzalez.com ▪ €
This charming hotel typifies the old houses of the Jewish Quarter, with a central patio and an elegant marble entrance replete with antiques and high ceilings. Free Wi-Fi.

Hotel Palacio de Hemingway

MAP D5 ▪ C/Tenorio 1, Ronda ▪ 952 87 01 01 ▪ €
This elegant mansion was once the home of the poet Pedro Pérez Clotet. The 12 rooms house hand-made Andalucían-style furniture. The terrace-restaurant offers great city views. Free Wi-Fi.

La Casa Campana, Arcos de la Frontera

MAP C5 ▪ Nuñez de Prado 4 ▪ www.casacampana.com ▪ €
This hotel features seven en-suite rooms (one of them an apartment) and a terrace offering city and river views. Breakfast is not included in the price of stay. Free Wi-Fi.

La Casa Grande, Arcos de la Frontera

MAP C5 ▪ C/Maldonado 10 ▪ 956 70 39 30 ▪ www.lacasagrande.net ▪ Closed 6 Jan–6 Feb ▪ €
In 1729, the Nuñez de Prado family erected this mansion. Perched over the cliff of La Peña, it features ceramic tiles, stone columns, wood beams and antiques. Free Wi-Fi.

Pensión Sevillano, Nerja

MAP E5 ▪ C/Almirante Ferrandiz 31 ▪ 952 52 15 23 ▪ €
A family-run hostel in the heart of Nerja, it is taste-fully decorated with a Moroccan theme. Rooms are comfortable and have ceiling fans, fridges and are en-suite. There is a delightful roof terrace.

Hotel Argantonio, Cádiz

MAP B5 ▪ C/Argantonio 3, Cádiz ▪ 956 21 16 40 ▪ www.hotelargantonio.es ▪ €€
Located in the old town, each floor of this hotel is decorated with a different theme. All rooms have a bath, a flat-screen TV and free Wi-Fi. Some rooms have balconies.

Hotel TRH, Baeza

MAP F2 ▪ C/Concepción 3 ▪ 953 74 81 30 ▪ www.trhbaeza.com ▪ €€
Right in the heart of this Renaissance town is this oasis of quiet beauty. It's part of a chain, with all the conveniences, yet evokes timeless style.

For a key to hotel price categories see p140

Rural Retreats

Alcázar de la Reina, Carmona
MAP C3 ▪ Hermana Concepción Orellana 2 ▪ 954 19 62 00 ▪ www.alcazar-reina.es ▪ €

In the historic centre of this small town, the façade of this hotel stands out, while the interior reflects Mudéjar craftsmanship. No two rooms are alike, but they all have marble bathrooms and many offer spectacular views.

Alquería de los Lentos, Nigüelas
MAP F4 ▪ Camino de los Molinos ▪ 958 77 78 50 ▪ www.alqueriadeloslentos.com ▪ €

Surrounded by orchards at the foothills of the Sierra Nevada, this 16th-century mill has been lovingly transformed into a small hotel and organic restaurant. There is a swimming pool, and most rooms have terraces.

Antonio, Zahara de los Atunes
MAP C6 ▪ Atlanterra km 1 ▪ 956 43 91 41 ▪ www.antoniohoteles.com ▪ €

This seaside retreat is decorated in a traditional style, with whitewashed walls, and there's a nice pool. Most rooms have terraces with sea views.

Casa Don Carlos, Alhaurin el Grande
MAP D5 ▪ Ctra Coin Churriana km 3.5, Alhaurin el Grande ▪ 669 94 50 46 ▪ www.casadoncarlos.com ▪ €

This award-winning, adults only bed and breakfast, facing Alhaurin el Grande, has magnificent views of the countryside.

The rooms are clean and comfortable. Guests can hire cars and motorcycles.

Casas Cuevas La Tala, near Guadix
MAP F4 ▪ A-92N km 1.5, Camino de La Tala al Perro ▪ 958 58 61 04 ▪ www.casascuevalatala.com ▪ €

A complex of stylishly preserved cave dwellings and an 18th-century manor house, some with hydro-massage tubs. Outdoor pool, barbecue and lovely grounds provide the perfect setting for relaxation.

Casona de Calderón Hotel, Osuna
MAP D4 ▪ Plaza Cervantes 16 ▪ 954 81 50 37 ▪ €

Set in a historic town near Seville, this exquisite boutique hotel offers a calming ambience. Along with rooms that feature a vintage flair and antique-style decorations, there's a lovely patio with an outdoor pool and an excellent restaurant.

Hotel Villa Maria, Cabra
MAP E3 ▪ C/Antonio Povedano 23 ▪ 857 89 40 40 ▪ www.villamariacabra.com ▪ €

Set on the edge of the Subbética mountain range, this restored manor house offers 12 beautifully furnished rooms. The on-site restaurant can prepare picnic lunches.

Cortijo El Sotillo, San José
MAP H5 ▪ Ctra Entrada a San José ▪ 950 61 11 00 ▪ www.playasycortijos.com ▪ €

A tranquil base from which to explore the beaches of Cabo de Gata. The rooms here are spacious and have large terraces with beautiful views.

Finca Buen Vino, Sierra de Aracena
MAP B3 ▪ Los Marines, N433 km 95 ▪ 959 12 40 34 ▪ www.fincabuenvino.com ▪ €€

A converted ranch, set amid green hills, this bed and breakfast is filled with an eclectic mix of furniture, paintings, pottery and books. Rooms are all distinctive, and there are self-catering cottages with a private pool available, too. Check the website for special activities.

La Almendra y el Gitano, Agua Amarga
MAP G4 ▪ Camino Cala del Plomo, Agua Amarga ▪ 678 50 29 11 ▪ www.laalmendrayelgitano.com ▪ €€

In the heart of a natural park, close to unspoiled beaches, and with no phones or Internet, this is a haven of tranquillity. There's a community kitchen for guests' use.

Hostels, Camping and Self-Catered

Albergue Inturjoven, Marbella
MAP D5 ▪ C/Trapiche 2 ▪ 955 18 11 81 ▪ www.inturjoven.com ▪ €

Double rooms, some with adjoining bath, a pool and recreational options make this an excellent youth hostel. It's just north of the lovely Casco Antiguo (old quarter), where you can see the real Marbella. Walk through its narrow, cobbled streets to get to the beach and the port.

Camping Cabo de Gata, Cabo de Gata
MAP H5 ▪ Ctra Cabo de Gata, Cortijo Ferrón ▪ 950 16 04 43 ▪ www.campingcabodegata.com ▪ €
This campsite offers shady areas for tents, trailers and RV hookups, as well as bungalows. Facilities include a pool, access to pristine beaches and a reception centre with safes.

Camping Conil, Conil de la Frontera
MAP B5 ▪ Carril Hijuela de la Mirla 86 ▪ 956 92 24 18 ▪ www.campingconil.es ▪ €
Set in a tranquil pine forest close to the coast, this campsite features a swimming pool, tennis courts, a mini-mart, bar, restaurant and laundry facilities.

Camping El Sur, Ronda
MAP D5 ▪ Ctra Ronda-Algeciras km 1.5 ▪ 952 87 59 39 ▪ www.campingelsur.com ▪ €
Camping and bungalows with kitchen and bathroom are available here. It's a chance to take beautiful walks or horse ride in the countryside around Ronda.

Hostal la Fuente, Córdoba
MAP D3 ▪ C/San Fernando 51 ▪ 957 48 78 27 ▪ www.hostallafuente.com ▪ €
A charming budget hotel in the centre of Córdoba, offering single, double, triple and quadruple rooms as well as some apartments. There's a rooftop terrace with an adjoining café, a central courtyard and a large communal lounge.

Hostal La Malagueña, Estepona
MAP D5 ▪ C/Raphael 1 ▪ 952 80 00 11 ▪ www.hlmestepona.com ▪ €
Although it isn't an official hostel or even aimed at backpackers, the price doesn't get any better than this. The airy rooms have balconies facing the square. You can stroll along the sandy beaches or wander around the shops of this old and still authentic fishing village.

Hostal La Posada, Mijas
MAP D5 ▪ C/Coin 47 & 49 ▪ 952 48 53 10 ▪ €
Rent a fully equipped apartment in this white village and sample a bit of the real Andalucía. Not all have air conditioning.

Instalación Juvenil, Sol y Nieve, Sierra Nevada
MAP F4 ▪ C/Peñones 22 ▪ 955 18 11 81 ▪ www.inturjoven.com ▪ €
Located near the top of the ski station, with rooms holding two to six, this place is ideal for skiers in the winter or trekkers during summer. Skis and other equipment for hire.

Los Castillarejos Apartamentos Rurales, Luque
MAP D3 ▪ Ctra CO-6203 km 5.7, Luque ▪ 957 09 00 12 ▪ www.loscastillarejos.com ▪ €
A set of 14 modern apartments decorated using natural materials and local stone. Kitchens are fully equipped; there's a pool and free Wi-Fi.

Cantueso, Periana
MAP E4 ▪ Periana, Málaga ▪ 699 94 62 13 ▪ www.cantueso.net ▪ €€
Ten whitewashed cottages with private terraces enjoy a splendid mountainside setting. Lush gardens provide tranquillity. Not all have air conditioning.

Casas Karen, Costa de la Luz
MAP C6 ▪ Camino del Monte 6, nr Cabo Trafalgar ▪ 956 43 70 67 ▪ www.casaskaren.com ▪ €€
Typical Andalucían *chozas* (traditional, thatched straw bungalows) and converted farm buildings between pine woods and the beach. Follow signs to Faro de Trafalgar.

Casas Rurales Benarum, Mecina Bombarón
MAP F4 ▪ C/Casas Blancas 1 ▪ 958 85 11 49 ▪ www.benarum.com ▪ €€
Twelve rural cabins, each accommodating two to five people, nestle in this quiet mountain town. The cabins are fully equipped and there is a pool and spa on site.

Torre de la Peña, Tarifa
MAP C6 ▪ Ctra N340, Tarifa ▪ 956 68 49 03 ▪ www.campingtp.com ▪ €€
This lovely site offers beachfront camping and bungalows, with spectacular views. It is perfect for watersports such as windsurfing, kitesurfing and snorkelling. There's a good restaurant on site serving Spanish cuisine made from fresh, locally produced ingredients.

For a key to hotel price categories see p140

General Index

Acknowledgments

Author
American-born Jeffrey Kennedy now lives mainly in Italy and Spain. A graduate of Stanford University, he divides his time between producing, acting and writing. He is the co-author of *Top 10 Rome* and the author of the Top 10 guides to *Mallorca*, *Miami and the Keys* and *San Francisco*.

Additional contributor
Chris Moss

Publishing Director Georgina Dee

Publisher Vivien Antwi

Design Director Phil Ormerod

Editorial Michelle Crane, Rachel Fox, Freddie Marriage, Jayne Miller, Sally Schafer

Cover Design Bess Daly, Maxine Pedliham

Design Marisa Renzullo, Vinita Venugopal

Picture Research Susie Peachey, Ellen Root, Lucy Sienkowska, Oran Tarjan

Cartography Zafar-ul Islam Khan, Suresh Kumar, James Macdonald, Casper Morris

DTP Jason Little, George Nimmo

Production Nancy-Jane Maun

Factchecker Lynnette McCurdy

Proofreader Kathryn Glendenning

Indexer Helen Peters

Illustrator chrisorr.com

First edition created by Sargasso Media Ltd, London

Revisions Ashif, Parnika Bagla, Dipika Dasgupta, Ben Hinks, Nayan Keshan, Shikha Kulkarni, Suresh Kumar, Bandana Paul, Kanika Praharaj, Vagisha Pushp, Lucy Richards, Zoë Rutland, Anuroop Sanwalia, Avijit Sengupta, Azeem Siddiqui, Beverly Smart, Hollie Teague, Priyanka Thakur, Stuti Tiwari, Tanveer Abbas Zaidi

Commissioned Photography Neil Lukas, Rough Guides/Demetrio Carrasco, Clive Streeter, Peter Wilson

Picture Credits

32-3, 58cl, 74tr, 119clb; Aitor Muñoz Muñoz 127cl; Carlos Neto 31bl; Pathastings 75cla; Sean Pavone 2tl, 3tl, 4cl, 8-9, 30cl, 82-3, 85tl, 108br, 114-5; Perseomedusa 6cra; Pigprox 45tl, 89cra; Yuan Ping 11tl; Ppy2010ha 75clb; Quintanilla 37crb; Rangpl 32br; Alvaro Trabazo Rivas 107cl; Fesus Robert 103tl; Paloma Rodriguez De Los Rios Ramirez 118t; Rubenconpi 12cla; Sborisov 12-3, 19br; Jozef Sedmak 25tc, 49tl, 52b, 84tl, 88tl, 118cl; Sergeialyoshin 10-1; Iryna Soltyska 23bl, 33cr; Jose I. Soto 13clb, 15cr, 16br; Alena Stalmashonak 20r; Nick Stubbs 39tl, 64b; Jan Sučko 11cra; Titelio 10cla; Aleksandar Todorovic 20cl, 42b, 85br; Typhoonski 27bl, 73br; Txematrull 11br; Venemama 68br; Alvaro German Vilela 10clb; Yury 124cl; Natalia Zakharova 99tr; Vladimir Zhuravlev 71t; Zoom-zoom 45br.

El Camborio: 121tr.

El Rinconcillo: 92t.

Getty Images: DEA/C. SAPPA 96c; e55evu 1; Imagno 43clb; Moment 67cl; NIS/Diego Lopez Alvarez 36-7; David Ramos 81cl; UIG/Editorial Education Images 36b; Universal Images Group / Sepia Times 55tc.

Ministerio de Agricultura, Alimentación y Medio Ambiente

Gabinete de la Ministra: 11clb, 36cl; CENEAM - MMA/J.M. Reyero 36crb, 37tc.

Museo Torre de la Calahorra: 23cb.

Real Alcázar de Sevilla: 21clb.

Robert Harding Picture Library: age fotostock/Daniel Sanz 6br; J.D. Dallet 22cl; Anna Elias 126tr; Jose Fuste Raga 126b; Sylvain Grandadam 93clb; Guy Heitmann 102tl; Jose Lucas 120cr; Guy Thouvenin 89bl; Ben Welsh 66bl

Sollo: Food & Groove 113ca.

SuperStock: Iberfoto 124tr.

Real Club Valderrama: 109tr.

Cover

Front and spine: **Getty Images:** e55evu.

Back: **AWL Images:** Matteo Colombo crb, Stefano Politi Markovina cla; **Dreamstime. com:** Tatiana Bralnina tl; **iStockphoto.com:** SeanPavonePhoto tr; **Getty Images:** e55evu b.

Pull Out Map Cover

Getty Images: e55evu.

All other images © Dorling Kindersley

For further information see:
www.dkimages.com

DK | Penguin Random House

First edition 2004

First published in Great Britain by
Dorling Kindersley Limited
DK, One Embassy Gardens, 8 Viaduct Gardens, London, SW11 7BW, UK

The authorised representative in the EEA is Dorling Kindersley Verlag GmbH. Arnulfstr. 124, 80636 Munich, Germany

Published in the United States by DK US, 1450 Broadway, Suite 801, New York, NY 10018, USA

Copyright © 2004, 2022 Dorling Kindersley Limited

A Penguin Random House Company

21 22 23 24 10 9 8 7 6 5 4 3 2 1

Reprinted with revisions 2006, 2008, 2010, 2012, 2014, 2016, 2019, 2022

All rights reserved.

No part of this publication may be reproduced, stored in or introduced into a retrieval system, or transmitted in any form, or by any means (electronic, mechanical, photocopying, recording or otherwise) without the prior written permission of the copyright owner.

The publishers cannot accept responsibility for any consequences arising from the use of this book, nor for any material on third party websites, and cannot guarantee that any website address in this book will be a suitable source of travel information.

A CIP catalogue record is available from the British Library.

A catalogue record for this book is available from the Library of Congress.

ISSN 1479-344X

ISBN 978-0-2414-6268-3

Printed and bound in China

www.dk.com

As a guide to abbreviations in visitor information blocks: **Adm** = *admission charge;* **D** = *dinner;* **L** = *lunch.*

MIX
Paper from responsible sources
FSC™ C018179

This book was made with Forest Stewardship Council ™ certified paper – one small step in DK's commitment to a sustainable future. For more information go to www.dk.com/our-green-pledge

Phrase Book

In an Emergency

Help!	¡Socorro!	soh-koh-roh
Stop!	¡Pare!	pah-reh
Call…	¡Llame a…	yah-meh ah
…a doctor!	…un médico!	oon meh-dee-koh
…an ambulance!	…una ambulancia!	oonah ahm-boo-lahn-thee-ah
…the police!	…la policía!	lah poh-lee-thee-ah
…the fire brigade!	…los bomberos!	lohs bohm-beh-rohs
Where is…	¿Dónde está…	dohn-deh ehs-tah
…the nearest telephone?	…el teléfono más próximo?	ehl teh-leh-foh-noh mahs prohx-ee-moh
…the nearest hospital?	…el hospital más próximo?	ehl ohs-pee-tahl mahs prohx-ee-moh

Communication Essentials

Yes	Sí	see
No	No	noh
Please	Por favor	pohr fah-vohr
Thank you	Gracias	grah-thee-ahs
Excuse me	Perdone	pehr-doh-neh
Hello	Hola	oh-lah
Goodbye	Adiós	ah-dee-ohs
Good night	Buenas noches	bweh-nahs noh-chehs
Morning	La mañana	lah mah-nyah-nah
Afternoon/Evening	La tarde	lah tahr-deh
Yesterday	Ayer	ah-yehr
Today	Hoy	oy
Tomorrow	Mañana	mah-nya-nah
Here	Aquí	ah-kee
There	Allí	ah-yee
What?	¿Qué?	keh
When?	¿Cuándo?	kwahn-doh
Why?	¿Por qué?	pohr-keh
Where?	¿Dónde?	dohn-deh

Useful Phrases

How are you?	¿Cómo está usted?	koh-moh ehs-tah oos-tehd
Very well, thank you	Muy bien, gracias	mwee bee-ehn grah-thee-ahs
Pleased to meet you.	Encantado de conocerle.	ehn-kahn-tah-doh deh thehr-leh
See you soon	Hasta pronto	ahs-tah-prohn-toh
That's fine	Está bien	ehs-tah bee-ehn
Where is/are…?	¿Dónde está/están…?	dohn-deh ehs-tah/ehs-tahn
How far is it to…?	Cuántos metros/kilómetros hay de aquí a…?	kwahn-tohs meh-trohs/kee-loh-meh-trohs eye deh ah-kee ah
Which way to…?	¿Por dónde se va a…?	pohr dohn-deh seh bah ah
Do you speak English?	¿Habla inglés?	ah-blah een-glehs
I don't understand	No comprendo	noh kohm-prehn-doh
Could you speak more slowly please?	¿Puede hablar más despacio por favor?	pweh-deh ah-blahr mahs dehs-pah-thee-oh pohr fah-vohr
I'm sorry	Lo siento	loh see-ehn-toh

Useful Words

big	grande	grahn-deh
small	pequeño	peh-keh-nyoh
hot	caliente	kah-lee-ehn-teh
cold	frío	free-oh
good	bueno	bweh-noh
bad	malo	mah-loh
well	bien	bee-ehn
open	abierto	ah-bee-ehr-toh
closed	cerrado	thehr-rah-doh
left	izquierda	eeth-key-ehr-dah
right	derecha	deh-reh-chah
straight on	todo recto	toh-doh rehk-toh

near	cerca	thehr-kah
far	lejos	leh-hohs
up	arriba	ah-ree-bah
down	abajo	ah-bah-hoh
early	temprano	tehm-prah-noh
late	tarde	tahr-deh
entrance	entrada	ehn-trah-dah
exit	salida	sah-lee-dah
toilet	servicios	sehr-bee-thee-ohs
more	más	mahs
less	menos	meh-nohs

Shopping

How much does this cost?	¿Cuánto cuesta esto?	kwahn-toh kwehs-tah ehs-toh
I would like…	Me gustaría…	meh goos-ta-ree-ah
Do you have…?	¿Tienen…?	tee-yeh-nehn
Do you take cards?	¿Aceptan tarjetas?	ah-thehp-tahn tahr-heh-tahs
What time do you open/close?	¿A qué hora abren/cierran?	ah keh oh-rah ah-brehn/thee-ehr-rahn
This one	Éste	ehs-teh
That one	Ése	eh-seh
expensive	caro	kahr-oh
cheap	barato	bah-rah-toh
size, clothes	talla	tah-yah
size, shoes	número	noo-mehr-oh
antiques shop	la tienda de antigüedades	tee-ehn-dah deh ahn-tee-gweh-dah-dehs
bakery	la panadería	pah-nah-deh ree-ah
bank	el banco	bahn-koh
bookshop	la librería	lee-breh-ree-ah
cake shop	la pastelería	pahs-teh-leh-ree-ah
chemist's	la farmacia	ahr-mah-thee-ah
grocer's	la tienda de comestibles	tee-yehn-dah deh koh-mehs-tee-blehs
market	el mercado	mehr-kah-doh
newsagent's	el kiosko de prensa	kee-ohs-koh deh prehn-sah
post office	la oficina de correos	oh-fee-thee-nah deh kohr-reh-ohs
shoe shop	la zapatería	thah-pah-teh-ree-ah
supermarket	el super-mercado	soo-pehr-mehr-kah-doh
travel agency	la agencia de viajes	ah-hehn-thee-ah -deh beeah-hehs

Sightseeing

art gallery	el museo de arte	moo-seh-oh deh ahr-teh
cathedral	la catedral	kah-teh-drahl
church	la iglesia, la basílica	ee-gleh-see-ah bah-see lee-kah
garden	el jardín	hahr-deen
library	la biblioteca	bee-blee-oh-teh-kah
museum	el museo	moo-seh-oh
tourist information office	la oficina de turismo	oh-fee-thee-nah deh too-rees-moh
town hall	el ayunta-miento	ah-yoon-toh mee-ehn-toh
bus station	la estación de autobuses	ehs-tah-thee-ohn deh owtoh-boo-sehs
railway station	la estación de trenes	ehs-tah-thee-ohn deh treh-nehs

Staying in a Hotel

Do you have a vacant room?	¿Tiene una habitación libre?	tee-eh-neh oo-nah ah-bee- tah-thee-ohn lee-breh
double room	habitación doble	ah-bee-tah-thee-ohn doh-bleh
with double bed	con cama de matrimonio	kohn kah-mah deh mah-tree-moh-nee-oh
twin room	habitación con dos camas	ah-bee-tah-thee-ohn kohn dohs kah-mahs

single room	habitación individual	ah-bee-tah-thee-ohn een-dee-vee-doo-ahl
room with a bath	habitación con baño	ah-bee-tah-thee-ohn kohn bah-nyoh
porter	el botones	boh-toh-nehs
key	la llave	yah-veh
I have a reservation	Tengo una habitación reservada	tehn-goh oo-na ah-bee-tah-thee-ohn reh-sehr-bah-dah

Eating Out

Have you got a table for…?	¿Tiene mesa para…?	tee-eh-neh meh-sah pah-rah
I want to reserve a table	Quiero reservar una mesa	kee-eh-roh reh-sehr-bahr oo-nah meh-sah
the bill	La cuenta	kwehn-tah
I am a vegetarian	Soy vegetariano/a	soy beh-heh-tah-ree-ah-no/na
waitress/ waiter	camarera/ camarero	kah-mah-reh-rah/ kah-mah-reh-roh
menu	la carta	kahr-tah
fixed-price menu	menú del día	meh-noo dehl dee-ah
wine list	la carta de vinos	kahr-tah deh bee-nohs
glass	un vaso	bah-soh
bottle	una botella	boh-teh-yah
knife	un cuchillo	koo-chee-yoh
fork	un tenedor	teh-neh-dohr
spoon	una cuchara	koo-chah-rah
breakfast	el desayuno	deh-sah-yoo-noh
lunch	la comida/ el almuerzo	koh-mee-dah/ ahl-mwehr-thoh
dinner	la cena	theh-nah
main course	el primer plato	pree-mehr plah-toh
starters	los entremeses	ehn-treh-meh-ses
dish of the day	el plato del día	plah-toh dehl dee-ah
coffee	el café	kah-feh
rare (meat)	poco hecho	poh-koh eh-choh
medium	medio hecho	meh-dee-oh eh-choh
well done	muy hecho	mwee eh-choh

Menu Decoder

al horno	ahl ohr-noh	baked
asado	ah-sah-doh	roast
el aceite	ah-thee-eh-teh	oil
las aceitunas	ah-theh-toon-ahs	olives
el agua mineral	ah-gwa mee-neh-rahl	mineral water
sin gas/con gas	seen gas/kohn gas	still/sparkling
el ajo	ah-hoh	garlic
el arroz	ahr-rohth	rice
el azúcar	ah-thoo-kahr	sugar
la carne	kahr-neh	meat
la cebolla	theh-boh-yah	onion
el cerdo	therh-doh	pork
la cerveza	thehr-beh-thah	beer
el chocolate	choh-koh-lah-teh	chocolate
el chorizo	choh-ree-thoh	spicy sausage
el cordero	kohr-deh-roh	lamb
frito	free-toh	fried
la fruta	froo-tah	fruit
los frutos secos	froo-tohs seh-kohs	nuts
las gambas	gahm-bahs	prawns
el helado	eh-lah-doh	ice cream
el huevo	oo-eh-voh	egg
el jamón serrano	hah-mohn sehr-rah-noh	cured ham
la langosta	lahn-gohs-tah	lobster
la leche	leh-cheh	milk
el limón	lee-mohn	lemon
la mantequilla	mahn-teh-kee-yah	butter
la manzana	mahn-thah-nah	apple
los mariscos	mah-rees-kohs	seafood
la naranja	nah-rahn-hah	orange
el pan	pahn	bread

el pastel	pahs-tehl	pastry
las patatas	pah-tah-tahs	potatoes
el pescado	pehs-kah-doh	fish
la pimienta	pee-mee-yehn-tah	pepper
el plátano	plah-tah-noh	banana
el pollo	poh-yoh	chicken
el postre	pohs-treh	dessert
el queso	keh-soh	cheese
la sal	sahl	salt
la salsa	sahl-sah	sauce
seco	seh-koh	dry
el solomillo	soh-loh-mee-yoh	sirloin
la sopa	soh-pah	soup
la tarta	tahr-tah	pie/cake
el té	teh	tea
la ternera	tehr-neh-rah	beef
el vinagre	bee-nah-greh	vinegar
el vino blanco	bee-noh blahn-koh	white wine
el vino rosado	bee-noh roh-sah-doh	rosé wine
el vino tinto	bee-noh teen-toht	red wine

Numbers

0	cero	theh-roh
1	uno	oo-noh
2	dos	dohs
3	tres	trehs
4	cuatro	kwa-troh
5	cinco	theen-koh
6	seis	says
7	siete	see-eh-teh
8	ocho	oh-choh
9	nueve	nweh-veh
10	diez	dee-ehth
11	once	ohn-theh
12	doce	doh-theh
13	trece	treh-theh
14	catorce	kah-tohr-theh
15	quince	keen-theh
16	dieciséis	dee-eh-thee-seh-ees
17	diecisiete	dee-eh-thee-see-eh-teh
18	dieciocho	dee-eh-thee-oh-choh
19	diecinueve	dee-eh-thee-nweh-veh
20	veinte	beh-een-teh
21	veintiuno	beh-een-tee-oo-noh
22	veintidós	beh-een-tee-dohs
30	treinta	treh-een-tah
31	treinta y uno	treh-een-tah ee oo-noh
40	cuarenta	kwah-rehn-tah
50	cincuenta	theen-kwehn-tah
60	sesenta	seh-sehn-tah
70	setenta	seh-tehn-tah
80	ochenta	oh-chehn-tah
90	noventa	noh-vehn-tah
100	cien	thee-ehn
101	ciento uno	thee-ehn-toh oo-noh
200	doscientos	dohs-thee-ehn-tohs
500	quinientos	khee-nee-ehn-tohs
700	setecientos	seh-teh-thee-ehn-tohs
900	novecientos	noh-veh-thee-ehn-tohs
1,000	mil	meel

Time

one minute	un minuto	oon mee-noo-toh
one hour	una hora	oo-na oh-rah
half an hour	media hora	meh-dee-a oh-rah
Monday	lunes	loo-nehs
Tuesday	martes	mahr-tehs
Wednesday	miércoles	mee-ehr-koh-lehs
Thursday	jueves	hoo-weh-vehs
Friday	viernes	bee-ehr-nehs
Saturday	sábado	sah-bah-doh
Sunday	domingo	doh-meen-goh

First

and Ten

FOOTBALL FUN, FACTS, AND TRIVIA

Compiled by
Daniel Partner

BARBOUR
PUBLISHING, INC.
Uhrichsville, Ohio

© MCMXCIX by Barbour Publishing, Inc.

ISBN 1-57748-435-5

Published by Barbour Publishing, Inc., P.O. Box 719, Uhrichsville, OH 44683, http://www.barbourbooks.com

ecpa Member of the
Evangelical Christian
Publishers Association

Printed in the United States of America.

The nice thing about football is that you have a scoreboard to show how you've done. In other things in life, you don't. At least, not one you can see.

CHUCK NOLL,
Pittsburgh Steelers coach (1969–91)

You love football—the roar of the crowd, the chill in the air, the smell of hot dogs wafting out of the concession stand. You love the sound of crunching shoulder pads, the thrill of a receiver dashing downfield, the joy of a victory for the home team. You love to see those big, strong men battling it out on the gridiron.

Football's a great game, with a fascinating story and a great cast of characters. Read *First and Ten* to relive some of the most exciting moments of football, learn the history of the sport, and meet many of the colorful personalities of the game. Read on, too, for an introduction to some of the many Christians who've made professional football their career. They're the guys who best understand Coach Noll's "unseen scoreboard"—*God's* scoreboard of life.

Be encouraged by the player testimonies from *Sports Spectrum,* the premier Christian sports magazine. Enjoy the facts and figures, the quips and quotes, the terms and timelines. *First and Ten* is a crash course in football fandom. Read on, then watch your favorite game with a whole new perspective!

from SPORTS SPECTRUM

Christian's Faith

Bob Christian could wallow in how frustrating his career has been. Instead, the Atlanta Falcons' fullback is enjoying having the turf as his mission field again—after being cut three times and missing the 1996 season with an injury.

This season Christian is sharing his faith and favorite Bible verse, Romans 8:28, in public service announcements (PSAs) filmed for an Atlanta television station and for use in the Georgia Dome. "During football games, if we make a good play, they can use it in the stadium on big screens," he says. "It's a way to get the gospel out to people who might not go to church."

Fans who see the PSAs may recognize Christian's favorite verse, "And we know that in all things God works for the good of those who love him, who have been called according to his purpose." The verse jumped out at him when he first accepted Jesus as Savior and started reading the Bible, he says. But it has meant even more during his career struggles.

"I can look back and see how every situation in my life has worked for my good, from injuries to getting cut to sitting at home trying to figure out what I'm going to do," he says.

4 FIRST AND TEN

The former Northwestern standout was cut by the Falcons in 1991 and by the London Monarchs of the WFL and San Diego in 1992. He made the practice squad with Chicago that year, playing in the last two games and two more seasons with the Bears. He became a Carolina Panther in 1995 and was signed by the Falcons as a free agent in 1997.

"The main reason God has me playing football in Atlanta is to be a witness for Him to the other guys on the team," says the five-foot-eleven-inch, 230-pound fullback. "They're bleeding and sweating alongside me in the battle. Those are the people I love dearly."

—by LORI WIECHMAN

Pro football is like nuclear warfare. There are no winners, only survivors.

FRANK GIFFORD,
announcer and former
New York Giants running back (1952–64)

I played football before they had headgear, and that's how I lost my mind.

CASEY STENGEL,
New York Yankees manager (1949–61)

A Pro Football Chronology
Part 1

1869

- Rutgers and Princeton play the first ever college soccer-football game.
- Rugby gains favor over soccer in eastern schools. Modern football begins to develop from rugby.

1876

- The first rules for American football are written at the Massasoit Convention.
- Walter Camp, the father of American football, becomes involved with the game.

1892

- Football is a major attraction of Pittsburgh-area athletic clubs. The Allegheny Athletic Association (AAA) and the Pittsburgh Athletic Club (PAC) are rivals.
- Former Yale All-America guard Pudge Heffelfinger is paid $500 by the AAA to play in a game against the PAC. He is the first person to be paid to play football.

1893

- The Pittsburgh Athletic Club signs halfback Grant Dibert for all its games—the first pro football contract.

1896

- The Allegheny Athletic Association team fields the first completely professional team for its two-game season.

- The Latrobe Athletic Association football team goes entirely professional—the first team to play a full professional season.

- The value of a touchdown is changed from four points to five.

- Chris O'Brien forms the Morgan Athletic Club on Chicago's south side. The team is later known as the Normals, the Racine Cardinals, the Chicago Cardinals, the St. Louis Cardinals, the Phoenix Cardinals, and, presently, the Arizona Cardinals. This team is the oldest continuing pro football organization.

- William Temple takes responsibility for paying the Duquesne Country and Athletic Club—the first known individual club owner.

- Baseball's Philadelphia Athletics and Philadelphia Phillies both form professional football teams. With the Pittsburgh Stars they attempt the first pro football league—the National Football League.
- The Athletics win the first night football game, 39–0 over Kanaweola AC at Elmira, New York.
- All three Pennsylvania teams claim the championship. The Stars are named champions by the league president.
- Hall of fame pitcher Christy Mathewson plays fullback for Pittsburgh.

- The first World Series of pro football—a five-team tournament—is played at New York's original Madison Square Garden. Here, New York and Syracuse play the first indoor football game. Syracuse, with Pop Warner at guard, wins 6–0 and eventually wins the tournament.

1903
- The Franklin (Penn.) Athletic Club wins the second (and last) World Series of pro football.
- Pro football is popularized in Ohio by the Massillon Tigers, who hire four Pittsburgh pros to play in the season's final game against Akron.

1904
- The value of a field goal is changed from five points to four.
- Ohio has seven pro teams.
- Massillon wins the Ohio Independent Championship, the current pro title.
- Halfback Charles Follis signs with the Shelby (Ohio) AC—the first African-American pro football player.

It's a very interesting game. They have big bears up front and little rabbits in the back. The idea is for the bears to protect the rabbits.

VIKTOR TIKHONOV,
National Soviet hockey coach,
seeing American football for the first time

Gridiron Glossary
The Odd Language of Football
Part 1

AUDIBLE: A play called by the quarterback at the line of scrimmage that changes the play that was previously called in the huddle; a change of plans in game play, just before the ball goes into play. Also called an automatic.

BALANCED LINE: A formation with an equal number of linemen on either side of the center.

BIRDCAGE: The face mask, donned by linemen, which has extra vertical and horizontal bars.

BLIND SIDE: The side opposite the side a player is looking toward.

BLITZ: An all-out run by linebackers and defensive backs, charging through the offensive line in an effort to sack the quarterback before he can hand off the ball or pass it. Also called red dogging.

BUTTONHOOK: A pass route in which the receiver heads straight downfield, then abruptly turns back toward the line of scrimmage.

CHAIN CREW: Three assistants to the officials whose job it is to handle the first down measuring chain and the down box.

CHEAP SHOT: A deliberate foul or other violent act against an unsuspecting player.

CHECK OFF: Calling an audible.

CLIPPING: Blocking an opponent from behind, typically at leg level. Clipping is a foul with a fifteen-yard penalty.

CLOTHESLINE: A foul. To clothesline is to strike another player across the face with one's extended arm.

COFFIN CORNER: One of the four corners of the field. A punter often tries to kick the ball out of bounds near a "coffin corner" to stop the other team from returning the ball and make them put the ball back into play close to their own goal line.

CONVERSION: A point after a touchdown.

CRACKBACK: A foul. Blocking by an offensive player who goes downfield, then turns back to the middle to block a player from the side.

CURL/CURL IN: A maneuver where the receiver runs downfield before turning back to run toward the line of scrimmage.

CUT: To suddenly change direction to lose a pursuing player. Also, to drop a prospective player from the team roster.

If you can count to eleven you'll have no trouble playing football. Count to twenty-two and you can play quarterback.

DARYLE LAMONICA,
Oakland quarterback (1963–74)

It's bad luck to be behind at the end of the game.
HUGH "DUFFY" DAUGHERTY

Stats
7+ Reception Games (1998)

Games	Player	Team
7	Herman Moore	Detroit
6	Marshall Faulk	Indianapolis
6	O. J. McDuffie	Miami
5	Antonio Freeman	Green Bay
5	Keyshawn Johnson	New York Jets
5	Carl Pickens	Cincinnati
5	Frank Sanders	Arizona
5	Jimmy Smith	Jacksonville
5	Rod Smith	Denver
4	Tim Brown	Oakland
4	Ben Coates	New England
4	Terry Glenn	New England
4	Keenan McCardell	Jacksonville
4	Frank Wycheck	Tennessee
3	Kimble Anders	Kansas City
3	Cris Carter	Minnesota
3	Larry Centers	Arizona
3	Marvin Harrison	Indianapolis
3	Michael Irvin	Dallas
3	Tony Martin	Atlanta
3	Ed McCaffrey	Denver
3	Rob Moore	Arizona
3	Johnnie Morton	Detroit
3	Muhsin Muhammad	Carolina
3	Ricky Proehl	St. Louis
3	Jerry Rice	San Francisco
3	Duce Staley	Philadelphia
3	Cameron Cleeland	New Orleans
2	Isaac Bruce	St. Louis
2	Wayne Chrebet	New York Jets

Games	Player	Team
2	Sean Dawkins	New Orleans
2	Joey Galloway	Seattle
2	Courtney Hawkins	Pittsburgh
2	Raghib Ismail	Carolina
2	Charles Johnson	Pittsburgh
2	Dorsey Levens	Green Bay
2	Terance Mathis	Atlanta
2	Mike Pritchard	Seattle
2	Andre Reed	Buffalo
2	Andre Rison	Kansas City
2	J.J. Stokes	San Francisco
2	Ricky Watters	Seattle
2	Michael Westbrook	Washington
2	Amp Lee	St. Louis
2	Randy Moss	Minnesota
2	Fred Taylor	Jacksonville
1	Derrick Alexander	Kansas City
1	Reidel Anthony	Tampa Bay
1	Tiki Barber	New York Giants
1	Chris Calloway	New York Giants
1	Albert Connell	Washington
1	Stephen Davis	Washington
1	Warrick Dunn	Tampa Bay
1	Quinn Early	Buffalo
1	Bert Emanuel	Tampa Bay
1	Bobby Engram	Chicago
1	Terrell Fletcher	San Diego
1	Oronde Gadsden	Miami
1	William Henderson	Green Bay
1	Ike Hilliard	New York Giants
1	Priest Holmes	Baltimore
1	Michael Jackson	Baltimore
1	Brian Mitchell	Washington

GAMES	PLAYER	TEAM
1	Eric Moulds	Buffalo
1	Terrell Owens	San Francisco
1	Bill Schroeder	Green Bay
1	Darnay Scott	Cincinnati
1	Leslie Shepherd	Washington
1	Torrance Small	Indianapolis
1	Bryan Still	San Diego
1	Yancey Thigpen	Tennessee
1	Wesley Walls	Carolina
1	Andrew Glover	Minnesota
1	Tony Gonzalez	Kansas City
1	Stephen Alexander	Washington
1	Jerome Pathon	Indianapolis
1	Floyd Turner	Baltimore

On the first day of rookie camp Floyd Peters came in and told the defensive linemen, "The number one rule is this—tackle the man with the ball." That immediately cleared things up.

BUBBA BAKER,
St. Louis defensive end (1980–88)

Bruce Matthews's Be-all, End-all

The careers of Tennessee Oilers' all-purpose offensive lineman Bruce Matthews and Denver's Hall of Fame-bound quarterback John Elway draw interesting parallels.

Matthews and Elway both broke into the NFL in 1983 as first-round draft choices. Both are Pac 10 products (Matthews played at Southern California; Elway at Stanford). Both have been named to just about every all-NFL team you can think of. And both have remained with the same club their entire professional careers.

But Matthews's and Elway's paths took a fork in the road last January as Elway finally captured a Super Bowl title. Getting fitted for a Super Bowl ring is certainly something that Matthews hopes will take place before he retires.

Although the Oilers failed to make the playoffs for four straight years (1994–1997), they're well acclimated to postseason pressure. With Matthews spearheading their offensive line—he's played all five positions in his career—the Oilers qualified for the playoffs seven straight seasons from 1987–1993. Unfortunately, Houston (now Tennessee) either bowed out in the wild-card game or never made it past the divisional playoffs.

Elway had a hand in ending Houston's season twice—in 1987 and 1991. Still, Matthews's respect for his long-time rival runs deep.

"I was glad to see that he got one [a Super Bowl ring]," says Matthews. "You can say it's not that big of a deal, but when you see somebody win it, it's special."

Matthews, who has been around for sixteen NFL campaigns, is well aware that the clock is winding down on his dream to play for the Lombardi Trophy. What if he falls short? Well, he'll be disappointed, but he'll never feel empty inside, thanks to his relationship with God through Jesus Christ—a relationship he began to develop during his rookie year.

Things couldn't have worked out better for Matthews that first season. He made the big time, but he also realized something was missing. A few of his Christian teammates encouraged Matthews to let Christ fill that void inside him.

"I was always spiritually inclined, but I never dedicated my life to the Lord," he says. "[I said] this [football] can't be the be-all, end-all. It became very apparent to me that God had a plan for my life.

"It doesn't matter what the situation is, winning or losing, as long as you're playing hard for the Lord and glorifying Him," says Matthews. "[Getting to] the Super Bowl would be a great honor, but I can be happy using the talents and abilities that God has blessed me with."

—by MIKE SANDROLINI

A Pro Football Chronology
Part 2

1905
- Canton AC (later, the Bulldogs) go professional. Massillon again wins the Ohio League championship.

1906
- The forward pass is legalized.
- George (Peggy) Parratt of Massillon throws a completion to Bullet Riley—the first pass completion in a pro game.
- Rivals Canton and Massillon vie for the championship. They play twice—Canton wins the first game, but Massillon wins the second and the Ohio League championship.
- A betting scandal combines with huge player salaries to cause a decline in interest in pro football in Ohio.

1909
- The value of a field goal drops from four points to three.

1912
- The value of a touchdown is increased from five points to six.
- Jack Cusack revives a pro team in Canton.

1913
- Jim Thorpe, double gold medal winner at the 1912 Olympics in Stockholm, plays for the Pine Village (Indiana) Pros.

1915
- Massillon fields a strong team. The rivalry with Canton is renewed.

- Jack Cusack signs Thorpe to play for Canton for $250 a game.

1916
- Thorpe and teammate Pete Calac lead Canton to a 9–0–1 season and the pro football championship.

1917
- Canton wins the Ohio League championship again.

1919
- Canton again wins the Ohio League championship.
- Earl (Curly) Lambeau and George Calhoun organize the Green Bay Packers when Lambeau's employer, the Indian Packing Company, provides $500 for equipment and the company field for practices. The team goes 10–1.

1920
- Akron Pros, Canton Bulldogs, Cleveland Indians, and Dayton Triangles hold an organizational meeting at the Jordan and Hupmobile auto showroom in Canton, Ohio, and form the American Professional Football Conference.
- A second organizational meeting is held in Canton. The league name is changed to the American Professional Football Association. Jim Thorpe is elected president of the league.

1921
- The 1920 season championship is awarded by the league to the Akron Pros. The league is reorganized, with Joe Carr as president. Carr moves the Association's headquarters to Columbus, drafts a league constitution and by-laws, and generally organizes the league.

- The Association is composed of twenty-two teams, including the Green Bay Packers.
- A.E. Staley turns the Decatur Staleys over to George Halas, who moves the team to Chicago.
- Player-coach Fritz Pollard of the Akron Pros is the first African-American head coach.
- The Staleys are the APFA champions with a 9–1–1 record—George Halas's first championship.

1922

- Bad weather and low attendance plague the Packers. Head coach and manager Curly Lambeau goes broke. Green Bay merchants arrange a $2,500 loan for the club and set up a public nonprofit corporation to operate the team.
- The American Professional Football Association changes its name to the National Football League on June 24. The Chicago Staleys are renamed the Chicago Bears.
- The NFL is composed of eighteen teams, including the new Oorang Indians of Marion, Ohio, an all-Indian team featuring Thorpe. The team is sponsored by the Oorang Dog Kennels.
- Canton finishes the season 10–0–2.

Pro football gave me a good sense of perspective to enter politics. I'd already been booed, cheered, cut, sold, traded, and hung in effigy.

JACK KEMP,
US Congressman and former quarterback (1957–62)

Gridiron Glossary
Part 2

DEAD BALL: A ball that is no longer in play, that is, a ball that is not held by a player or loose from a kick, fumble, or pass.

DELAY OF GAME: A delay caused by a team using or requesting excessive time-outs, resulting in a five-yard penalty.

DOWN AND IN: A maneuver where the receiver runs straight downfield, then suddenly cuts toward the middle of the field.

DOWN AND OUT: The opposite of the above maneuver. In a down and out, the receiver runs downfield then turns out, toward the sideline.

DOWN BOX (DOWN INDICATOR): A seven-foot metal rod, on the end of which are four cards (numbered one to four), used to keep track of the number of the down being played.

DRAFT: The selection of new players into the pro ranks from among the various top college players. Teams doing poorly are allowed to choose before those doing well.

ELIGIBLE: An offensive player who is able (by the rules) to catch a forward pass; "eligible" to receive the pass.

ENCROACH: Contacting an opposing player before the snap. Encroaching is illegal, with a five-yard penalty.

END LINE: The very end of the field in either direction. There are two end lines (one at each end of the field).

END ZONE: The area between the goal lines and the end lines; the last ten yards at either end of the field.

EXTRA POINT: After scoring a touchdown, a team can earn one more point by making a successful place-kick.

FAIR CATCH: When there is a punt and a receiver fielding the ball signals that he will not advance after catching it (by raising his hand), this is a fair catch. Opposing players may not tackle the receiver making the fair catch.

FLANKER: An offensive player on the right or left side of the formation. A flanker usually plays as a receiver.

FLAT: The field on either side of the formation.

FLOOD: An attempt to swamp the opposition or an area of the field with sheer numbers of players.

FREE AGENT: A professional athlete who is not constrained to deal with one team. Rather, a free agent may sign with any team he or she chooses.

FREE SAFETY: One of the two defensive backs deepest in the field who isn't assigned a particular area or player to cover and is thus free to follow the play anywhere it goes.

FREEZE: Holding on to the ball for a long time without scoring or attempting to score, to "freeze" the game.

FRONT FOUR: The defensive front line; made up of two ends and two tackles.

FULLBACK: A position used in college and high school football. A member of the offense whose job it is to run the ball, receive passes, and block for a teammate running the ball.

FUMBLE: A ball that is dropped while in play.

Tom Landry is a perfectionist. If he was married to Raquel Welch, he'd expect her to cook.

DON MEREDITH,
Dallas Cowboys quarterback (1960–68)

Stats
100-Yard Rushing Games (1998)

GAMES	PLAYER	TEAM
12	Jamal Anderson	Atlanta
11	Terrell Davis	Denver
8	Curtis Martin	New York Jets
8	Barry Sanders	Detroit
7	Emmitt Smith	Dallas
6	Jerome Bettis	Pittsburgh
6	Gary Brown	New York Giants
6	Eddie George	Tennessee
6	Garrison Hearst	San Francisco
6	Fred Taylor	Jacksonville
5	Robert Smith	Minnesota
4	Corey Dillon	Cincinnati
4	Marshall Faulk	Indianapolis
4	Priest Holmes	Baltimore
4	Napoleon Kaufman	Oakland
4	Natrone Means	San Diego
4	Ricky Watters	Seattle
4	Robert Edwards	New England
3	Karim Abdul-Jabbar	Miami
3	Adrian Murrell	Arizona
3	Antowain Smith	Buffalo
2	Mike Alstott	Tampa Bay
2	Tim Biakabutuka	Carolina
2	Warrick Dunn	Tampa Bay
2	Terrell Fletcher	San Diego
2	Darick Holmes	Green Bay
2	Fred Lane	Carolina
2	James Stewart	Jacksonville
1	James Allen	Chicago
1	Donnell Bennett	Kansas City

Games	Player	Team
1	Charlie Garner	Philadelphia
1	Greg Hill	St. Louis
1	Dorsey Levens	Green Bay
1	Bam Morris	Kansas City
1	Lamar Smith	New Orleans
1	Duce Staley	Philadelphia
1	Kordell Stewart	Pittsburgh
1	Chris Warren	Dallas
1	Ahman Green	Seattle

Defensive backs. Nothing but reactions. You train 'em like seals.

SAM BAKER,
Washington Redskins
fullback/kicker (1953–59)

In life, as in a football game, the principle to follow is: Hit the line hard.

THEODORE ROOSEVELT,
twenty-sixth President of the United States

Trying to Find a Way to Give God the Glory

Arizona Cardinals all-pro cornerback Aeneas Williams spent his first two years at Southern University living the life of a model student-athlete.

Wanting to follow in the footsteps of his older brother Achilles—who was also attending Southern at the time—Williams got involved in student government, like his brother, and was on a fast track to graduation.

Williams held his own on the gridiron over that span, too—the intramural gridiron.

Aeneas had enjoyed a fine prep career at Fortier High School in New Orleans, which has produced a handful of NFL players, but he failed to land a football scholarship. Yet Williams wasn't heartbroken. He was content with completing his class requirements, playing intramural football, and looking up to his brother.

But things would change. Achilles Williams graduated from Southern in 1988, leaving his little brother to fend for himself. Aeneas seized the moment. "My brother graduating from college that particular year gave me an opportunity to find out who Aeneas was," he says.

And find out he did. That summer, Williams tried out for the other football program at Southern—the one that sports helmets and shoulder pads. Williams not only made the team; he went on to play three collegiate seasons and intercepted eleven passes his senior year alone. Over the years, Williams hasn't missed a beat, nor many opposing quarterbacks' errant passes, as a pro.

A Pro Bowl starter every year since 1994, Williams has been the NFL's co-leader in interceptions four times. Now the eight-year pro is setting his sights on helping the improved Cardinals get into the NFC playoffs with an eventual goal of making it to the Super Bowl.

"One of the things I've seen and [has] stuck in my mind is seeing [Green Bay's] Reggie White win it," says Williams. "It ignited something even more in me to get into the Super Bowl and win it. If I don't win a Super Bowl, the only question I want to ask myself is this: Did I do my best? I want to leave the game with no regrets."

From Williams's perspective, however, being a part of a Super Bowl-winning club in Arizona wouldn't be the highlight of his career. "I get the most fulfillment leading my teammates and friends throughout the league to the Lord and discipling them," he says. "I am still in awe of what the Lord has done in my life. My heart's desire is to disciple young believers and to give them the heart I've been given."

"A lot of times the interviewers [from the media] want me to give myself the credit," says Williams. "I'm always trying to find a way to give God the glory."

—by MIKE SANDROLINI

A Pro Football Chronology
Part 3

1923

- Jim Thorpe, playing for the Toledo Maroons, fumbles. The Bears' George Halas picks up the ball and returns it ninety-eight yards for a touchdown—a record that lasts until 1972.
- Canton has its second consecutive undefeated season, going 11–0–1 and winning the NFL title.

1924

- The league has eighteen franchises.
- League champion Canton is purchased by the owner of the Cleveland franchise, who takes the best players for the Cleveland Bulldogs.
- Cleveland wins the title with a 7–1–1 record.

1925

- Five new franchises are admitted to the NFL.
- The New York Giants are awarded to Tim Mara and Billy Gibson for $500.
- The NFL establishes its first player limit—sixteen.
- All-America halfback Harold (Red) Grange signs to play with the Chicago Bears.
- On Thanksgiving Day, a crowd of 36,000—the largest yet in pro football—sees Red Grange and the Bears play the Chicago Cardinals to a scoreless tie.
- The Chicago Cardinals, with the best record in the league, are named the 1925 champions.

1926

- Grange bolts the Bears over a salary/ownership dispute.

- Grange's manager starts the first American Football League. It lasts one season.
- A new rule prohibits any team from signing a player whose college class has not graduated.
- The NFL grows to twenty-two teams, including the Duluth Eskimos with All-America fullback Ernie Nevers of Stanford. "The Iron Men of the North" play twenty-nine exhibition and league games, twenty-eight on the road. Nevers plays in all but twenty-nine minutes of the season.
- Frankford (Pennsylvania) beats the Bears for the championship.

1927

- The NFL is reorganized into twelve teams.
- The league's center shifts from the Midwest to the cities of the East.
- The championship goes to the New York Giants, with ten shutouts in thirteen games.

1928

- Grange and Nevers retire from pro football.
- The NFL is reduced to ten teams.
- The Providence Steam Rollers win the championship in the Cycledrome, a ten thousand-seat oval built for bicycle races.

1929

- A fourth official, the field judge, is added.
- Grange and Nevers return to the NFL.
- Nevers scores six rushing touchdowns and four extra points for the Cardinals to beat Grange's Bears 40–6.
- Providence becomes the first NFL team to host a game at night under floodlights.

- The Packers, with back Johnny Blood (McNally), tackle Cal Hubbard, and guard Mike Michalske, win their first NFL championship.

1930
- Dayton, the last of the NFL's original franchises, is purchased, moved to Brooklyn, and renamed the Dodgers.
- The Packers edge the Giants for the title.
- George Halas retires as a player.
- Rookie All-America fullback-tackle Bronko Nagurski joins the Bears.
- The Giants defeat a team of former Notre Dame players coached by Knute Rockne 22–0 at the Polo Grounds. The proceeds go to help those suffering because of the Great Depression.

1931
- The Bears, Packers, and Portsmouth are each fined $1,000 for using players whose college classes had not graduated.
- The Packers win an unprecedented third consecutive title.

1932
- The Boston Braves join the league.
- NFL membership drops to eight teams, the lowest in history.
- Official statistics are kept for the first time.
- The Bears and the Spartans finish the season in the first tie for first place.
- The resulting first playoff game in NFL history is held indoors at Chicago Stadium because of bitter cold and heavy snow. The arena allows only an eighty-yard field so the rules are adjusted: The goal posts are moved from the end lines to the

goal lines, inbounds lines (hash marks) where the ball is put in play are drawn ten yards from the walls that butt against the sidelines.

- The Bears win 9–0.

1933

- The NFL makes significant changes from the college game for the first time.
- The adjustments from the 1932 championship game are adopted—hash marks and goal posts on the goal lines. The forward pass is legalized from anywhere behind the line of scrimmage.
- The NFL divides into two divisions. The winners are to meet in an annual championship game.
- New franchises join the league—the Pittsburgh Pirates, the Philadelphia Eagles, and the Cincinnati Reds.
- Halas becomes sole owner of the Bears and reinstates himself as head coach.
- The Boston Braves name is changed to the Redskins.
- In the first NFL Championship Game, the Western Division Bears defeat the Eastern Division Giants 23–21.

1934

- The Portsmouth Spartans move to Detroit and become the Lions.
- The Bears play the best college football players. The game ends in a scoreless tie before 79,432 at Soldier Field.
- Rookie Beattie Feathers of the Bears is the NFL's first 1,000-yard rusher, gaining 1,004 yards on 101 carries.

- Graham McNamee, announcer for NBC radio, calls the Thanksgiving Day game between the Bears and the Lions—the first NFL game broadcast nationally.
- The championship game occurs on an extremely cold and icy day at the Polo Grounds. The Giants trail the Bears 13–3 in the third quarter, change to basketball shoes for better footing, and win 30–13. The contest becomes known as the "Sneakers Game."
- The player waiver rule is adopted.

My parents sent me to Harvard to be a specialist. I don't think they were thinking of this.

PAT MCINALLY,
Cincinnati Bengals punter (1976–85)

I remember one time when Bronko Nagurski was horsing around in a second-floor hotel room with a teammate, and Bronko fell out of the window. A crowd gathered and a policeman came up and said, "What happened?" "I don't know," said Nagurski. "I just got here myself."

RONNIE GIBBS,
former referee

Gridiron Glossary
Part 3

GAME BALL: The ball given to a winning team's player or coach considered to have made the most contribution to their win. (It is supposed to be the ball or a ball used in the game.)

GOAL LINE: The line over which the ball must pass to score a touchdown. There are two goal lines, one at each end of the field, ten yards from the ends of the field.

GOAL-LINE STAND: Making a tough defensive effort against the opposition at or near one's goal line.

GRIDIRON: A football field.

HAIL MARY: The quarterback throwing the ball up in the air without really targeting any particular receiver, hoping someone on his side catches it. Typically done when the quarterback's about to get sacked!

HALFBACK: A position in college and high school football. A member of the offense whose job it is to run the ball, receive passes, or block for another teammate running the ball.

HAND OFF: Quite literally what it says: to hand the ball off to a teammate.

HANG TIME: The time a punt remains in the air.

HASH MARKS: These marks divide the field into thirds. Whenever the ball becomes dead on or outside one of these marks, it is placed on its respective hash mark.

HITCH AND GO: A maneuver where a runner runs downfield to catch a pass, fakes a quick turn (as if to catch), then continues downfield for a deeper pass.

HOLDER: A player who holds the ball during a place kick.

HOLDING: Keeping another player from advancing by literally holding him back with one's hand(s). Usually illegal.

HOTDOG: A player who uses theatrics and "hams it up" for the camera.

HUDDLE: The action of the players grouping together to plan the next play(s). As a noun, the group itself.

ILLEGAL MOTION: Movement by an offensive player before the snap. Illegal motion is, obviously, illegal and yields a five-yard penalty.

ILLEGAL PROCEDURE: Used to indicate a number of infractions, including an illegal snap, having less than seven players on the offense's line of scrimmage, and taking more than two steps after making a fair catch.

INCOMPLETE: A forward pass that is not caught or intercepted.

INTENTIONAL GROUNDING: The quarterback purposefully throwing the ball out of bounds or into the ground to avoid throwing a bad pass (which might be intercepted). Intentional grounding can be difficult to call, but a referee may assign the offending team a five-yard penalty and the loss of a down.

KEY: Watching a player to try to determine the direction in which he is going to be moving. A player may make small movements, such as foot placement, that can give away his next move to an observant player who is "keying" him.

Everyone has some fear. A man without fear belongs in a mental institution. . .or on special teams, either one.
WALT MICHAELS,
Cleveland Browns linebacker (1951–63)

Stats
Multiple Interception Games (1998)

Games	Player	Team
2	Percy Ellsworth	New York Giants
2	Robert Griffith	Minnesota
2	Ty Law	New England
2	Sam Madison	Miami
1	Jay Bellamy	Seattle
1	Jeff Brady	Carolina
1	Zack Bronson	San Francisco
1	Terrell Buckley	Miami
1	LeRoy Butler	Green Bay
1	Mark Carrier	Detroit
1	Ray Crockett	Denver
1	Charles Dimry	San Diego
1	Cris Dishman	Washington
1	Darrien Gordon	Denver
1	Victor Green	New York Jets
1	Henry Jones	Buffalo
1	Robert Jones	Miami
1	Sammy Knight	New Orleans
1	Kwamie Lassiter	Arizona
1	Ray Lewis	Baltimore
1	John Lynch	Tampa Bay
1	Ronald McKinnon	Arizona
1	Lawyer Milloy	New England
1	Kurt Schulz	Buffalo
1	Phillippi Sparks	New York Giants
1	Shawn Springs	Seattle
1	Zach Thomas	Miami
1	Brian Walker	Miami
1	Darnell Walker	San Francisco
1	Dewayne Washington	Pittsburgh

Games	Player	Team
1	Darryl Williams	Seattle
1	Rod Woodson	Baltimore
1	Artrell Hawkins	Cincinnati
1	Fred Weary	New Orleans

The idea is to have a plan and still allow for the unforeseeable. I've been reading about Nelson's battle with the Franco-Spanish fleet at Trafalgar in 1805. He had twenty-five days to make his plan. He was outnumbered, but his plan worked. He had steps prepared for the contingencies, and the plan left a certain flexibility in the choices of his captains. That is the basis of football.

BILL WALSH,
San Francisco 49ers coach (1979–88)

Nobody in football should be called a genius. A genius is a guy like Norman Einstein.

JOE THEISMANN,
Washington Redskins quarterback (1974–85)

SPORTS
spectrum

A Good Name and Loving Esteem

"If you must choose, take a good name rather than great riches; for to be held in loving esteem is better than silver and gold" (Proverbs 22:1 TLB).

King Solomon didn't have professional athletes in mind when he dispatched this scriptural morsel of wisdom—but it fits. In an age of continual fiscal selfishness and personal gratification, it has become common for pro sports figures to ignore this exhortation and choose silver and gold above a good name. So what happens when a player chooses both: to be held in loving esteem and obtain riches?

The answer can be found in the form of five-time Pro Bowl receiver Cris Carter—a player snatched by the Minnesota Vikings for a meager $100 when he was waived by the Philadelphia Eagles in 1990. Once in Minnesota, Carter became a Christian, and it showed both on and off the field. He has developed a "good name" and is held in "loving esteem" by fans, players, and coaches. Carter's good name, coupled with his great skills, has parlayed itself into great riches as he is in the midst of a substantial four-year contract.

With both proverbial components intact, one would

think Carter's career was complete. However, football-related fullness eludes him as he has yet to compete for a Super Bowl crown—an opportunity he contends would be an answer to prayer.

Now in his twelfth NFL season, Carter feels he has learned what it takes to realize his gridiron goal. "I've always wanted to make it, but I never really understood what it took to win it all," he says. Carter learned the value of experiencing rough times while watching former Eagle teammate and fellow believer Reggie White hoist the Lombardi Trophy after Super Bowl XXXI with the Green Bay Packers. "I've learned a lot from Reggie, and I realized that he had a lot of failures along the way. Regardless of whether he ever won a title, he's still had a tremendous career," Carter says.

Despite his arduous drive to claim the ultimate football prize, Carter, thirty-two, realizes that becoming a champion does not define him as a person. "Just because I am not in a Super Bowl doesn't make me a loser," he explains. "My life does not revolve around the Super Bowl."

The sure-handed receiver's professional ambition does less to define him than does his personal mission. Carter is unmistakably a preacher who contends that an NFL locker room is "not a place to preach Christianity; it is a place to live it. My number one job is to live a life that people would see me and know that there is something different," he says.

That difference is a name that will be recorded in the Book of Life long after any on-field accomplishments are forgotten and eternal riches that will outlast even the most lucrative contract.

—by TROY PEARSON

A Pro Football Chronology
Part 4

1935

- An annual draft of college players is scheduled to begin in 1936.
- The inbounds line, or hash marks, are moved nearer the center of the field, fifteen yards from the sidelines.
- The Lions defeat the Giants 26–7 in the NFL Championship Game.

1936

- All NFL member teams play the same number of games.
- The Eagles sign University of Chicago halfback and Heisman Trophy winner Jay Berwanger—the first player ever selected in the NFL draft.
- A rival league, the American Football League, forms. The Boston Shamrocks are its champions.
- In the NFL Championship Game, Green Bay defeats the Redskins 21–6 on December 13.

1937

- A new Cleveland franchise is named the Rams.
- The Redskins move to Washington, D.C. and sign TCU All-America tailback Sammy Baugh.
- Baugh leads the Redskins to a 28–21 victory over the Bears in the NFL Championship Game.
- The 8–0 Los Angeles Bulldogs win the AFL title, but the league soon folds.

1938

- Hugh (Shorty) Ray becomes technical advisor on rules and officiating.
- A new rule is implemented: a fifteen-yard penalty for roughing the passer.
- Rookie Byron "Whizzer" White of the Pittsburgh

Pirates leads the NFL in rushing. White later becomes a justice of the U.S. Supreme Court.
- The Giants defeat the Packers 23–17 for the NFL title.
- The Pro Bowl game is established between the NFL champion and a team of pro all-stars.

1939

- The New York Giants defeat the Pro All-Stars 13–10 in the first Pro Bowl.
- NBC broadcasts the Brooklyn Dodgers–Philadelphia Eagles game from Ebbets Field to approximately 1,000 sets in New York—the first NFL game to be televised.
- Green Bay defeats New York 27–0 in the NFL Championship Game.
- For the first time, NFL attendance exceeds one million in a season—1,071,200.

1940

- A rival league, the third to call itself the American Football League, is formed with six teams. The Columbus Bullies are its champions.
- The Bears defeat the Redskins 73–0 in the NFL Championship Game—the most decisive victory in NFL history.
- This is the first championship to be carried on network radio, broadcast by Red Barber.

1941

- The league by-laws provide for playoffs in case of ties in division races and sudden-death overtimes in case a playoff game is tied after four quarters.
- An official NFL Record Manual is published for the first time.
- Columbus again wins the AFL championship—but the two-year-old league folds.
- The Bears and the Packers tie for the Western

Division championship. The Bears win the first divisional playoff game in league history, 33–14.
- The Bears defeat the Giants 37–9 for the NFL championship.

1942

- Players depart for service in World War II, depleting the rosters of NFL teams.
- With George Halas in the Navy, the Bears go 11–0 in the regular season.
- The Redskins defeat the Bears 14–6 in the NFL Championship Game.

1943

- The Cleveland Rams co-owners join the armed forces, and the team is granted permission to suspend operations for the season.
- The league adopts free substitution, makes the wearing of helmets mandatory, and approves a ten-game schedule for all teams.
- Philadelphia and Pittsburgh merge for one season.
- Sammy Baugh (league leader in passing, punting, and interceptions) leads the Redskins to a tie with the Giants for the Eastern Division title. The Redskins win the divisional playoff game, 28–0.
- The Bears beat the Redskins 41–21 in the championship game.

1944

- A new franchise in Boston is named the Yanks.
- The Brooklyn Dodgers change their name to the Tigers.
- Coaching from the bench is legalized.
- The Cardinals and the Steelers merge for one year under the name Card-Pitt.
- Green Bay defeats the New York Giants 14–7 in the NFL Championship.

1945

- The inbounds lines (hash marks) are moved from fifteen yards away from the sidelines to twenty yards from the sidelines.
- Brooklyn and Boston merge and become the Boston Yanks.
- Steve Van Buren of Philadelphia leads the NFL in rushing, kickoff returns, and scoring.
- World War II ends, with 638 NFL players having served in the war. Twenty-one died in action.
- Rookie quarterback Bob Waterfield leads Cleveland to a 15–14 victory over Washington in the NFL Championship Game.

1946

- The free substitution rule is withdrawn. Substitutions are limited to no more than three men at a time.
- The NFL champion Rams move to Los Angeles.
- The rival All-America Football Conference begins play with eight teams. The Cleveland Browns, coached by Paul Brown, win the AAFC's first championship.
- Giants players are questioned about an attempt to fix the championship game.
- Chicago beats New York for the championship, 24–14.

Gridiron Glossary
Part 4

LATERAL: As a forward pass, but not thrown in the direction of the opponents' goalpost. Rather, the ball is thrown in any direction other than toward the opponents' goal.

LINEBACKER: Defensive players placed behind the defensive linemen. Their job is to tackle runners and block or intercept passes. There are three or four linebackers.

LINE JUDGE: An official who keeps track of time and also watches for various violations, including the quarterback's position when passing (the quarterback isn't allowed to go past the line of scrimmage to pass).

LINE OF SCRIMMAGE: Before each play, a set of two imaginary lines are used to determine where the players will line up. These are the lines of scrimmage and pass through each tip of the ball, running parallel to the goal lines.

LIVE BALL: Opposite of a ball that is dead. A live ball is either loose as a result of a kick, fumble, or pass or is held by a player.

MAN IN MOTION: The player who turns and runs behind the line of scrimmage, parallel to it, as the signals are called. He then runs downfield just as the ball is snapped.

MAN-TO-MAN DEFENSE: Covering each member of the offense with a member of the defense. Also called player-to-player defense. See also "zone defense."

MIDDLE GUARD: The defensive lineman positioned between the tackles, opposite the offensive center. Also called the nose guard.

MOUSETRAP: A trap block.

MULTIPLE OFFENSE: Offense strategy using a number of formations.

NICKEL DEFENSE: A defensive formation involving five defensive backs, hence the name.

NOSE GUARD: The middle guard.

OFFENSE: The team with the ball; the offense attempts to run or pass the ball across the defense's goal line.

OFF SEASON: When football teams don't play; in the NFL, February through the middle of August.

OFFSIDE: When a player is over the line of scrimmage (on the opposing team's side) before the ball is snapped.

ONSIDE KICK: A short kick (though at least ten yards), with the plan being to recover the kick and thus regain possession.

OPTION PLAY: An offensive play wherein the player with the ball has the option of running or passing.

OUTSIDE: Toward the sideline.

Three hundred pounds of player and thirty-four pounds of equipment just teeing off.

DAVE BUTZ,
St. Louis Cardinals/Washington Redskins
lineman (1973–1988)

SUPER BOWL	MVP	WINNER
XXXIII	John Elway	Denver 34
XXXII	Terrell Davis	Denver 31
XXXI	Desmond Howard	Green Bay 35
XXX	Larry Brown	Dallas 27
XXIX	Steve Young	San Francisco 49
XXVIII	Emmitt Smith	Dallas 30
XXVII	Troy Aikman	Dallas 52
XXVI	Mark Rypien	Washington 37
XXV	Ottis Anderson	NY Giants 20
XXIV	Joe Montana	San Francisco 55
XXIII	Jerry Rice	San Francisco 20
XXII	Doug Williams	Washington 42
XXI	Phil Simms	NY Giants 39
XX	Richard Dent	Chicago 46
XIX	Joe Montana	San Francisco 38
XVIII	Marcus Allen	L.A. Raiders 38
XVII	John Riggins	Washington 27
XVI	Joe Montana	San Francisco 26
XV	Jim Plunkett	Oakland 27
XIV	Terry Bradshaw	Pittsburgh 31
XIII	Terry Bradshaw	Pittsburgh 35
XII	Harvey Martin & Randy White	Dallas 27
XI	Fred Biletnikoff	Oakland 32
X	Lynn Swann	Pittsburgh 21
IX	Franco Harris	Pittsburgh 16
VIII	Larry Csonka	Miami 24
VII	Jake Scott	Miami 14
VI	Roger Staubach	Dallas 24
V	Chuck Howley	Baltimore 16
IV	Len Dawson	Kansas City 23
III	Joe Namath	NY Jets 16
II	Bart Starr	Green Bay 33
I	Bart Starr	Green Bay 35

—Winners and Losers

Loser	Location	Attendence	Date
Atlanta 19	Miami	74,803	1/31/99
Green Bay 24	San Diego	68,912	1/25/98
New England 21	New Orleans	72,301	1/26/97
Pittsburgh 17	Tempe	76,347	1/28/96
San Diego 26	Miami	74,107	1/29/95
Buffalo 13	Atlanta	72,817	1/30/94
Buffalo 17	Pasadena	98,374	1/31/93
Buffalo 24	Minneapolis	63,130	1/26/92
Buffalo 19	Tampa	73,813	1/27/91
Denver 10	New Orleans	72,919	1/28/90
Cincinnati 16	Miami	75,179	1/22/89
Denver 10	San Diego	73,302	1/31/88
Denver 20	Pasadena	101,063	1/25/87
New England 10	New Orleans	73,818	1/26/86
Miami 16	Stanford	84,059	1/20/85
Washington 9	Tampa	72,920	1/22/84
Miami 17	Pasadena	103,667	1/30/83
Cincinnati 21	Pontiac	81,270	1/24/82
Philadelphia 10	New Orleans	76,135	1/25/81
L.A. Rams 19	Pasadena	103,985	1/20/80
Dallas 31	Miami	79,484	1/21/79
Denver 10	New Orleans	75,583	1/15/78
Minnesota 14	Pasadena	103,438	1/9/77
Dallas 17	Miami	80,187	1/18/76
Minnesota 6	New Orleans	80,997	1/12/75
Minnesota 7	Houston	71,882	1/13/74
Washington 7	Los Angeles	90,182	1/14/73
Miami 3	New Orleans	81,023	1/16/72
Dallas 13	Miami	79,204	1/17/71
Minnesota 7	New Orleans	80,562	1/11/70
Baltimore 7	Miami	75,389	1/12/69
Oakland 14	Miami	75,546	1/14/68
Kansas City 10	Los Angeles	61,946	1/15/67

from
SPORTS
spectrum

Those Trusty Placekickers

Part I

Muddy, sweaty, Behemoth-sized men. Guys so big they need two zip codes. Scale-tippers who run the forty-yard dash in 4.5 seconds. Men of extraordinary size, strength, speed, and endurance. These are football players!

Grown men who dent the scales at a mere 170. Former soccer stars. Men who carry little orange tools onto the field to assist them. Guys who don't even wear shoes that match. These are not football players!

Think again.

These are football players. Players of a different breed—these are placekickers.

While they obviously don't fit the stereotypical model of today's NFL star, kickers are just as important to the success of a team on a Sunday afternoon as any 300-pound lineman. Perhaps even more important.

If there's one player who gets stuck with the "hero" or the "goat" tag more than any other, it's the kicker. On a field full of muscled-up mortals it's these little giants who loom large. The guy who makes a living with a swift kick of his foot and tacks on three points at a time.

You know the scenario: The team is down by a point with seven ticks on the game clock. The two minute offense has just stalled at the thirty-three-yard-line. Who gets the call? It's the smallest guy in uniform, that's who. It's show time!

With the pressure of teammates, coaches, fans, and the media, it's the job of these little big men to come through.

Amid this pressure, more than a handful of the NFL's finest kickers find a peace that transcends the success/failure balance they often hang in. These strong-legged heroes have an inner peace they receive from only one place—their relationship with Jesus Christ.

Matt Stover of the Baltimore Ravens is one such kicker. Matt's world isn't wrapped up in a field goal. "I look at it like this: 'Okay this is an opportunity God's given me, and I'm gonna give it everything I've got.' When the failures happen, I look at them and say, 'Lord, help me through this. I know You can work this out for good.' I trust in that, and then I move on. Because life does go on. Football is not my life, it's not even my priority."

And Stover's not alone. Many of Matt's NFL kicking brethren also gain their strength and their focus from their personal relationship with Jesus.

Norm Johnson, a sixteen-year NFL veteran now with the Pittsburgh Steelers, says his faith in Christ is crucial to the mental aspect of kicking. It helps him focus and not get down on himself.

"In our job, things are up-and-down all of the time," explains Johnson. "Faith in Christ helps us get through the down times. It helps us deal with the fact that we lost a game or missed a kick. We know that not only our family still loves us, but so does Jesus. And when you know that, what's said about you in the newspapers or what fans yell at you has very little consequence. It doesn't affect you. If you don't have that kind of faith, a lot of those outside factors may get to you and overcome you."

(to be continued)

A Pro Football Chronology
Part 5

1947
- The NFL adds a fifth official, the back judge.
- The Cleveland Browns again win the AAFC title, defeating the New York Yankees 14–3.
- The Cardinals win the NFL Championship Game 28–21 over the Philadelphia Eagles.

1948
- Plastic helmets are prohibited. A flexible artificial tee is permitted at the kickoff. Officials other than the referee are equipped with whistles, not horns.
- Halfback Fred Gehrke of the Los Angeles Rams paints horns on the Rams' helmets—the first modern helmet emblems in pro football.
- The 14–0 Cleveland Browns win their third straight championship in the AAFC, defeating the Buffalo Bills 49–7.
- The Eagles defeat the Cardinals 7–0 in the championship game, which takes place in a blizzard.

1949
- The Boston Yanks become the New York Bulldogs.
- Free substitution is adopted for one year.
- For the first time the NFL has two 1,000-yard rushers in the same season—Steve Van Buren of Philadelphia and Tony Canadeo of Green Bay.
- AAFC franchises Cleveland, San Francisco, and Baltimore are scheduled to join the NFL in 1950.
- The Browns win their fourth consecutive AAFC title, defeating the 49ers 21–7.
- In a heavy rain, the Eagles defeat the Rams 14–0 in the NFL Championship Game.

- Unlimited free substitution is restored, opening the era of two platoons and specialization.
- Curly Lambeau, founder of the franchise and Green Bay's head coach since 1921, resigns under fire.
- The American and National conferences are created to replace the Eastern and Western divisions.
- The Los Angeles Rams have all of their games televised—the first team to do so.
- In the first game of the season, former AAFC champion Cleveland defeats NFL champion Philadelphia 35–10.
- Deadlocks in both conferences occur for the first time. In the playoffs the Browns defeat the Giants in the American and the Rams defeat the Bears in the National.
- Cleveland defeats Los Angeles 30–28 in the NFL Championship Game.

1951

- The Pro Bowl game, dormant since 1942, is revived matching the all-stars of each conference. The American Conference defeats the National Conference 28–27.
- Rulesmakers decree that no tackle, guard, or center is eligible to catch a forward pass.
- The Rams reverse their television policy and televise only road games.
- The NFL Championship Game is televised coast-to-coast for the first time—the DuMont Network pays $75,000 for the rights to the game.
- The Rams defeat the Browns, 24–17, to become champions.

1952

- A new franchise in Dallas—the Texans—goes 1–11.

The owners turn the franchise back to the league in midseason. The commissioner's office operates the Texans as a road team. At the end of the season the franchise is canceled. This is the last time an NFL team will fail.

- The Detroit Lions win their first NFL championship in seventeen years, defeating the Browns 17–7.

1953

- The defunct Dallas organization becomes the Baltimore Colts.
- The names of the American and National conferences are changed to the Eastern and Western conferences.
- Jim Thorpe dies.
- The Lions defeat the Browns for the championship, 17–16.

1954

- Fullback Joe Perry of the 49ers is the first player in league history to gain 1,000 yards rushing in consecutive seasons.
- Cleveland defeats Detroit 56–10 in the NFL Championship Game.

1955

- The sudden-death overtime rule is used for the first time in a pre-season game. The Rams beat the Giants 23–17 three minutes into overtime.
- Rule change: The ball is immediately dead if the ball carrier touches the ground with any part of his body except his hands or feet while in the grasp of an opponent.
- The Baltimore Colts spend eighty cents on a phone call to Johnny Unitas and sign him as a free agent.

- Quarterback Otto Graham plays his last game as the Browns defeat the Rams 38–14 in the NFL Championship Game. Graham quarterbacked the Browns to ten championship game appearances in ten years.

1956

- The NFL Players Association is founded.
- New rules: Grabbing an opponent's face mask (other than the ball carrier's) is illegal. Using radio receivers to communicate with players on the field is prohibited. A natural leather ball with white end stripes replaces the white ball with black stripes for night games.
- George Halas retires as coach of the Bears.
- The Giants rout the Bears 47–7 in the championship game.

1957

- Pete Rozelle is named general manager of the Rams.
- Detroit defeats Cleveland 59–14 in the championship game.

1958

- Halas reinstates himself as coach of the Bears.
- Jim Brown of Cleveland gains 1,527 yards rushing—an NFL record.
- Baltimore, coached by Weeb Ewbank, defeats the Giants 23–17 in the first sudden-death overtime in an NFL Championship Game.

Gridiron Glossary
Part 5

PASS PATTERN: The specific route run by a receiver to catch a pass.

PASS RUSH: The rush by the defense to try to tackle the quarterback before he can complete a pass.

PENALTY: Punishment for a foul. Can consist of losing a down or even the ball, but usually sets back the penalized team five to fifteen yards.

PIGSKIN: Old term for a football.

PILING ON: Several players jumping on the player with the ball after he's been tackled. Also called "dogpiling." Piling on is illegal, with a fifteen-yard penalty.

PLACEKICK: A kick made while the ball is held in place on the ground (either with a tee or by another player).

PLAYBOOK: A notebook containing a team's terms, strategies, plays, etc., issued to each player.

PLAYMAKER: One skilled in helping their team score with winning strategy.

POCKET: The area where the quarterback sets up his pass. Guarded against the opposition to form a safe "pocket" for the quarterback.

POINT AFTER TOUCHDOWN: After scoring a touchdown, a team may score an extra point for a successful placekick through the opposition's goal post.

POINT SPREAD: The projected difference in scores between two teams about to play.

POST PATTERN: A pass pattern where the receiver runs ten to fifteen yards downfield before turning toward the middle of the field, but at a forty-five-degree angle (in the direction of the goal post).

POSTSEASON: The time when a tournament is played leading up to the Super Bowl. Also called the playoffs.

PRESEASON: The time during which teams play exhibition games and check out new talent, from August through Labor Day, when the regular season starts.

PRIMARY: The receiver who was chosen by the quarterback in the huddle to receive the ball.

PULLING: Leaving one's position to move elsewhere to block.

PUNT: A play in which the ball is dropped from the kicker's hands and kicked before hitting the ground.

QUARTER: A football game is divided into four quarters of fifteen minutes each (twelve minutes in high school football).

QUARTERBACK SNEAK: A play wherein the quarterback receives the ball after the snap and immediately runs forward through the opposition, with his own team blocking for him.

QUICK COUNT: When the quarterback calls the signals at the line of scrimmage very rapidly so as to throw off the other team.

QUICK KICK: A surprise punt.

I've got bruises all over my body from bumping into Dan around the kitchen or taking a gouge from him while he's asleep.

DIANE BIRDWELL,
wife of DAN BIRDWELL,
Oakland Raiders defensive end (1962–69)

The Big Bucks and Jerry Kramer,

Green Bay Packers offensive guard (1958–68)

In 1967, I had earned $27,500 for my regular season pay. In 1968, I negotiated a pretty unusual deal. I started with a salary of $26,000, but I also got a $2,500 bonus for signing and $3,500 for scouting, and that made my actual base pay $32,000. In addition, I was to get $500 extra for each field goal I kicked. . . , plus a $3,000 bonus if we won eight games, another $2,000 if we won ten games, and another $2,000 if we won our division. I thought I was a cinch to earn at least $43,000. I figured I had to kick at least fourteen field goals, an average of one a game, and I figured there was no way we could lose our division, no way we could win fewer than eight games. That meant $11,000 plus my $32,000 base. And if everything went well, I thought I had a reasonable chance of kicking eighteen field goals and the team had a reasonable chance of winning ten games. Including a potential $25,000 from the playoff and Super Bowl games, I calculated that my purely football income for the 1968 season could climb as high as $74,000, way up in the quarterback brackets.

> *If you'd ask me, what's the common religion among scouts, I'd have to say Hindu. They all believe in reincarnation. You're always hearing, "This guy's another Dick Butkus, this guy's another Willie Brown."*
>
> GEORGE YOUNG

Those Trusty Placekickers

Part 2

For most kickers the game is as much mental as it is physical. There's no time for self-doubt or worry. No time to contemplate the magnitude of the upcoming attempt. A kicker is focused on one thing and one thing alone—kicking the football. They shut out the world around them and do their job.

"I can't hear the crowd," says New England Patriots placekicker Adam Vinatieri. "I'm focusing in on kicking the football. I don't even think of the game situation too much. I try to make every kick exactly the same and focus on the fundamentals, not on the consequences."

Norm Johnson takes it one step further.

"If I can get to the point where I'm not thinking of anything, that's the best situation for me to be in. You've done this motion so often that it becomes almost a reaction and a muscle reflex. Many times I'll come off the field, having just made a successful field goal, and I'll have to ask how everything went because it was almost blank."

Matt Stover adds, "Our game is so mental. You've got to relax back there and say, 'Hey, just kick it normal.'

You don't need to change anything, just continue to kick the same way and make sure you're mentally sharp."

Detroit Lions kicker Jason Hanson says he practices mentally. "I think kicking is seventy-five to ninety percent mental. So I mentally rehearse kicks. I'll sometimes do field goals without a ball."

A different breed of football player indeed. While the men in the trenches battle it out with brawn, the kicker wages war against his own mind.

Ryan Longwell of the Green Bay Packers credits his faith in Christ for his mental toughness.

"My faith keeps me at such an even keel," explains Longwell. "In what could be high-pressure situations, I'm usually the calmest guy on the field because I realize it's all in God's great plan."

While all of these kickers are quick to give God credit for their current position in the NFL, they don't use their faith as a crutch. They have a healthy balance of respect for God's sovereignty and for their responsibility to be good stewards of the exceptional physical and mental gifts He has given them.

"He's blessed me with a healthy leg and a great mind," explains Longwell. "But I think it's a two-way street. I've got to do my job working out and getting in shape to glorify Him by bringing the best I have to the table."

Stover says, "Prior to the game, I lift the game up [in prayer] to the Lord. But I don't send up too many prayers on the field. He's not going to kick the ball for me."

While you may never see our small wonders land a bone-jarring shot on an unsuspecting kick-returner, the placekickers of today are far from weak. They take their workout regimen seriously.

Stover uses a specifically designed workout put together by a kinesiologist.

Vinatieri does the same workout as the "little" guys

on his team. You can find Adam pumping iron with any New England teammate who isn't a lineman, a linebacker, or a tight end.

"You build team camaraderie when the guys see you working out," says Vinatieri. "And if you're in good shape, you have less chance of injury."

Longwell considers his workout routine as one of the keys to gaining the respect of his teammates.

"I know that if I was a big lineman or a quarterback getting beat up on every play and I saw some kid come in with a clean uniform and miss a kick, I'd be mad at him. So I'm in the weight room with the guys. I run with the guys. They see I'm putting in the effort to be successful and to help them win."

But try as they might, placekickers are still very different than the rest of their gridiron contemporaries. That's why there's such a strong bond among kickers across the league. Think about it—when was the last time you watched an NFL game when at its conclusion, one kicker didn't shake hands with the opposing team's kicker first? It's a fraternity!

But Vinatieri, Hanson, Stover, Longwell, and Johnson have a stronger, more important tie that binds them away from football. Their faith in Christ truly sets these men apart.

"Football is so temporary—the money, the fame—it's so temporary," says Hanson. "My life is centered around Jesus Christ. That's what life is about, not the football field!"

Vinatieri adds, "To God, I don't think the most important thing in our lives is to play football. It's about being a Christian, and being a disciple, and bringing other people to Him."

—by ROB BENTZ

A Pro Football Chronology
Part 6

1959
- Vince Lombardi is named head coach of the Green Bay Packers.
- A second pro football league is organized and named the American Football League.
- The Colts again defeat the Giants in the NFL Championship Game.

1960
- Pete Rozelle is elected NFL Commissioner.
- The AFL adopts the two-point option on points after touchdown.
- The Boston Patriots defeat the Buffalo Bills 28–7 in the first AFL preseason game.
- The Denver Broncos defeat the Patriots 13–10 in the first AFL regular-season game.
- Philadelphia defeats Green Bay 17–13 in the NFL Championship Game.

1961
- The Houston Oilers defeat the Los Angeles Chargers 24–16 in the first AFL Championship Game.
- Canton, Ohio, where the league that became the NFL was formed in 1920, is chosen as the site of the Pro Football Hall of Fame.
- Houston defeats San Diego 10–3 for the AFL championship.
- Green Bay wins its first NFL championship since 1944, defeating the New York Giants 37–0.

1962
- Both leagues prohibit grabbing any player's face mask.

- The AFL makes the scoreboard clock the official timer of the game.
- The Dallas Texans defeat the Oilers 20–17 for the AFL championship. After 17 minutes, 54 seconds of overtime, the game lasted a record 77 minutes, 54 seconds.
- The Packers beat the Giants 16–7 for the NFL title.

1963
- Rozelle suspends indefinitely Green Bay halfback Paul Hornung and Detroit defensive tackle Alex Karras for placing bets on their own teams and on other NFL games.
- Paul Brown, head coach of the Browns since their inception, is fired.
- The Pro Football Hall of Fame is dedicated at Canton, Ohio.
- Jim Brown of Cleveland rushes for an NFL single-season record 1,863 yards.
- Boston defeats Buffalo 26–8 in the first divisional playoff game in AFL history.
- The Bears defeat the Giants 14–10 in the NFL Championship Game. This is the record sixth and last title for George Halas in his thirty-sixth season as the Bears' coach.

1964
- The Chargers defeat the Patriots 51–10 in the AFL Championship Game.
- Hornung and Karras are reinstated.
- Pete Gogolak of Cornell signs with Buffalo—the first soccer-style kicker in pro football.
- Buffalo defeats San Diego 20–7 in the AFL Championship Game.
- Cleveland defeats Baltimore 27–0 in the NFL Championship Game.

1965

- The NFL adds a sixth official, the line judge. The color of the officials' penalty flags is changed from white to bright gold.
- Field Judge Burl Toler is the first African-American official in NFL history.
- Green Bay defeats Baltimore 13–10 in sudden-death overtime in a Western Conference playoff game.
- The Packers defeat the Browns 23–12 in the NFL Championship Game.
- In the AFL Championship Game, the Bills again defeat the Chargers, 23–0.

1966

- Buddy Young is named Director of Player Relations—the first African-American to work in the league office.
- In the NFL, goal posts are offset from the goal line, painted bright yellow, with uprights twenty feet above the crossbar.
- The AFL–NFL merger is announced. Pete Rozelle is named Commissioner of the expanded league.

1967

- Green Bay defeats Dallas 34–27 in the NFL championship.
- Kansas City defeats Buffalo 31–7 in the AFL.
- The Packers defeat the Chiefs 35–10 in the first game ever between AFL and NFL teams.
- The "slingshot" goal post and a six-foot-wide border around the field are made standard in the NFL.
- Baltimore picks Bubba Smith, a Michigan State defensive lineman, as the first choice in the first combined AFL–NFL draft.
- Defensive back Emlen Tunnell of the New York

Giants is the first African-American player to enter the Pro Football Hall of Fame.

- Denver beats Detroit 13–7 in a preseason game—the first time an AFL team has defeat an NFL team.
- Green Bay defeats Dallas 21–17 for the NFL championship on a last-minute one-yard quarterback sneak by Bart Starr in thirteen-below-zero temperatures at Green Bay.
- Oakland defeats Houston 40–7 for the AFL championship.

1968

- Green Bay defeats Oakland 33–14 in Super Bowl II at Miami, January 14.
- Vince Lombardi resigns as head coach of the Packers, but remains as general manager.
- George Halas retires for the fourth and last time as head coach of the Bears.
- The Oilers play in the Astrodome—the first NFL team to play its home games in a domed stadium.
- NBC drops the last 1:05 of a Jets–Raiders game in order to begin the movie *Heidi* on time. The Raiders scored two touchdowns in the last forty-two seconds to win 43–32.
- Weeb Ewbank becomes the first coach to win titles in both the NFL and AFL—his Jets defeat the Raiders 27–23 for the AFL championship.
- Baltimore defeats Cleveland 34–0 in the NFL championship.

1969

- An AFL team wins the Super Bowl for the first time—the Jets defeat the Colts 16–7 in Super Bowl III.
- Monday Night Football is signed for 1970.

- The NFL marks its fiftieth year.

1970

- Kansas City defeats Minnesota 23–7 in Super Bowl IV.
- The merged twenty-six-team league adopts rules changes: names on the backs of players' jerseys, value of a point after touchdown worth one point, the scoreboard clock the official timing device of the game.
- Vince Lombardi dies of cancer at fifty-seven.
- Tom Dempsey of New Orleans kicks an NFL-record, game-winning, sixty-three-yard field goal against Detroit.

1971

- Baltimore defeats Dallas 16–13 on Jim O'Brien's thirty-two-yard field goal with five seconds to go in Super Bowl V.
- Miami defeats Kansas City 27-24 in sudden-death overtime in the AFC Divisional Playoff Game. After 22 minutes, 40 seconds of overtime, the game lasts 82 minutes, 40 seconds overall—the longest game in history.

This is a game for madmen.

VINCE LOMBARDI,
Green Bay Packers coach (1959–69)

Gridiron Glossary
Part 6

READY LIST: A list of several plays ready to be used in an upcoming game, tailored to an opposing team's strengths and weaknesses.

RECEIVER: A receiver, or pass receiver, is a member of the offense whose job it is to get into the open to catch a pass from the quarterback and then run with the ball. Additionally, in professional football, the end on the left is referred to as a "wide" receiver.

RECOVER: Grabbing a ball that has been fumbled (whether the recovering player's side initially had the ball or not).

RED DOG: A blitz.

REGULAR SEASON: A time period of seventeen weeks during which a team plays sixteen games to determine their ranking going into the postseason tournament.

RETURNER: A player who runs back kickoffs and punts.

REVERSE: A type of offensive play. In a reverse, the player with the ball runs in one direction, then hands off the ball to another player going the opposite direction, reversing the ball's direction of travel.

ROLL: The quarterback rolls when he moves left or right with the ball before throwing it.

ROSTER: A list of the members of a team.

ROUGHING: A personal foul with a fifteen-yard penalty. Called when a player illegally contacts another player, as in roughing the punter, when a player tackles the punter without touching the ball, or roughing the passer, where a defensive player attempts to tackle the quarterback after the ball has been thrown.

RUNBACK: Returning a kickoff, punt, or interception.

RUNNING BACK: Positioned behind the quarterback, there are two running backs, whose job it is to run with the ball, which is typically handed off by the quarterback. Part of the offensive backfield. In college and high school football, there are halfbacks and fullbacks in these positions, but in professional football they are simply the two running backs.

RUSH: To run from the scrimmage line with the ball.

SACK: Tackling the quarterback before he can throw a pass.

SAFETY: When a team forces the opposition to down the ball in their own end zone, the defense receives two points, called a safety. Also, the player position called safety is a defensive backfield position, the deepest in the backfield. There are two safeties.

SAFETY BLITZ: A charge by one or both safeties in an attempt to tackle the quarterback.

SAFETY VALVE: A short pass thrown to a running back when the wide receivers are covered.

SCRAMBLE: An unplanned offensive play in which a quarterback runs behind the line of scrimmage to elude tacklers.

SCRAMBLER: A quarterback who has earned a reputation for scrambling.

SCREEN PASS: A pass from behind the line of scrimmage in a play that allows the rushers to charge through as the offensive linemen fake blocking them, only to set up a wall for a receiver for the pass.

SCRIMMAGE: The action between two teams, starting when the ball is snapped.

SECONDARY: The defensive backfield, or second line of defense.

SHIFT: The movement of two (or more) offensive players between positions.

SIGNAL CALLER: The quarterback.

SIGNALS: The quarterback tells the other players, with signals, what the next play will be. Signals are also used at the line of scrimmage to tell the center when to snap the ball.

SLANT: Running, with the ball, at an angle.

Once, after a long gain, I was walking by the Eagles' huddle and I reached out and pinched Bill Bradley as hard as I could on the arm. He ran to the referee, screaming that I had pinched him and the ref told him they didn't have a penalty for that.

CONRAD DOBLER,
St. Louis Cardinals offensive guard
(1972–81)

Nothing devastates a football team like a selfish player. It's a cancer. The greatest back I ever had was Marion Motley. You know why? The only statistic he ever knew was whether we won or lost. The man was completely unselfish.

PAUL BROWN,
Cleveland Browns coach (1946–62)

Stats

300-Yard Passing Games (1998)

GAMES	PLAYER	TEAM
7	Steve Young	San Francisco
4	Drew Bledsoe	New England
4	Randall Cunningham	Minnesota
4	Brett Favre	Green Bay
4	Dan Marino	Miami
4	Peyton Manning	Indianapolis
2	Mark Brunell	Jacksonville
2	Kerry Collins	New Orleans
2	John Elway	Denver
2	Trent Green	Washington
2	Jake Plummer	Arizona
2	Doug Flutie	Buffalo
1	Troy Aikman	Dallas
1	Jeff Blake	Cincinnati
1	Chris Chandler	Atlanta
1	Glenn Foley	New York Jets
1	Rich Gannon	Kansas City
1	Jeff George	Oakland
1	Brad Johnson	Minnesota
1	Erik Kramer	Chicago
1	Neil O'Donnell	Cincinnati
1	Steve Stenstrom	Chicago
1	Vinny Testaverde	New York Jets
1	Billy Joe Tolliver	New Orleans
1	Craig Whelihan	San Diego

Cunningham Alone Can't Do It

Randall Cunningham believes God has led him to the Twin Cities for a simple two-word reason: Super Bowl.

Cunningham's football career has been "born again." After a dozen seasons that saw him become the NFL's all-time leading rusher among quarterbacks, he scrambled completely out of the game, leaving the pocket to retire following the 1995 campaign. Cunningham, 35, contends that not taking a snap in '96 helped get him centered.

"My time away from football got me back in line with what God would have me to do," says Cunningham. "I had to sit back and think. I was really humbled as a person."

Admittedly, this fleet-footed player could no longer run from his Heavenly Pursuer. "Sometimes you get outside God's will, and you don't realize it," he says. "I look at things now as, 'What is God saying to me?' In the past I cared about what the world was saying." That gameless season allowed him to focus on a new strategy for his life and career.

With his personal priorities properly placed, Cunningham felt a fresh focus on football. This newfound perspective is evident as much on the field as off.

The one-time league MVP (1990) is staying in the pocket and using his teammates more than ever before. "I've learned that it's done as a team," he says. "There were times when I thought I could lead a team to a Super Bowl, but now I realize that one person can't do it."

Vikings coach Dennis Green echoes Cunningham's revolutionary realization. "We're not expecting Randall to be our savior. We've got other guys who have to play and hold up their end of the bargain. We're confident that Randall will do the same," says Green.

Cunningham is convinced that he was not ready to experience winning an NFL championship. . .until now. "As a non-Christian, I handled not winning a Super Bowl without a problem. But as a Christian, I believe that God has put me here to play football with a purpose," he explains. "I have to make sure that I stay in His will so He can allow me the time to do it [win a title]. I am just going to have to wait on it."

Does he think it is time for him to claim the NFL crown with the Vikings? "All I know is that it's God's will for me to be here," he says with a smile.

—by TROY PEARSON

The harder we work, the luckier we get.
VINCE LOMBARDI,
Green Bay Packers coach (1959–69)

A Pro Football Chronology
Part 7

1972

- Dallas defeats Miami 24–3 in Super Bowl VI.
- The inbounds lines (hash marks) are moved nearer the center of the field, twenty-three yards, one foot, nine inches from the sidelines.
- Franco Harris's "Immaculate Reception" gives the Steelers their first postseason win ever, 13–7 over the Raiders.

1973

- Miami defeats Washington 14–7 in Super Bowl VII, completing a 17–0 season, the first perfect-record regular-season and postseason mark in NFL history.
- The jersey numbering system is adopted.
- O. J. Simpson of Buffalo is the first player to rush for more than 2,000 yards in a season, gaining 2,003.

1974

- Miami defeats Minnesota 24–7 in Super Bowl VIII at Houston, the second consecutive Super Bowl championship for the Dolphins.
- Rules changes: one sudden-death overtime period added for preseason and regular-season games; the goal posts moved from the goal line to the end lines; kickoffs moved from the forty- to the thirty-five-yard line; after missed field goals from beyond the twenty, the ball to be returned to the line of scrimmage; restrictions placed on members of the punting team to open up return possibilities; roll-blocking and cutting of wide receivers eliminated;

the extent of downfield contact by a defender on an eligible receiver restricted; the penalties for offensive holding, illegal use of the hands, and tripping reduced from fifteen to ten yards; wide receivers blocking back toward the ball within three yards of the line of scrimmage prevented from blocking below the waist.

1975

- Pittsburgh defeats Minnesota 16–6 in Super Bowl IX—the Steelers' first championship since entering the NFL in 1933.
- Referees are equipped with wireless microphones for all games.

1976

- Pittsburgh defeats Dallas 21–17 in Super Bowl X. The Steelers, Green Bay, and Miami are the only teams to win two Super Bowls.
- New rule: adoption of two thirty-second clocks for all games, visible to both players and fans to note the official time between the ready-for-play signal and snap of the ball.

1977

- Oakland defeats Minnesota 32–14 in Super Bowl XI—the fifth consecutive victory for the AFC in the Super Bowl.
- Rules changes: defenders permitted to make contact with eligible receivers only once; the head slap outlawed; offensive linemen prohibited from thrusting their hands to an opponent's neck, face, or head; and wide receivers prohibited from clipping, even in the legal clipping zone.
- Chicago's Walter Payton sets a single-game rushing

record with 275 yards (on forty carries) against Minnesota, November 20.

1978

- Dallas defeats Denver 27–10 in Super Bowl XII— the first victory for the NFC in six years.
- A seventh official, the side judge, is added to the officiating crew.
- Rules changes permit a defender to maintain contact with a receiver within five yards of the line of scrimmage, but restrict contact beyond that point. The pass-blocking rule is interpreted to permit the extending of arms and open hands.
- A study on the use of instant replay as an officiating aid is made during seven nationally televised preseason games.

1979

- Pittsburgh defeats Dallas 35–31 in Super Bowl XIII—becoming the first team ever to win three Super Bowls.
- Rules changes prohibit players on the receiving team from blocking below the waist during kickoffs, punts, and field-goal attempts; prohibit the wearing of torn or altered equipment and exposed pads that could be hazardous; extend the zone in which there could be no crackback blocks; and instruct officials to quickly whistle a play dead when a quarterback is clearly in the grasp of a tackler.

1980

- Pittsburgh defeats the Los Angeles Rams 31–19 in Super Bowl XIV—becoming the first team to win four Super Bowls.

- Rules changes: restrictions on contact in the area of the head, neck, and face; players prohibited from directly striking, swinging, or clubbing on the head, neck, or face.

1981

- Oakland defeats Philadelphia 27–10 in Super Bowl XV—becoming the first wild-card team to win a Super Bowl.

1982

- San Francisco defeats Cincinnati 26–21 in Super Bowl XVI.
- The season is reduced from a sixteen-game schedule to nine as the result of a fifty-seven-day players' strike.

1983

- Because of the shortened season, the NFL adopts a format of sixteen teams in a Super Bowl Tournament for the 1982 playoffs. The NFC's number-one seed, Washington, defeated the AFC's number-two seed, Miami, 27–17 in Super Bowl XVII.
- George Halas, the owner of the Bears and the last surviving member of the NFL's second organizational meeting, dies at 88.

1984

- The Los Angeles Raiders defeat Washington 38–9 in Super Bowl XVIII.
- Many all-time records are set: Dan Marino of Miami passes for 5,084 yards and 48 touchdowns; Eric Dickerson of the Los Angeles Rams rushes for 2,105 yards; Art Monk of Washington catches 106

passes; and Walter Payton of Chicago breaks Jim Brown's career rushing mark, finishing the season with 13,309 yards.

I remember in one game, head down, charging like a bull, [Bronko] Nagurski blasted through two tacklers at the goal line as if they were a pair of old-time saloon doors, through the end zone, and full speed into the brick retaining wall behind it. The sickening thud reverberated throughout the stadium. "That last guy really gave me a good lick," he said to me when he got back to the sideline.

GEORGE HALAS,
Chicago Bears founder,
owner, player, coach (1920–68)

Football is a game played with arms, legs, and shoulders; but mostly from the neck up.

KNUTE ROCKNE,
Notre Dame coach (1918–30)

Gridiron Glossary
Part 7

SLOT: A gap in the offensive line between a receiver and a tackle.

SNAP: The handing of the ball by the center, reaching back between his legs, to the quarterback or punter.

SPEARING: Contacting another player with one's head; a foul in college football.

SPECIAL TEAMS: A special group, or "platoon," of players specializing in one particular maneuver, such as punts or kick-offs. When the maneuver is about to be done, the coach will substitute the special team. Special teams give their all to their specialties and consequently suffer higher injury rates than the rest of the team. That's why they are also called bomb squads or suicide squads.

SPIRAL: The football's rotation, about its longitudinal axis, when it's thrown.

SPLIT END: A receiver who lines up several yards away from the next player along the line of scrimmage.

SQUARE IN/OUT: A pass route where the runner goes downfield, then turns "in" at a "square" or right angle to the center of the field or "out" to the sideline.

STRAIGHTARM: To defend against an opposing tackler by using the hand and arm.

STRONG SIDE: In an unbalanced line, the side with the most players.

STUNT: An unusual charge by the offensive linemen, sometimes in concert with the linebackers, in which they loop around each other during the charge instead of running straight ahead.

SUICIDE SQUAD: See "special teams."

SUBSTITUTION: Putting a player into the game as a

substitute for another. For example, a play requiring a very fast player may cause the coach to bring out one player and replace him with another, faster player.

SUPER BOWL: The National Football League's championship game.

I considered naming the team the Chicago Cubs. . . . But I noted football players are bigger than baseball players; so if baseball players are cubs, then certainly football players must be bears!

George Halas,
Chicago Bears founder, owner,
player, coach (1920–68)

"Trent Dilfer has been saved by Jesus Christ"

Trent Dilfer has just endured the day's first two hours of practice in the Florida sun. He's tired, the sun has scorched his head, and he misses his wife and two children, who are out of town. He doesn't complain. You won't hear him do that. His withered blue eyes tell the story.

He smiles and looks sheepishly at a reporter as they sit in the University of Tampa cafeteria. "Can we maybe do this tomorrow? I'm just really tired, and I'd like to collect my thoughts and do this right."

Dilfer, who in 1997 enjoyed his first Pro Bowl season with the Tampa Bay Buccaneers, realizes that just about every writer in the greater Tampa–St. Petersburg area, and many from across the country, wants to talk to him about the most-anticipated season in franchise history.

He offers to do part of the interview then and there, but continue the rest of it another day—when he's better rested and at a time when he promises he'll be a better interview.

The difference between Trent Dilfer and the average multimillion-dollar athlete is that he cares. He doesn't tell you he won't, he doesn't tell you he can't, and when something changes he asks, "Is that okay?" An unlikely response from a guy who makes more than $4 million a season and has the future of the NFL's most resurgent franchise at his fingertips.

"The interviews aren't that hard," he says about his life as a football star. "Dealing with the kids and the autographs is not that hard. What's difficult is dealing with the parents. The grown-ups are the people that really ruin it for us. They should understand what we're going through in our busyness and our lifestyle, yet they continue to criticize us for not giving all of our free time to be with them and sign their autographs."

Tired as he might be, Dilfer can still talk. And what he enjoys talking about most is his faith and the difference it makes in his life.

"Trent Dilfer has been saved by Jesus Christ," he says. "And all of that other stuff doesn't really matter. That's where my value comes from, and that's why I can handle being criticized in the media. That's why I can handle people calling radio shows and lying about me. That's why I can handle some of the adverse situations I face, and that's why I can handle success.

"Throwing an interception does not change where I stand with God—it's how I deal with the interception that counts. Winning a Super Bowl will not mean anything eternally—it's how I deal with winning the Super Bowl that will make me the kind of person I am."

It may sound as if Dilfer doesn't care what people think, but he does. He cares what people—especially children—think. He's already the center of attention, especially after last season's franchise record twenty-one touchdown passes, but being liked and accepted is something that's important to him. It has been ever since he was a youngster.

Just listen to his mother: "When he was in high school and was probably a much better basketball player than a football player, the first time he was named Player of the Game, when they turned on the TV lights, he was just like a natural," says Marcie Lynch, who suffered through a divorce from Trent's father, Doug, when Trent was just two years old. She married Frank Lynch three years later. "He's always liked the limelight," says Mom.

He grew up looking out for number one and would do anything to become more popular. Dilfer was restless, and although athletics brought him attention, he yearned for more. He was a self-described "show-off."

Trent says it was more about being liked than popular, but it's a different story today. As far as his Buccaneer teammates are concerned, he says, he wants to be respected. "I want to do whatever it takes for them to achieve what we're all trying to achieve, and that's a championship. I don't necessarily get caught up in whether they like me or not, because personalities conflict. But I want them to respect me and I want them to know I'm here for them. I really am. I will be selfless in order to win, if that's what it takes. I'll make the sacrifices, both personally and professionally, to ensure our success as a football team."

It's a different perspective from the one he had as a rookie.

When Dilfer came into the league in 1994, Coach Sam Wyche handed the Bucs' top draft pick (sixth overall) the starting quarterback job over Craig Erickson early in his first year. Yet Erickson still had something that Dilfer wanted—the support of his teammates. Erickson's demotion led to resentment in the locker room, not necessarily because Erickson was the better man for the job, but because the guys liked Erickson. Dilfer has decided that respect is a better way to impress his teammates.

Trent grew up in a Christian home and went to church, but although he played the game of being a Christian, he didn't allow matters of faith to influence his life until the summer before his sophomore year of college at Fresno State University. It was 1992, and Trent was at a Fellowship of Christian Athletes camp in Thousand Oaks, California, where he was a "huddle leader" for ten underprivileged children. Even the camp leaders thought he was a Christian. At the camp, Trent ended up being the pupil instead of the teacher.

As he observed the other counselors, he was impressed with their love for Jesus Christ. He knew he didn't have that love. "These guys just loved me to death," he says. "I saw Christ through them."

At that camp, where he had been brought in to be a counselor, Dilfer prayed a sincere prayer of faith, asking Jesus Christ to be his Savior. "I confessed everything to Him and made a decision to trust Him," he says.

He returned home and told his mother that he'd had a change in his life.

"He lay on the sofa in the family room and cried," says Lynch of her son. "He said he never really realized how much he had." Finally, he was experiencing real faith in Christ.

Trent's life changed in another way around that time as well. He had met and befriended Fresno State swimmer and classmate Cassandra Franzman before attending the FCA camp. Later, regular Bible study brought the couple together, and they were married in July 1993. They've since added to the flock with children Madeleine and Trevin.

"I want to raise kids that are blessings to God," says Trent. "That's the bottom line. That's our goal as parents— to raise children who are blessings to God, who know

Him personally, and who serve Him diligently throughout their life.

"The biggest people I want to be a witness to in my life are my kids. When they're asked about their dad they can say, 'Oh yeah, he played in the NFL, but I want them to say first, 'He loves Jesus.' That's a great, great challenge."

In the past, Trent and Cassandra's Christian lifestyle kept Dilfer from being "one of the guys," but now having the guys' respect and being a righteous man takes precedence.

He won't change. He won't go against his beliefs, but there's still a big part of Trent that wants to be embraced by his teammates. He so much wanted to be accepted that in his second season he went along with teammates to a handful of bars, but he found himself feeling like a fish out of water. His prayer life, studying God's Word, being discipled, and fellowship with other believers have helped him to achieve the consistency that is now so evident in his life.

"It's hard, but I want to be real," says Dilfer. "They all know where I stand and there are certain things I won't compromise, but at the same time I don't mind being real."

Football Fortunes

Since Trent was the son of a physical education teacher and coach, it would seem only natural that he would excel on the gridiron. As a preadolescent, he was a waterboy and ballboy for Aptos High School near Santa Cruz, California, where he understood the offense better than the quarterbacks.

"He was a student of every game he's been involved

in. He knew the offense better than my college quarter-backs," says Frank Lynch, Dilfer's mentor and stepfather, who coached for both Aptos High and Cabrillo College, a community college in Aptos. "He and I used to banter back and forth about what to do in certain situations when we were watching games. He enjoys the mental part of the game and the logistics and dissecting the game."

After a successful football career at Aptos High, where he was a two-time All-Conference selection in both basketball and football, Dilfer headed to one of the three schools that recruited him. Santa Clara and Northern Arizona also offered the four-sport letterman (golf, basketball, football, baseball) a scholarship, but Dilfer decided to play for the Bulldogs in the Western Athletic Conference.

At Fresno State, he got his first chance as a redshirt freshman when starting quarterback Mark Barsotti was injured. As expected, Dilfer was nervous, but he stepped in, started the final four games of the season, and helped his club to a berth in the California Raisin Bowl.

In Dilfer's sophomore year, Fresno State was playing at San Diego State for the right to go to the Freedom Bowl. Fresno State led in the fourth quarter, but SDSU scored and took the lead with just three minutes left in the game. Dilfer drove the Bulldogs the length of the field before facing a fourth-and-goal on the six-yard line with ten seconds left. The sophomore then promptly tossed a perfect fade to Tydus Winans in the corner of the end zone for the winning score.

Former Fresno State teammate and current Buccaneer teammate Lorenzo Neal says, "In that play, he showed some leadership, and he showed poise as a sophomore and in a game of that magnitude. I was like, 'Boy, this kid can play.' To do that in that type of game and that type of environment you just say, 'Hey, this guy's arrived.' "

From there, Dilfer truly typified the excellence of execution. In 1993, his junior and final year of college, Dilfer set an NCAA record by throwing 318 passes without an interception. In just his second full season starting, he drew the interest of pro scouts by running the Bulldogs' pro-style offense to perfection and throwing for twenty-eight touchdowns with just four interceptions.

Dilfer's first two years in the NFL weren't so glorious. Doubts began to surface among some experts about his ability to get the job done in the big time. But then along came Tony Dungy and the new "plan" the man brought to the team.

"We wanted to build from the ground up," Dungy says of his plan. "But there was a lot of foundation here. I just felt that if the guys believed in what we were trying to do, it would go well. We got some guys to believe that, and it's starting to come."

Dungy surprised Dilfer in their first year together by telling him that he would have to win the starting job in training camp, but that if he did, he was their guy. He was the one they would stick with, win or lose. Dilfer respected that, and he responded by recording career highs in passing yardage (2,859), completions (267), and attempts (482), even though the Bucs went 6–10.

Tampa Bay ended the 1996 season winning five of its last seven games, catapulting the Buccaneers and Dilfer into 1997, the most successful season in franchise history. The Bucs opened the season by winning their first five games, and the team went on to the playoffs for the first time in fifteen years. The end came in a disappointing 21–7 loss to the Green Bay Packers, but Tampa Bay showed it had arrived when a league-high eight players, including Dilfer, were named to the Pro Bowl.

The Pro Bowl selection followed a year that saw

Dilfer start every game for the third consecutive season, connect on 217 of 386 passes for a career-best 56.2 completion percentage, and throw a team-record 152 passes without an interception.

The numbers, accolades, and life he keeps in perspective.

"I've learned some very valuable lessons through football. I'm at the point now where I'm excited about how I'm going to grow spiritually," says Dilfer. "I'm excited because I know the Lord's going to make me richer spiritually. I don't know if it's going to be through failure, I don't know if He's going to do it through success—but I know I'm going to grow."

—by BUDDY SHACKLETTE

They say I teach brutal football, but the only thing brutal about football is losing.

PAUL "BEAR" BRYANT,
University of Alabama coach (1958–82)

A Pro Football Chronology
Part 8

1985

- San Francisco defeats Miami 38–16 in Super Bowl XIX.

1986

- Chicago defeats New England 46–10 in Super Bowl XX. The Patriots are the first wild card team to win three consecutive games on the road.
- Limited use of instant replay as an officiating aid is adopted.
- Players are prohibited from wearing or otherwise displaying equipment, apparel, or other items that carry commercial names, names of organizations, or personal messages of any type.
- Instant replay is used to reverse two plays in thirty-one preseason games. During the regular season, 374 plays are closely reviewed by replay officials, leading to 38 reversals in 224 games. Eighteen plays are closely reviewed by instant replay in ten postseason games with three reversals.

1987

- The New York Giants defeat Denver 39–20 in Super Bowl XXI—their first NFL title since 1956.
- The 1987 season is reduced from a sixteen-game season to fifteen as the result of a twenty-four-day players' strike.
- Instant replay is used to reverse eight plays in fifty-two preseason games. During the strike-shortened 210-game regular season, 490 plays are closely reviewed by replay officials, leading to fifty-seven

reversals. Eighteen plays are closely reviewed by
instant replay in ten postseason games, with three
reversals.

1988

- Washington defeats Denver 42–10 in Super Bowl
  XXII.
- The instant replay system is retained for the third
  consecutive season; the instant replay official is
  assigned to a regular seven-man, on-the-field crew.
  A forty-five-second clock is approved to replace
  the thirty-second clock. The interval between plays
  is changed to forty-five seconds from the time the
  ball is signaled dead until it is snapped on the succeeding play.
- Johnny Grier becomes the first African-American
  referee in NFL history.

1989

- San Francisco defeats Cincinnati 20–16 in Super
  Bowl XXIII.
- Commissioner Pete Rozelle announces his
  retirement.
- The instant replay system continues for the fourth
  straight season. The policy regarding anabolic
  steroids and masking agents is strengthened. NFL
  clubs called for strong disciplinary measures in
  cases of feigned injuries.
- Art Shell is named head coach of the Los Angeles
  Raiders, making him the NFL's first African-
  American head coach since Fritz Pollard coached
  the Akron Pros in 1921.
- Paul Tagliabue becomes the seventh chief execu-
  tive of the NFL.

- San Francisco defeats Denver 55–10 in Super Bowl XXIV—making the 49ers and Pittsburgh the only teams to win four Super Bowls.
- A limited system of instant replay is adopted.
- Dr. John Lombardo appointed as the league's Drug Advisor for Anabolic Steroids. Dr. Lawrence Brown named as the league's Advisor for Drugs of Abuse.
- For the first time since 1957, every NFL club won at least one of its first four games.

1991

- New York defeats Buffalo 20–19 in Super Bowl XXV—the Giants' second title in five years.
- Instant replay continues for the sixth consecutive year.
- Paul Brown, founder of the Cleveland Browns and Cincinnati Bengals, dies at age eighty-two.

1992

- Washington defeats the Buffalo Bills 37–24 in Super Bowl XXVI—the Redskins' third championship in ten years.
- The use of a limited system of instant replay is rejected.

1993

- Dallas defeats the Buffalo Bills 52–17 in Super Bowl XXVII—the Cowboys' first NFL title since 1978.
- Don Shula becomes the winningest coach in NFL history with 325 victories, one more than George Halas.

1994

- Dallas defeats the Buffalo Bills 30–13 in Super Bowl XXVIII—as the Cowboys become the fifth team to win back-to-back Super Bowl titles.
- Rules changes: modifications in line play, chucking rules, and the roughing-the-passer rule; adoption of the two-point conversion and moving the spot of the kickoff back to the thirty-yard line.
- The NFL celebrates its seventy-fifth anniversary.

1995

- The San Francisco 49ers become the first team to win five Super Bowls by defeating the San Diego Chargers 49–26 in Super Bowl XXIX.
- Rules changes adopted primarily relate to the use of the helmet against defenseless players.
- Many significant records and milestones are achieved: Miami's Dan Marino surpasses Pro Football Hall of Famer Fran Tarkenton in four major passing categories—attempts, completions, yards, and touchdowns—to become the NFL's all-time career leader. San Francisco's Jerry Rice becomes the all-time reception and receiving-yardage leader with career totals of 942 catches and 15,123 yards. Dallas's Emmitt Smith scores twenty-five touchdowns, breaking the season record of twenty-four set by Washington's John Riggins in 1983.

1996

- The Dallas Cowboys win their third Super Bowl title in four years by defeating the Pittsburgh Steelers 27–17 in Super Bowl XXX.
- Former NFL Commissioner Pete Rozelle dies.

Rozelle, regarded as the premiere commissioner in sports history, led the NFL for twenty-nine years, from 1960–1989.

1997

- The Green Bay Packers win their first NFL title in twenty-nine years by defeating the New England Patriots 35–21 in Super Bowl XXXI.
- The ten-thousandth regular-season game in NFL history is played when the Seattle Seahawks defeat the Tennessee Oilers 16–13 at the Kingdome in Seattle.

1998

- The Denver Broncos win their first Super Bowl by defeating the defending champion Green Bay Packers 31–24 in Super Bowl XXXII.

1999

- The Denver Broncos again win the Super Bowl, defeating Atlanta 34–19 in Super Bowl XXXIII.

I once asked [offensive lineman] Dave Herman how his wife enjoyed coming to the games. "All she looks for," he said, "is to see whether I get up or not."

PAUL ZIMMERMAN,
Sports Illustrated writer

Gridiron Glossary
Part 8

TACKLE: To bring down another player. For example, to sack the quarterback is to tackle him. Also an offensive position. There are two tackles, one outside each guard, whose job is to block the onrushing defensive line and open up holes for a runner.

TAILBACK: A member of the offensive backfield whose job is to run with the ball. Also called a running back or halfback.

THREE-POINT STANCE: The position players at the line of scrimmage take before the snap, leaning forward on one hand with their feet spread.

TIME: In professional and college football, the game is limited to sixty minutes (forty-eight minutes in high school football). This is divided into two thirty-minute halves, each of which is divided into two fifteen-minute quarters, or "periods." In between the two halves is halftime, which lasts fifteen minutes. If the teams are tied at the end of the time limit, the game goes into overtime, continuing until one of the teams pulls ahead.

TOUCHBACK: A touchback occurs when the defensive team gains possession of the ball in their own end zone on the same play in which the offensive team caused the ball to cross the goal line.

TOUCHDOWN: Carrying the ball into or catching the ball in the opposition's end zone. Worth six points.

TRAP BLOCK: When a player is allowed through the enemy line only to be blocked by surprise from another player behind the line. Also called a mousetrap.

TURN IN/OUT: A pass route where the player runs

downfield, then turns in toward the middle of the
   field or out toward the sidelines.
TURNOVER: Losing possession of the ball, typically
   by error.

UNBALANCED LINE: A formation with more players
   on one side of the center than the other.
UPRIGHTS: Vertical posts supporting the crossbar in
   the goalpost.

WEAK SIDE: The side of an unbalanced line with the
   least players.

ZONE DEFENSE: A defense strategy where each
   player has an area, or "zone," of the field to
   defend. See also "man-to-man defense."

*When we had the head slap, that's when they
had some real football. Blood and stuff trickling
down your legs. You don't hardly see no snaggle-
toothed linemen anymore. Everything's changed.
All of 'em got teeth.*

CHARLIE JOHNSON,
San Francisco 49ers noseguard (1966–68)

Boom Town Eisenhauer

Larry Eisenhauer was the defensive end for the Patriots in the old AFL. One afternoon a San Diego Charger public relations man stopped by and handed the Boston players a bunch of "Charley Charger" coloring books. The Patriots took them over to poolside, and the rumor that night was the Eisenhauer had spent the rest of his day coloring his Charley Charger book.

"It's a lie," he said later. "I wasn't coloring the thing. I was just reading it."

Before games Eisenhauer was one of the noted dressing room maniacs. He'd attack walls, lockers, anything that got in his way. On the field he played with a wild intensity seldom seen today. Boston used to have a daytime kiddie show in those days called "Boom Town," featuring Rex Trailer and his sidekick, Pablo. One day they decided to film a show at Fenway Park, and the action would center around the Patriots football team. Pablo would grab the ball and run for a TD, with all the Patriots chasing him. Eisenhauer was picked to be one of the chasers.

Once the action started, though, a hidden bell clanged and all the 6'5", 250-pounder saw was an enemy player running for a touchdown, a guy who had to be stopped. So he stopped him.

"I'm kind of ashamed of it now," he said later. "Pablo was only about 5'3", and he was slow, so it wasn't any trick catching him. I didn't really hurt him; I just sort of jumped on his back. Why give the guy a free touchdown?"

Stats
100-Yard Receiving Games (1998)

GAMES	PLAYER	TEAM
6	Antonio Freeman	Green Bay
5	Wayne Chrebet	New York Jets
5	Tony Martin	Atlanta
5	Frank Sanders	Arizona
5	Jimmy Smith	Jacksonville
4	Joey Galloway	Seattle
4	Terry Glenn	New England
4	Keyshawn Johnson	New York Jets
4	Ed McCaffrey	Denver
4	Herman Moore	Detroit
4	Eric Moulds	Buffalo
4	Rod Smith	Denver
4	Michael Westbrook	Washington
4	Randy Moss	Minnesota
3	Tim Brown	Oakland
3	Cris Carter	Minnesota
3	Sean Dawkins	New Orleans
3	Bobby Engram	Chicago
3	Marshall Faulk	Indianapolis
3	Michael Irvin	Dallas
3	Raghib Ismail	Carolina
3	Terance Mathis	Atlanta
3	O. J. McDuffie	Miami
3	Johnnie Morton	Detroit
3	Muhsin Muhammad	Carolina
3	Jerry Rice	San Francisco
2	Derrick Alexander	Kansas City
2	Isaac Bruce	St. Louis
2	Marvin Harrison	Indianapolis
2	Garrison Hearst	San Francisco

GAMES	PLAYER	TEAM
2	Shawn Jefferson	New England
2	James Jett	Oakland
2	Jermaine Lewis	Baltimore
2	Keenan McCardell	Jacksonville
2	Rob Moore	Arizona
2	Terrell Owens	San Francisco
2	Carl Pickens	Cincinnati
2	Darnay Scott	Cincinnati
2	Torrance Small	Indianapolis
2	Bryan Still	San Diego
2	J.J. Stokes	San Francisco
2	Floyd Turner	Baltimore
1	Reidel Anthony	Tampa Bay
1	Brett Bech	New Orleans
1	Brandon Bennett	Cincinnati
1	Ben Coates	New England
1	Albert Connell	Washington
1	Stephen Davis	Washington
1	Rickey Dudley	Oakland
1	Bert Emanuel	Tampa Bay
1	Oronde Gadsden	Miami
1	Andre Hastings	New Orleans
1	Courtney Hawkins	Pittsburgh
1	Ike Hilliard	New York Giants
1	Charles Johnson	Pittsburgh
1	James McKnight	Seattle
1	Ernie Mills	Dallas
1	Keith Poole	New Orleans
1	Ricky Proehl	St. Louis
1	Andre Reed	Buffalo
1	Jake Reed	Minnesota
1	Chris Sanders	Tennessee
1	Bill Schroeder	Green Bay

GAMES	PLAYER	TEAM
1	Leslie Shepherd	Washington
1	Yancey Thigpen	Tennessee
1	Lamar Thomas	Miami
1	Chris Penn	Chicago
1	Mark Carrier	Carolina
1	Cameron Cleeland	New Orleans
1	Tony Simmons	New England

Question to Norm Van Brocklin, Los Angeles
    Rams quarterback (1949–60): What's your
    favorite play?
Answer: "Our Town" by Thornton Wilder.

*I've compared offensive linemen to the story of
Paul Revere. After Paul Revere rode through
town everybody said what a great job he did.
But no one ever talked about the horse. I know
how Paul Revere's horse felt.*

GENE UPSHAW,
Oakland Raiders offensive guard
(1967–81)

References

Christian's Faith—from *Sports Spectrum*, December 1998.

Pro Football Chronology—adapted from *NFL Record & Fact Book*, http://www.nfl.com

Gridiron Glossary—adapted from *Football Dictionary*, http://www.football.com.

The Stats—compiled from http://www.nfl.com.

Bruce Matthews' Be-all, End-all—from *Sports Spectrum*, January/February 1999.

Trying to Find a Way to Give God the Glory—from *Sports Spectrum*, January/February 1999.

A Good Name and Loving Esteem—from *Sports Spectrum*, January/February 1999.

Those Trusty Placekickers—from *Sports Spectrum*, November 1998.

The Big Bucks and Jerry Kramer—from *Farewell to Football* by Jerry Kramer. World Publishing, 1969.

Cunningham Alone Can't Do It—from *Sports Spectrum*, January/February 1999.

Trent Dilfer has been saved by Jesus Christ—from *Sports Spectrum*, November 1998.

Boom Town Eisenhauer—from *The Fireside Book of Pro Football*, Richard Whittingham, ed. Simon and Schuster, 1989.